D0073209

PENSION MATHEMATICS
with Numerical Illustrations

Howard E. Winklevoss, Ph.D.

Associate Professor of Insurance and Actuarial Science
Wharton School

Published for the

Pension Research Council

Wharton School
University of Pennsylvania

by

RICHARD D. IRWIN, INC.   Homewood, Illinois   60430
Irwin-Dorsey Limited   Georgetown, Ontario   L7G 4B3

© *Copyright 1977 by the*
Pension Research Council
of the
Wharton School
University of Pennsylvania

All Rights Reserved

First Printing, January 1977

ISBN 0-256-01886-3
Library of Congress Catalog Card No. 76–22249

Printed in the United States of America

To my parents
Marion and Howard Winklevoss

PENSION RESEARCH COUNCIL

DAN M. McGILL, *Chairman and Research Director*
Chairman, Insurance Department
Wharton School of the University of Pennsylvania

Verne Arends, *Superintendent of Pension Research*, Northwestern Mutual
    Life Insurance Company, Milwaukee
Robert A. Albright, *Assistant to Vice President and Comptroller*, U.S.
    Steel and Carnegie Pension Fund, Pittsburgh
Preston C. Bassett, F.S.A., *Vice President and Actuary*, Towers, Perrin,
    Forster & Crosby, New York City
Herman C. Biegel, Esq., *Senior Partner*, Lee, Toomey and Kent,
    Washington, D.C.
Edwin F. Boynton, F.S.A., *Consulting Actuary*, The Wyatt Company,
    Washington, D.C.
Laurence E. Coward, F.S.A., *Executive Vice President and Director*,
    William M. Mercer, Ltd., Toronto
John K. Dyer, Jr., F.S.A., *Independent Actuary*, Beach Haven, New Jersey
Robert Ellis, *Manager, Employee Benefits*, Owen-Illinois, Toledo
Donald S. Grubbs, Jr., F.S.A., *Consulting Actuary*, George B. Buck
    Consulting Actuaries, Washington, D.C.
Ernest L. Hicks, C.P.A., *Partner*, Arthur Young and Company,
    New York City
Russell H. Hubbard, Jr., Esq., *Corporate Employee Relations*,
    General Electric Company, Fairfield, Connecticut
Arthur Levitt, *Comptroller of the State of New York*, Albany
George M. Lingua, *Senior Vice President*, First National City Bank,
    New York City
Dudley M. Mason, *General Manager*, Personnel Research Department,
    Armstrong Cork Company, Lancaster, Pennsylvania
Meyer Melnikoff, F.S.A., *Senior Vice President and Actuary*, Prudential
    Insurance Company, Newark
Roger F. Murray, *Colt Professor of Banking and Finance*, Columbia
    University, New York City
Robert J. Myers, F.S.A., *Professor of Actuarial Science*, Temple University,
    Philadelphia

Bert Seidman, *Director, Department of Social Security*, AFL–CIO, Washington, D.C.

Robert Tilove, *Senior Vice President*, Martin E. Segal Company, New York City

Charles L. Trowbridge, F.S.A., *Senior Vice President*, Bankers Life Company, Des Moines

L. Edwin Wang, *Executive Secretary*, Board of Pensions of Lutheran Church in America, Minneapolis

Howard E. Winklevoss, *Associate Professor of Insurance and Actuarial Science*, University of Pennsylvania, Philadelphia

Howard Young, F.S.A., *Special Consultant to the President*, United Automobile Workers, Detroit

PURPOSE OF THE COUNCIL

The Pension Research Council was formed in 1952 in response to an urgent need for a better understanding of the private pension mechanism. It is composed of nationally recognized pension experts representing leadership in every phase of private pensions. It sponsors academic research into the problems and issues surrounding the private pension institution and publishes the findings in a series of books and monographs. The studies are conducted by mature scholars drawn from both the academic and business spheres.

Foreword

This book is the culmination of ten years of intensive inquiry by Howard Winklevoss into the intricacies of pension costs and actuarial liabilities. It is a welcome and much needed addition to pension literature.

When I began my pension research activities in the early 1950s, I sought in vain for explanations of pension cost behavior of the type that abound in this book. I suspect that many of these relationships were known, perhaps intuitively, by actuaries actively engaged in pension consulting or the pension operations of life insurance companies. If so, their insights and perceptions were apparently treated as proprietary information, to be confined to internal communications or the inner recesses of their minds. With some notable exceptions, the ideas did not find their way into published pension literature.

To a considerable degree, knowledge of pension cost behavior was constrained by the technology of the day. Pension cost calculations were laborious and many shortcuts and approximations were used. With the development of sophisticated, high-speed computers, it has become feasible to refine pension actuarial techniques and assumptions. In particular, it has become feasible through the construction of computer models to simulate the experience of a pension plan over many years, with a changing population mix and a variety of actuarial assumptions, especially those of an economic nature. The fruit of this improved technology and refined actuarial approaches is a keener perception of pension cost behavior under varied circumstances.

To a large extent this book simply quantifies and provides new or improved actuarial notation for long recognized pension cost concepts and procedures. In certain areas, however, new insights and techniques have been developed. Both types of contributions are useful and innovative. The book should serve the needs of pension actuaries of all persuasions, pension consultants, management and labor pension specialists, governmental officials with pension responsibilities, students, and others interested in the dynamics of pensions. Dr. Winklevoss is to be commended for having completed this prodigious and scholarly task.

On a more personal note, it has been an intellectually rewarding experience to work with Dr. Winklevoss on this project and other academic undertakings.

Philadelphia, Pa.   DAN M. McGILL
December 1976

Preface

Nearly ten years ago while I was studying at the University of Oregon, Mark Greene, now at the University of Georgia, encouraged me to combine my mathematical and computer interests and develop a computer model to investigate pension costs for my doctoral dissertation. My enthusiasm for the task was immediately dampened when I discovered that a comprehensive text on pension mathematics did not exist. The best piece of literature on the subject at the time was an article written by Charles Trowbridge more than 15 years earlier in the *Transactions of the Society of Actuaries*. To make matters even more difficult, this article and others I found on the subject were written under the presumption that the reader was well-grounded in actuarial concepts and, particularly, in actuarial notation. In short, my development of the computer model and the subsequent investigation of pension costs turned out to be less formidable than sorting out the mathematics of pensions.

After joining the Wharton School faculty, my colleague Dan McGill encouraged me to continue my research into pension costs. It was his belief that considerably more published information was needed on the sensitivity of pension costs to different actuarial assumptions, to various plan designs, and to alternative actuarial cost methods.

This book has been written to help fill the mathematical and numerical gap in the pension cost literature. The mathematical material presented in the book, while conforming to standard actuarial notation, begins with basic definitions and principles so that mathematicians in fields other than actuarial science, as well as actuaries, will have a comprehensive source on pension mathematics. Chapters 2 and 3 give the basic definitions of various actuarial functions, while

Chapters 5 through 9 give the mathematics of various actuarial cost methods. Much of the material presented in Chapters 10 and 11 on the mathematics of ancillary benefits is new to the actuarial science literature, as is the mathematics on early retirement given in Chapters 11 and 12.

The usefulness of the book, however, is not restricted to mathematically oriented readers. Chapter 1 introduces the subject of pension costs; parts of Chapters 2 and 3 discuss various aspects of actuarial assumptions; Chapter 4 provides background on pension plan populations; and parts of Chapter 5 deal conceptually with basic pension cost concepts, all of which will be of interest to non-mathematically oriented readers. Chapters 14 through 17 consist entirely of numerical illustrations of pension costs and are almost entirely independent of the mathematics presented in earlier chapters. Chapter 14 investigates the sensitivity of pension costs to various pension plan designs; Chapter 15 shows the sensitivity of pension costs to different actuarial assumptions; Chapter 16 gives the results of using alternative actuarial cost methods on a hypothetical pension plan population simulated over a 50-year forecast period; and Chapter 17 presents the results of numerous pension cost forecasts under different assumptions as to interest yields, salary increases, and so forth. Thus, a substantial portion of the book provides information which will be helpful to plan administrators, corporate treasurers, and other management personnel concerned with pension costs.

The author wishes to pay special tribute to Dan McGill, Professor at the Wharton School and Chairman of the Pension Research Council, for the guidance and help he offered in writing this book. My association with him over the past seven years has had a profound effect on both my knowledge of the pension institution and my interest in pension research. His careful review of several earlier versions of the book improved its quality measurably.

Cecil J. Nesbitt, Professor at the University of Michigan, reviewed two earlier versions of the book in painstaking detail, recommending both conceptual and technical improvements in the material. Glenn D. Allison, Vice President and Actuary of Winklevoss and Associates, made a significant contribution to the book. In addition to his exhaustive review of the material, my association with him as a consultant in building computer models of various pension systems has been most helpful in designing the computer model used to present the numerical illustrations in the book. Roy S. Neff, also an Actuary at Winklevoss and Associates, provided a candid and insightful analysis of the material which led to many improvements.

Other extremely valuable reviews of the book were given by Kenneth Altman, Executive Director of the New York State Employees' Retirement Systems; Gerald Cook, Supervising Actuary for the New York State Systems; Laurence E. Coward, Executive Vice President and Director, William M. Mercer, Ltd.; Donald S. Grubbs, Jr., George Buck Consulting Actuaries; Paul H. Jackson, The Wyatt Company; William F. Marples, Consulting Actuary; Charles L. Trowbridge, Senior Vice President and Chief Actuary, Bankers Life Company; Preston C. Bassett, Vice President and Actuary, Towers, Perrin, Forster & Crosby; and Blackburn H. Hazlehurst, Hazlehurst & Associates.

I am particularly indebted to my Administrative Assistant, Sandra Costantino who typed the manuscript, with all of its equations and tables, more times than either of us would like to remember. Last, and most important, is my gratitude to my wife, Carol, whose encouragement and support permitted me to immerse myself into the writing of this book to a far greater extent than a husband has a right to ask.

In spite of all of the generous help that was given to me over the past five years in the preparation of the book, I remain solely responsible for any conceptual or technical errors that may remain.

Philadelphia, Pa.   HOWARD E. WINKLEVOSS
December 1976

Contents

List of Tables

Table

Table

Table

List of Figures

Figure

Chapter 1

Pension Plan Benefits

The primary function of a pension plan is to provide income to employees in their retirement. Pension plans are not limited to providing retirement income, however, and all plans provide at least some of the following types of benefits: (1) vested termination benefits (2) disability benefits, and (3) death benefits, the latter consisting of either a lump sum death benefit or an annuity to a surviving spouse or other dependents. In this chapter, the eligibility requirements and benefit formulas typically associated with each of these various pension plan benefits are discussed, and those assumed in the numerical illustrations presented throughout this book are given.[1]

At this point it is important to distinguish between a *defined contribution* and a *defined benefit* pension plan. A defined contribution pension plan, as the name implies, is one under which a certain (defined) amount of employer (and sometime employee) contributions is set aside each year for each plan participant on a systematic basis, usually as a specified percentage of salary. The employee's pension benefit under this approach is whatever amount the contributions accumulated on the employee's behalf (with interest) will provide at retirement, taking into account the probability that the individual will survive to receive successive benefit payments and the expected investment earnings that can be made on the accumulated funds during the benefit payment period.

A defined benefit pension plan, on the other hand, is one under which the *retirement benefit* (as opposed to employer's contributions) is the defined quantity, generally related to the employee's length of service at retirement and his or her salary. A defined benefit pension

---

[1] For a comprehensive treatment of pension plan design, see Dan M. McGill, *Fundamentals of Private Pensions*, 3d ed. (Homewood, Ill.: Richard D. Irwin, 1975).

1

plan causes employer contributions to be the dependent variable, whereas under a defined contribution plan the retirement benefit is the dependent variable. The subject matter of this book deals with the defined benefit type of pension plan, but many of the underlying mathematical principles apply equally well to the defined contribution pension plan.

RETIREMENT BENEFITS

The discussion begins with the eligibility requirements and benefit formulas typically associated with retirement benefits, the most important of the benefits provided under a pension plan.

Eligibility Requirements

There are two fundamental types of eligibility requirements related to retirement benefits, one denoting the requirements for plan membership and the other denoting the requirements for retirement under the plan after membership status is attained.

The Employee Retirement Income Security Act of 1974 (ERISA) places a limit on the age and service requirements for plan membership. The law states that an employee must be eligible to join the pension plan when an age requirement of 25 *and* a service requirement of one year are satisfied.[2] Naturally, a plan can provide more liberal eligibility requirements than those specified under ERISA, and some plans have no waiting period whatsoever. Unless the plan is contributory, in which case the employee may elect not to participate, benefits usually begin to accrue at the time these membership eligibility requirements are met.

In some cases benefit accruals are granted retroactively to the employee's date of employment, but the law does not require that pre-eligibility service be included for benefit accrual purposes.

In the interest of simplicity, the pension cost data presented in this book are based on the assumption of no age or service requirement for plan membership, that is, plan membership is automatic at the date of hire.[3]

At the other end of the employment cycle are the eligibility requirements for retirement. The normal retirement age of the plan—an age stated in the plan document and frequently specified as age 65—

---

[2] If the plan provides full and immediate vesting, the eligibility requirements for plan participants can be extended to three years of service and age 25.

[3] ERISA permits the plan to exclude employees hired within five years of the plan's normal retirement age, but this provision is likewise not used for the analysis presented here.

defines early and late retirement under the plan. The traditional definition of the normal retirement age is the first age at which retirement can occur with *full* benefit accruals, however, this definition does not apply to many large corporate pension plans. Full benefit accruals are often provided at ages below the plan's normal retirement, for example, down to age 60 in a plan having age 65 as its normal retirement age. With respect to late retirement, the normal retirement age not only defines when late retirement begins, but is often the point at which benefit accruals are frozen. In addition, the normal retirement date is frequently used as the commencement date of a deferred pension benefit to a vested terminated employee and, in some cases, to a disabled employee.

The symbol r is used to denote the normal retirement age in the pension mathematics presented in later chapters, and r' is used to denote the earliest age at which an employee becomes eligible for early retirement, either with full benefit accruals or reduced benefits. Unless otherwise stated r is age 65 in the numerical examples of this book and r' is assumed to be based on the employee's age and service. The precise early retirement eligibility provision assumed is one permitting early retirement, on an actuarially reduced basis, upon the attainment of age 55 and the completion of 20 years of credited service. Thus, for most employees, r' will be age 55.

Benefit Amount

The most common type of benefit formula used in pension plans is the so-called unit benefit formula that provides a unit of benefit for each year of credited service. There are basically three such formulas associated with defined benefit plans: flat benefit, career average, and final average. The flat benefit formula is the simplest of the three, providing a flat dollar benefit, say $10 per month, for each year of service rendered by the employee. The flat unit is almost always increased at periodic intervals by plan amendment to maintain pace with the inflationary trends in the economy. Since it is not permissible under existing law to anticipate future benefit increases for funding purposes, the intermittent jumps in the unit benefit can cause some funding problems.[4]

---

[4] Although it would be possible for a firm to set its contributions according to an anticipated benefit unit increase, the minimum and maximum contribution limits must be determined without such consideration. A procedure sometimes used to solve the funding problem is to assume a noninflationary interest rate with the objective that excess investment returns will offset the cost of inflationary benefit improvements.

The second type of benefit formula, known as the career average, provides a pension benefit that is defined in terms of some stipulated percentage of the employee's career average salary. For example, a plan might define an employee's benefit accruals as 2 percent of each year's current salary.[5] It is permissible under the law to use a larger percentage for salary in excess of the average Social Security wage base than the percentage applied to salary under this level. The difference in the percentages, which is limited to a value of 1.4, is allowed so that an employer's plan can compensate for the fact that Social Security benefits are not based on total salary. Thus, if a plan were to use the maximum difference under a step rate benefit formula, in theory at least, total benefits (private pension benefits plus the portion of the Social Security benefit attributable to employer contributions) would constitute roughly the same percentage of salary for all employees regardless of their salary level. A plan using such a formula is said to be integrated with Social Security and is deemed under law not to be discriminatory in favor of highly paid employees. Although the benefit formula of the private pension plan does indeed discriminate in favor of employees whose salaries are in excess of the Social Security wage base, such discrimination is designed to offset the inherent discrimination in the benefits provided under Social Security, which favor lower-paid employees.

The third basic type of benefit formula is one that provides a given percentage of the employee's final average (or highest average) salary per year of service. Since the benefits derived from this type of benefit formula tend to be based on the employee's salary nearest retirement, the percentage provided in the formula need not be as high as that under the career average formula in order to provide the same benefit. A more precise relationship between these two benefit formulas is given in Chapter 14 under various assumptions as to salary increases.

The final average benefit formula can also be integrated with Social Security according to the step rate procedure, but in this case, the rate differential is limited to 1 percent. Moreover, the law requires that at least five consecutive years be used in determining the average salary to be used in determining the employee's benefit. For example, a plan could provide 1 percent of an employee's final five year average salary up to the applicable Social Security wage base and 2 percent on the excess salary.

---

[5] In practice, plans having a career average benefit formula are often updated by basing the past service benefits on the employee's current year's salary. Thus, an employee's retirement benefit under this formula may not represent a stipulated percentage of career average salary. The updating process causes funding problems with this benefit formula similar to those under the flat benefit formula.

Another procedure for integrating a plan with Social Security is known as the offset method. Under this procedure, which is generally used with the final average benefit formula, the retirement benefit of the plan is determined without regard to the Social Security wage base, but the benefit so determined is offset (reduced) by a certain portion of the retiring employee's primary insurance amount (PIA) under Social Security. The typical procedure is to deduct a certain percentage of the PIA, say $1\frac{1}{2}$ percent per year of service. However, no more than a total of $83\frac{1}{3}$ percent of the employee's PIA at retirement can be offset against the basic pension benefit. In addition, the provisions of ERISA require that the Social Security offset be frozen at retirement, allowing future increases in the Social Security PIA to inure entirely to the benefit of the retired employee.

The benefit formula used in this book to illustrate pension costs is one providing a benefit of $1\frac{1}{2}$ percent of the participant's final five year average salary for each year of credited service. The benefit formula is not assumed to be integrated with Social Security on either the step rate or offset basis. The latter assumption is made to simplify the various analyses, but it should be noted that many pension plans are indeed integrated with Social Security. The normal annuity form is assumed to be a straight life annuity and the benefits payable for early retirement are assumed to be actuarially reduced to reflect the cost of the early benefit payments.

VESTED BENEFITS

An employee is said to be vested in his or her accrued benefit when its payment at retirement is no longer contingent upon the employee remaining in the service of the employer. When an employee with vested benefits terminates employment, that employee is entitled to a benefit commencing at his or her early or normal retirement age in the amount of his or her vested accruals.

Eligibility Requirements

ERISA allows the sponsors of a pension plan to select one of three vesting provisions in satisfaction of the minimum vesting requirements.[6] The simplest one, and the one used to illustrate pension costs in this book, is full vesting after ten years of service. A second alternative involves graded vesting, providing 25 percent vesting after

---

[6] It is possible that a plan would be required to provide more liberal vesting than the minimum requirement under ERISA if the actual operation of the vesting provision appeared to favor highly paid employees.

five years of service, increasing by 5 percent per year for the next five years and 10 percent per year for the next five years. This schedule results in full vesting after 15 years of service. The third and final minimum vesting provision allowed under ERISA is known as the Rule of 45. This method provides for 50 percent vesting when the participant's age and years of service total 45, and an additional 10 percent for each of the five subsequent years. A plan using this standard may require a minimum of five years of service before the vesting schedule begins, but the 50 percent vesting and subsequent grading must begin after ten years of service irrespective of the age-service total. This is a complicated alternative indeed.

If the maximum eligibility requirements for plan membership (age 25 and one year of service) are used, only service rendered prior to age 22 can be excluded for determining an employee's vesting status (except under the Rule of 45). The relative cost of vesting among these three alternative vesting schedules is analyzed in Chapter 14.

Benefit Amount

In most cases, the benefit accruals used to determine the vested benefit are those defined by application of the basic benefit formula. The law has established guidelines to prevent "backloading," a pattern of attained age benefit accruals which could render the vesting provision virtually meaningless over most ages. In all cases benefits attributable to employee contributions are fully and immediately vested. At the time of termination, an employee may be entitled to a return of his or her contributions, usually with interest, instead of leaving them in the plan and receiving a deferred retirement benefit. Prior to the passage of ERISA, the employee's election to take back his contributions generally had the effect of forfeiting benefits associated with employer contributions.[7]

DISABILITY BENEFITS

There are fundamentally two types of disability benefits found in pension plans, one providing a deferred pension to a disabled employee beginning at age 65 and the second providing an annuity that begins after a specified waiting period. The former type is generally found in combination with a long-term disability (LTD)

---

[7] If an employee is vested in less than 50 percent of his or her benefit and withdraws his or her contributions at the time of termination, forfeiture of benefits associated with employer contributions may still be invoked, subject to a buy-back provision.

benefit program operating outside the pension plan, since the LTD policy usually provides the desired level of benefit from the point of disability up to the normal retirement age.

Eligibility Requirements

The eligibility provisions for disability benefits vary widely among plans, but a minimum age or service requirement, or both, usually exists. It is not uncommon to have the disability entitlement coincide with the eligibility for early retirement, for example, age 55 and 20 years of service. Or it may coincide with the eligibility for vesting. The provision used in this book is one that pays benefits equal to the employee's full accrued benefits if the employee is at least age 40 and has at least 15 years of service.

Benefit Amount

The most common procedure in determining the benefits payable upon disability is to apply the basic benefit formula of the plan to the employee's salary and years of service at the time of disability. Some plans use the total potential service of the employee up to age 65 instead of the service up to the data of disability. This is almost invariably the case if the disability pension is the deferred type. The benefit assumed throughout this book, however, is the full, unreduced accrued benefit of the employee payable immediately at the time of disability for life.

DEATH BENEFITS

The death benefit under a pension plan payable on behalf of active employees may consist of a lump sum distribution, such as the return of accumulated employee contributions or some multiple of the deceased employee's salary, or it may take the form of an annuity payable to a surviving spouse. This book considers only the latter type. Death benefits may also be associated with non-active employees, especially retired employees. The various types of annuity options that precipitate such a benefit upon the death of the pensioner are considered in Chapter 3.

Eligibility Requirements

The eligibility provision for a surviving spouse benefit is generally related to the early retirement eligibility requirements. In fact, ERISA requires that a spouse's option be made available to plan members at the later of the eligibility for early retirement or ten years prior to normal retirement. The benefit payable under this mandatory option, however, can be adjusted to cover the cost of providing the spouse's benefit.

The provision used to illustrate pension costs in this book is one that provides a surviving spouse benefit after qualification for early retirement has been met, that is, age 55 and 20 years of service.

Benefit Amount

One procedure for determining the surviving spouse's benefit is to provide some proportion of the deceased participant's benefit accruals. A common formula is one providing 50 percent of the participant's attained age accruals, and ERISA requires that an option of at least this amount be made available to employees. In the cost illustrations presented later, the benefit payable is assumed to be 50 percent of the employee's attained age benefit accruals without an actuarial reduction to reflect the cost of the surviving spouse benefit. This benefit is assumed to be payable for life or until the remarriage of the spouse.

SUMMARY OF PLAN PROVISIONS

The plan provisions assumed in the numerical illustrations presented in this book are summarized below.

I. Retirement Benefits
   A. Eligibility:
      1. Normal Retirement . . . . Age 65
      2. Early Retirement . . . . Age 55 and 20 years of service
      3. Late Retirement. . . . . Not applicable
   B. Benefit . . . . $1\frac{1}{2}$ percent of final five-year average salary per year of service, not integrated with Social Security, payable for life, actuarially reduced for early retirement

II. Vested Benefits
     A. Eligibility . . . .   Full vesting after
                                                  ten years of service
     B. Benefit . . . .   Accrued benefit
                                                  (determined by
                                                  applying the
                                                  retirement benefit
                                                  formula to current
                                                  salary and service),
                                                  payable at age 65
                                                  for life

III. Disability Benefits
     A. Eligibility . . . .   Age 40 and 15 years
                                                  of service
     B. Benefit . . . .   Accrued unreduced
                                                  benefit, payable
                                                  immediately for life

IV. Surviving Spouse Benefit (Pre-Retirement Only)
     A. Eligibility . . . .   Age 55 and 20 years
                                                  of service
     B. Benefit . . . .   50 percent of
                                                  accrued unreduced
                                                  benefit, payable
                                                  immediately for life
                                                  or until spouse
                                                  remarries

Chapter 2

Actuarial Assumptions

The purpose of this chapter is to set forth the basic actuarial assumptions required in analyzing pension costs. These include assumptions relating to the various rates of decrement applicable to plan members, assumptions used to estimate each member's future salary for plans that require such an estimate, and an assumption reflecting the time value of money.

In addition to a general discussion of actuarial assumptions, the specific assumptions that are used to illustrate pension costs throughout this text are presented. These assumptions, although referred to as "standard assumptions" for use in this book, are not in any sense standard for plans in practice. Notwithstanding this qualification, the assumptions used in this book are believed to be more or less typical of the large corporate plan.

DECREMENT ASSUMPTIONS

Pension plan participants in active service are exposed to the contingencies of death, disablement, early withdrawal from employment, and retirement, while nonactive members are exposed to death.[1] These various contingencies are considered in pension mathematics through the use of rates of decrement. A distinction must be made between a rate of decrement and a probability of decrement, with the latter being defined for both a single-decrement environment and a multiple-decrement environment.

---

[1] Technically, some classes of non-active participants are "exposed" to the contingency of re-entry into active status, or what one might term an incremental assumption. This contingency and a corresponding rate of increment are not considered in the mathematics developed in this book; however, increments to the entire active membership via new hires are considered in later chapters.

A rate of decrement refers to the proportion of participants leaving a particular status due to a given cause, under the assumptions that there are no other decrements applicable. If such a rate is used in a single-decrement environment (that is, where there are in fact no other decrements applicable), it is also equal to the probability of decrement. For example, retired employees exist in a single-decrement environment, being exposed only to mortality, and the applicable rate of mortality at a given age is identical to the probability of dying at that age. However, if the rate of decrement is used in a multiple-decrement environment (that is, where more than one decrement is operating), it is *not* equal to the probability of decrement. For example, active employees exist in a multiple-decrement environment, being exposed to mortality, withdrawal, disability, and retirement. The applicable rate of mortality is *not* equal to the probability of dying because other decremental rates prevent the participants from being exposed to the mortality decrement throughout the entire year.

A typical assumption for transforming a *rate* of decrement into a *probability* of decrement in a multiple-decrement environment is that all decrements occur on a uniform basis throughout the year. If $q'^{(k)}$ is the rate of decrement for cause k and $q^{(k)}$ is the probability of decrement, the transformation of a rate into a probability in a double-decrement environment ($k = 1,2$) under the uniform distribution of death (UDD) assumption is as follows:

$$q^{(1)} = q'^{(1)}[1 - \tfrac{1}{2}q'^{(2)}]. \tag{2.1a}$$

The value of $q^{(2)}$ would be found in an analogous way. The value of $q^{(1)}$ in a three decrement environment ($k = 1,2,3$) becomes

$$q^{(1)} = q'^{(1)}[1 - \tfrac{1}{2}(q'^{(2)} + q'^{(3)}) + \tfrac{1}{3}q'^{(2)}q'^{(3)}], \tag{2.1b}$$

and for a four-decrement environment ($k = 1,2,3,4$), we have

$$\begin{aligned} q^{(1)} = q'^{(1)}[1 &- \tfrac{1}{2}(q'^{(2)} + q'^{(3)} + q'^{(4)} \\ &+ \tfrac{1}{3}(q'^{(2)}q'^{(3)} + q'^{(2)}q'^{(4)} + q'^{(3)}q'^{(4)}) \\ &- \tfrac{1}{4}(q'^{(2)}q'^{(3)}q'^{(4)})]. \end{aligned} \tag{2.1c}$$

The mathematics and numerical analysis presented in this book are based on an approximation to the above UDD assumption in the case of more than two decrements. The value of $q^{(1)}$ in the three- and four-decrement environment is approximated by the following:

$$\begin{aligned} q^{(1)} &\doteqdot q'^{(1)}[1 - \tfrac{1}{2}q'^{(2)}][1 - \tfrac{1}{2}q'^{(3)}] \\ &\doteqdot q'^{(1)}[1 - \tfrac{1}{2}(q'^{(2)} + q'^{(3)}) + \tfrac{1}{4}q'^{(2)}q'^{(3)}] \end{aligned} \tag{2.2a}$$

$$q^{(1)} \doteqdot q'^{(1)}[1 - \tfrac{1}{2}q'^{(2)}][1 - \tfrac{1}{2}q'^{(3)}][1 - \tfrac{1}{2}q'^{(4)}]$$
$$\doteqdot q'^{(1)}[1 - (q'^{(2)} + q'^{(3)} + q'^{(4)})$$
$$+ \tfrac{1}{4}(q'^{(2)}q'^{(3)} + q'^{(2)}q'^{(4)} + q'^{(3)}q'^{(4)}) \qquad (2.2b)$$
$$- \tfrac{1}{8}q'^{(2)}q'^{(3)}q'^{(4)}].$$

The error involved with the above is quite small, causing $q^{(1)}$ to be understated by $\tfrac{1}{12}q'^{(2)}q'^{(3)}$ for the three-decrement case and by

$$\tfrac{1}{12}(q'^{(2)}q'^{(3)} + q'^{(2)}q'^{(4)} + q'^{(3)}q'^{(4)}) - \tfrac{1}{8}q'^{(2)}q'^{(3)}q'^{(4)}$$

for the four-decrement case.

The above shows, and general reasoning would suggest, that in a multiple-decrement environment the probability of decrement is *smaller* than the rate of decrement. The degree of reduction in the rate, of course, is dependent on the number and magnitudes of the competing decrements. In a pension plan environment the reduction can be substantial for active employees, owing both to the number of decrements and to the relative size of some decrements such as withdrawals and retirements.

The following discussion of the various decrements associated with pension plans is based on rates of decrement, and probabilities of decrements in a single-decrement environment, in spite of the fact that for active participants these decrements act together in a multiple-decrement environment. Chapter 3 considers the latter case.

As indicated above, a rate of decrement (or a probability of decrement in a single-decrement environment) is denoted by $q'^{(k)}$ while the corresponding probability of decrement in a multiple-decrement environment is denoted by this symbol without the prime. The following rates will be discussed in this chapter:

$$q'^{(m)} = \text{mortality rate}$$
$$q'^{(w)} = \text{withdrawal rate}$$
$$q'^{(d)} = \text{disability rate}$$
$$q'^{(r)} = \text{retirement rate.}$$

Mortality Decrement

Mortality among active employees prevents the attainment of a retirement status and hence the receipt of a pension benefit, while mortality among pensioners acts to terminate the payment of their pension benefit. Although mortality terminates the primary pension benefit, it often creates another form of benefit obligation. As noted in the previous chapter, it is not uncommon to find plans for which mortality prior to retirement causes a death payment to be made in the form of a lump sum based on a flat-dollar amount of some multiple of salary, or in the form of an annual payment to the surviving spouse either for a specified period of time or for life. Similarly, death in retirement quite frequently results in the continuation of all or some portion of the deceased's pension, either to his or her estate, to a surviving spouse, or to some other, third-party beneficiary.

Age is the most obvious factor related to mortality rates. Annual mortality rates become progressively higher as age increases, beginning at approximately 0.05 percent at age 20 and increasing to 100 percent at the end of the human life span, generally assumed to be age 100 or 110. A second factor related to mortality is the sex of the employee or pensioner. Females tend to have lower mortality rates than males at every age. It is not entirely clear what causes this result, but empirical studies have shown that for ages near retirement, a 5-year age setback in the male table allows one to achieve a reasonably good approximation to the female mortality rate, while a somewhat larger setback at younger ages and a smaller setback at older ages are required to achieve the same result. There are other factors, such as occupation, that tend to be related to mortality, but these usually are not taken into account unless the circumstances call for a more refined evaluation of employee mortality.

If the pension plan population is large, a mortality rate schedule based solely on its past experience may be developed. The construction of such a table normally involves some combination of the most recent mortality experience of the group, past trends in its mortality, and a subjective element reflecting anticipated future mortality. A somewhat more sophisticated approach is to develop a series of mortality rate schedules, one for each future calendar year. The theory underlying this procedure is that the mortality rate for an employee currently age x, for example, will be different from the mortality rate of an employee reaching this age 10 or 20 years from the present time.

The mortality rate assumption used to illustrate various pension costs throughout this book, and referred to hereafter as one of the book's standard assumptions, is the GAM–1971 male mortality schedule set out in Table 2–1.

The probability of an individual's surviving to age 65 is an important parameter of pension plan mathematics and costs. If the rate

TABLE 2–1

1971 Male Group Annuity Mortality Rates

x	$q_x^{\prime(m)}$	x	$q_x^{\prime(m)}$	x	$q_x^{\prime(m)}$	x	$q_x^{\prime(m)}$	x	$q_x^{\prime(m)}$
20	0.00050	40	0.00163	60	0.01312	80	0.08743	100	0.32983
21	0.00052	41	0.00179	61	0.01444	81	0.09545	101	0.35245
22	0.00054	42	0.00200	62	0.01586	82	0.10369	102	0.37722
23	0.00057	43	0.00226	63	0.01741	83	0.11230	103	0.40621
24	0.00059	44	0.00257	64	0.01919	84	0.12112	104	0.44150
25	0.00062	45	0.00292	65	0.02126	85	0.13010	105	0.48518
26	0.00065	46	0.00332	66	0.02364	86	0.13931	106	0.53934
27	0.00068	47	0.00375	67	0.02632	87	0.14871	107	0.60609
28	0.00072	48	0.00423	68	0.02919	88	0.15849	108	0.68747
29	0.00076	49	0.00474	69	0.03244	89	0.16871	109	0.78543
30	0.00081	50	0.00528	70	0.03611	90	0.17945	110	1.00000
31	0.00086	51	0.00587	71	0.04001	91	0.19049		
32	0.00092	52	0.00648	72	0.04383	92	0.20168		
33	0.00098	53	0.00713	73	0.04749	93	0.21299		
34	0.00105	54	0.00781	74	0.05122	94	0.22653		
35	0.00112	55	0.00852	75	0.05529	95	0.24116		
36	0.00120	56	0.00926	76	0.06007	96	0.25620		
37	0.00129	57	0.01004	77	0.06592	97	0.27248		
38	0.00140	58	0.01089	78	0.07260	98	0.29016		
39	0.00151	59	0.01192	79	0.07969	99	0.30912		

of mortality at age x is denoted by $q_x^{\prime(m)}$, the probability of a life age x living to age $x + 1$, assuming no other decrements, is given by the complement of the mortality rate and denoted by $p_x^{\prime(m)}$. For the general case, the probability of a life age x living n years is denoted by $_np_x^{\prime(m)}$ and may be expressed in terms of the specific rates of mortality at age x through age $x + n - 1$ as follows:

$$_np_x^{\prime(m)} = \prod_{t=0}^{n-1} (1 - q_{x+t}^{\prime(m)}) = \prod_{t=0}^{n-1} p_{x+t}^{\prime(m)}. \tag{2.3}$$

If we exclude consideration of other decrements, as in the above formulation, then pension costs are directly proportional to the probability of surviving to retirement. Similarly, once retirement is reached, the probability of surviving to each successive retirement age has a significant impact on the cost of providing a retirement pension. The probability of surviving to normal retirement age, $_{r-x}p_x^{\prime(m)}$ for $x \leqslant r$, and the probability of surviving beyond this age, $_{x-r}p_r^{\prime(m)}$ for $x \geqslant r$, are given in Table 2–2 for various values of x and $r = 65$.[2]

---

[2] Since retired employees exist in a single-decrement environment, the rate of mortality and the probability of mortality are identical, making the prime symbol on $_{x-r}p_r^{\prime(m)}$ unnecessary, but it is retained here for clarity.

TABLE 2–2

Mortality-Based Survival Probabilities

x	$_{65-x}p_x^{\prime(m)}$	x	$_{x-65}p_{65}^{\prime(m)}$
20	0.8099	65	1.0000
25	0.8121	70	0.8740
30	0.8149	75	0.6988
35	0.8187	80	0.4947
40	0.8241	85	0.2856
45	0.8326	90	0.1273
50	0.8485	95	0.0411
55	0.8767	100	0.0083
60	0.9225	105	0.0007
65	1.0000	110	0.0000

These probabilities illustrate that retirement-related pension costs are reduced by 10 to 20 percent by pre-retirement mortality. For example, if 40 were the average age of the typical group of active employees, pension costs would be reduced by approximately 18 percent due to the mortality assumption, since $_{25}p_{40}^{\prime(m)}$ is equal to 0.8241. This cost reduction, however, could be more than offset by a pre-retirement death benefit. Pension costs after retirement, of course, are affected significantly by the post-retirement survival probability, $_{x-r}p_r^{\prime(m)}$, which approaches zero at an ever-increasing rate as x increases.

Withdrawal Decrement

The withdrawal or termination decrement, like the mortality decrement, prevents employees from attaining retirement age and receiving benefits under the plan. An employee may not forfeit his entire pension upon withdrawal, however, if he has satisfied the plan's requirements for vesting.[3] Thus, while termination of employment acts to prevent the employee from receiving his normal retirement benefit, and in turn tends to lower pension costs, vesting allows the employee to maintain a claim against a portion of the pension benefit that he would receive if he were to remain in employment. This, of course, mitigates the full cost reduction that would otherwise be associated with the withdrawal decrement.

There are a multitude of factors entering into the determination of employee termination rates, but two factors consistently found to have

---

[3] In this and subsequent passages the male pronoun is used for succinctness; it is understood to include both males and females.

significant relationship are age and length of service. The older the employee and/or the longer his period of service, the less likely it is that he will terminate employment. Consequently, withdrawal rate schedules frequently have both an age and a service dimension. These schedules are called select and ultimate termination rates, the term "select" referring to the rates applicable for a period beyond the employee's entry age and the term "ultimate" referring to the rates applicable to ages beyond the point for which the length of service is important. Most schedules have a three or five year select period. It is not uncommon to find actuaries using a withdrawal schedule based on age alone for ease of computation, but this practice is gradually disappearing in favor of at least an age-service schedule for large corporate pension plans. In some cases, additional dimensions are used, such as sex, occupational level, and vesting status. Finally, just as the rates of mortality might change over time, the rates of termination may also change. In this case a series of termination rate schedules would be used, reflecting historical trends and subjective estimates of expected future trends in employee withdrawal.

Table 2–3 shows the age-service termination rate schedule to be used in illustrating pension costs in this book, given by quinquennial entry ages from 20 to 60. Since the plan to which these rates are applicable permits early retirement at age 55 with 20 years of service, the termination rates are zero at and beyond the first age for which a given entrant qualifies for early retirement.

The rate of withdrawal at age x for a participant entering the plan at age y is denoted by $q_x'^{(w)}$.[4] The probability that the employee will remain in service for one year, excluding consideration of other rates of decrement, is equal to the complement of this rate, that is, $p_x'^{(w)} = 1 - q_x'^{(w)}$. The probability of surviving n years may be found by taking the product of n such complements, from age x to age $x + n - 1$. Table 2–4 gives the probability of remaining in service until retirement age from each entry age shown, based on the standard termination rate schedule, and the probability of remaining in service until the first vesting age (or age 65 if sooner) under the full-vesting-in-ten-years provision.[5]

---

[4] It is assumed that this rate is also based on the employee's entry age y, although the symbol does not make this functional relationship explicit. An appropriate symbol might be $q_{y,x}'^{(w)}$, but this is not used in the interest of simplicity.

[5] Note the use of the symbol y in Table 2–4 to denote the employee's entry age, a convention used throughout this book.

TABLE 2–3

Termination Rates, $q_x^{'(w)}$

					Entry Ages, y				
x	20	25	30	35	40	45	50	55	60
20...	0.2431								
21...	0.2245								
22...	0.2071								
23...	0.1908								
24...	0.1757								
25...	0.1616	0.2119							
26...	0.1486	0.1749							
27...	0.1365	0.1506							
28...	0.1254	0.1340							
29...	0.1152	0.1207							
30...	0.1059	0.1059	0.1682						
31...	0.0974	0.0974	0.1397						
32...	0.0896	0.0896	0.1160						
33...	0.0827	0.0827	0.0966						
34...	0.0764	0.0764	0.0814						
35...	0.0708	0.0708	0.0708	0.1281					
36...	0.0658	0.0658	0.0658	0.1013					
37...	0.0614	0.0614	0.0614	0.0820					
38...	0.0575	0.0575	0.0575	0.0684					
39...	0.0541	0.0541	0.0541	0.0586					
40...	0.0512	0.0512	0.0512	0.0512	0.0942				
41...	0.0487	0.0487	0.0487	0.0487	0.0751				
42...	0.0466	0.0466	0.0466	0.0466	0.0616				
43...	0.0448	0.0448	0.0448	0.0448	0.0526				
44...	0.0433	0.0433	0.0433	0.0433	0.0466				
45...	0.0421	0.0421	0.0421	0.0421	0.0421	0.0686			
46...	0.0410	0.0410	0.0410	0.0410	0.0410	0.0547			
47...	0.0402	0.0402	0.0402	0.0402	0.0402	0.0463			
48...	0.0394	0.0394	0.0394	0.0394	0.0394	0.0420			
49...	0.0388	0.0388	0.0388	0.0388	0.0388	0.0399			
50...	0.0382	0.0382	0.0382	0.0382	0.0382	0.0382	0.0538		
51...	0.0376	0.0376	0.0376	0.0376	0.0376	0.0376	0.0462		
52...	0.0370	0.0370	0.0370	0.0370	0.0370	0.0370	0.0417		
53...	0.0362	0.0362	0.0362	0.0362	0.0362	0.0362	0.0391		
54...	0.0354	0.0354	0.0354	0.0354	0.0354	0.0354	0.0371		
55...	0.0000	0.0000	0.0000	0.0000	0.0345	0.0345	0.0345	0.0522	
56...	0.0000	0.0000	0.0000	0.0000	0.0333	0.0333	0.0333	0.0419	
57...	0.0000	0.0000	0.0000	0.0000	0.0319	0.0319	0.0319	0.0359	
58...	0.0000	0.0000	0.0000	0.0000	0.0302	0.0302	0.0302	0.0324	
59...	0.0000	0.0000	0.0000	0.0000	0.0281	0.0281	0.0281	0.0297	
60...	0.0000	0.0000	0.0000	0.0000	0.0000	0.0258	0.0258	0.0258	0.0500
61...	0.0000	0.0000	0.0000	0.0000	0.0000	0.0230	0.0230	0.0230	0.0343
62...	0.0000	0.0000	0.0000	0.0000	0.0000	0.0197	0.0197	0.0197	0.0258
63...	0.0000	0.0000	0.0000	0.0000	0.0000	0.0160	0.0160	0.0160	0.0199
64...	0.0000	0.0000	0.0000	0.0000	0.0000	0.0118	0.0118	0.0118	0.0127

TABLE 2–4

**Termination-Based Survival
Probabilities for Various Entry Ages**

Entry Age y	$_{10}p_y'^{(w)}$	$_{65-y}p_y'^{(w)}$
20	0.1481	0.0355
25	0.2618	0.1009
30	0.3813	0.2023
35	0.4961	0.3347
40	0.5781	0.4080
45	0.6400	0.4945
50	0.6815	0.6183
55	0.7457	0.7457
60	0.8648*	0.8648

*Equal to $_5p_{60}'^{(w)}$.

It is clear that retirement-related costs, especially for younger employees, are significantly reduced by the withdrawal assumption.[6] While it is true that vesting prevents a forfeiture of the employee's pension upon termination, the chances that an entrant at a young age will become vested are also rather small for this set of termination rates, and a vested benefit is generally much smaller than the employee's normal retirement benefit. Thus, the cost associated with vesting will not be nearly as great as the cost reduction due to the withdrawal assumption; hence, the withdrawal decrement reduces total pension costs in spite of the fact that vesting adds to the plan's costs. The relative cost associated with retirement and vesting is studied in Chapter 14.

Disability Decrement

Disability among active employees, like mortality and withdrawal, prevents qualification for a retirement benefit and, in turn, lowers the cost of retirement. This cost reduction, however, is offset to some extent if the plan provides a disability benefit. As noted in the previous chapter, a typical disability benefit might provide an annual pension, beginning after a waiting period, based on the employee's benefits accrued to data, or on his projected normal retirement benefit. When

---

[6] Pension liabilities for the entire plan may not be as sensitive to the withdrawal decrement as one might conclude from the probabilities given in Table 2–4. This is the case since older employees, for whom the termination decrements are small, make up a disproportionately large amount of the total liability.

TABLE 2–5

Disabled-Life Mortality Rates

x	$^dq_x'^{(m)}$	x	$^dq_x'^{(m)}$	x	$^dq_x'^{(m)}$	x	$^dq_x'^{(m)}$	x	$^dq_x'^{(m)}$
20	0.00840	40	0.01454	60	0.03488	80	0.09654	100	0.35919
21	0.00853	41	0.01151	61	0.03663	81	0.10171	101	0.40694
22	0.00872	42	0.01570	62	0.03847	82	0.10715	102	0.46409
23	0.00891	43	0.01633	63	0.04042	83	0.11287	103	0.53204
24	0.00910	44	0.01699	64	0.04248	84	0.11890	104	0.61229
25	0.00930	45	0.01770	65	0.04465	85	0.12524	105	0.07064
26	0.00951	46	0.01845	66	0.04695	86	0.13191	106	0.81619
27	0.00973	47	0.01924	67	0.04938	87	0.13893	107	0.94334
28	0.00996	48	0.02009	68	0.05195	88	0.14630	108	1.00000
29	0.01021	49	0.02097	69	0.05466	89	0.15404		
30	0.01048	50	0.02191	70	0.05754	90	0.16219		
31	0.01077	51	0.02290	71	0.06056	91	0.17094		
32	0.01108	52	0.02395	72	0.06375	92	0.18059		
33	0.01141	53	0.02506	73	0.06713	93	0.19154		
34	0.01177	54	0.02624	74	0.07069	94	0.20429		
35	0.01216	55	0.02749	75	0.07444	95	0.21944		
36	0.01258	56	0.02881	76	0.07841	96	0.23769		
37	0.01303	57	0.03020	77	0.08259	97	0.25984		
38	0.01351	58	0.03167	78	0.08700	98	0.28679		
39	0.01401	59	0.03323	79	0.09165	99	0.31954		

disability benefits are provided outside the pension plan, it is common to continue crediting the disabled employee with service until normal retirement, at which time the auxiliary plan's benefits cease and the employee begins receiving a normal pension. The mortality rate assumption under either type of benefit must be based on disabled-life mortality instead of the mortality rates applicable to other plan members.

The disabled-life mortality used in this book is given in Table 2–5, and survival probabilities based on these rates are given in Table 2–6,

TABLE 2–6

Disabled-Life Survival Probabilities

x	$^dp_{65-x}'^{(m)}$	x	$^dp_{x-65}'^{(m)}$
20	0.4234	65	1.0000
25	0.4424	70	0.7757
30	0.4646	75	0.5575
35	0.4913	80	0.3618
40	0.5246	85	0.2049
45	0.5659	90	0.0968
50	0.6238	95	0.0354
55	0.7044	100	0.0076
60	0.8214	105	0.0003
65	1.0000	110	0.0000

where $^dq_x^{\prime(m)}$ and $^dp_x^{\prime(m)}$ denote the disabled-life mortality rate and survival probability, respectively. Comparing these rates and probabilities with those in Tables 2–1 and 2–2 reveals that disabled-life mortality is significantly greater than the mortality rate of non-disabled lives.

There are several factors related to rates of disability among active employees, the most notable ones being age, sex, and occupation. In the interest of simplicity, and since disability benefits generally represent a relatively small portion of total pension plan costs, the standard disability assumption used to illustrate costs in this book is related to age alone. These rates are given in Table 2–7 and the corresponding symbol is $q_x^{\prime(d)}$. If one considers *only* the disability decrement, the probability of surviving n years is the product of n complements, $1 - q_x^{\prime(d)}$, for ages x through $x + n - 1$.

TABLE 2–7

Disability Rates

x	$q_x^{\prime(d)}$	x	$q_x^{\prime(d)}$	x	$q_x^{\prime(d)}$
20	0.0003	35	0.0004	50	0.0031
21	0.0003	36	0.0005	51	0.0034
22	0.0003	37	0.0006	52	0.0038
23	0.0003	38	0.0007	53	0.0042
24	0.0003	39	0.0008	54	0.0046
25	0.0003	40	0.0009	55	0.0050
26	0.0003	41	0.0010	56	0.0054
27	0.0003	42	0.0012	57	0.0060
28	0.0003	43	0.0014	58	0.0068
29	0.0003	44	0.0016	59	0.0080
30	0.0004	45	0.0018	60	0.0098
31	0.0004	46	0.0020	61	0.0124
32	0.0004	47	0.0022	62	0.0160
33	0.0004	48	0.0025	63	0.0208
34	0.0004	49	0.0028	64	0.0270

Table 2–8 illustrates disability-related survival probabilities by giving the probability of surviving to age 65 for quinquennial ages from 20 through 60. These rates indicate that retirement-related costs are reduced 10 to 15 percent as a result of the disability decrement, an effect quite similar to that of the mortality rate decrement. The added cost of providing disability benefits, relative to the reduced cost of retirement benefits, is studied at a later point in this book.

TABLE 2–8

Disability-Based Survival Probabilities

x	$_{65-x}p'^{(d)}_x$	x	$_{65-x}p'^{(d)}_x$
20	0.8498	45	0.8619
25	0.8511	50	0.8717
30	0.8524	55	0.8886
35	0.8541	60	0.9168
40	0.8567	65	1.0000

Retirement Decrement

Unlike the other decremental factors that prevent the receipt of a regular retirement pension, the retirement decrement among active employees initiates the pension payments.

Retirement prior to the plan's normal retirement age, as noted in the previous chapter, is called early retirement. The benefits paid to employees retiring early are generally less than the benefit accruals earned to date of early retirement. This reduction may be a flat percentage per year prior to normal retirement, such as 6 percent, or it may be what is known as an acturial equivalent reduction. The latter is a reduction reflecting as precisely as possible the loss of interest, the loss of the benefit of survivorship, and the longer life expectancy associated with early retirement.[7] The subject of actuarial equivalence and the financial implications of providing a greater-than-actuarially-equivalent early retirement benefit are taken up in considerable detail in Chapters 12 and 13.

The degree to which employees elect to retire early, given the fact that the plan permits early retirement, is a function of numerous economic and sociological factors. Length of service, health status, level of pension benefits, occupational status, sex, and the ages for which Social Security benefits are payable tend to be related to the incidence of early retirement. Other factors, no doubt, could be detected in a given plan, and since the basis of early retirement varies widely among plans, retirement rates are generally constructed from the experience of the particular plan under consideration. Although it has been customary to use an average retirement age as a surrogate for the more precise early (and late) retirement distribution, age-specific

---

[7] The benefit of survivorship is explained at a later point in this book. It essentially refers to the concept that a portion of the benefits of those employees who survive in service is provided by the forfeiture of contributions made on behalf of those who do not survive.

rates over the eligible retirement ages, for example, from age 55 through age 70, are frequently used in connection with large corporate plans. Since there has been a distinct trend toward increased early retirement in recent years, the early retirement assumption might have a larger subjective factor as to future rates of early retirement than is the case with the other actuarial assumptions discussed up to this point.

The retirement rate of decrement at age x is denoted by $q_x'^{(r)}$. Although the subject of early retirement is analyzed at various points in this book, pension costs are determined under a single retirement age for the book's standard assumptions, the single age being 65.

Figure 2–1 shows a graph of the mortality-based, withdrawal-based, and disability-based survival probabilities to age 65 from age x for an age-30 entrant under standard assumptions. The withdrawal-based survival probability is by far the most significant of the three at ages below 50, whereas the mortality-based and disability-based survival probabilities are quite similar, as noted earlier. Figure 2–1 does not portray the retirement-based survival probability, since this function would simply be unity at all ages under the standard assumption that retirement occurs at age 65.

FIGURE 2–1

Single Decrement Survival Probabilities from Age x to Age 65.

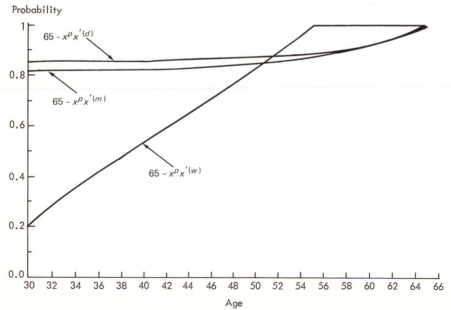

SALARY ASSUMPTION

The benefits of a pension plan and its contributions are often a function of the employee's salary. In these cases an estimate of the employee's future salary is required. This estimate involves consideration of three factors: (1) salary increases due to merit, (2) increases due to labor's share of productivity gains, and (3) increases due to inflation.[8]

Merit Component

Merit increases are those that an individual employee will receive as he progresses through his career and that are theoretically based on his ability to perform at a more competent or responsible level as he becomes older and accumulates more years of service with the firm. The percentage of pay increase from this source typically diminishes as the employee becomes older. Since such raises are exclusive of inflation or overall productivity gains achieved by the employment group as a whole, they are not likely to have much effect on the aggregate payroll of all employees over time, unless the distribution of employees by age and service changes significantly. In other words, as the existing group of employees grows older and earns larger salaries due to merit increases, there is a continual flow of new employees into the lower job classifications. The net result is a relatively stable year-to-year distribution of merit-related salaries for the entire group of active employees.

The merit scale used as a component in the projection of an employee's salary can be estimated from a homogeneous group of employees by comparing the differences in salaries among employees at various ages and with various periods of service for a given year. A cross-sectional analysis of this type eliminates the effect of inflation and productivity on the merit scale.

The merit scale used to illustrate pension costs in this book is given in Table 2–9. Since this scale is unity at age 20, an employee entering at this age will have an age-64 salary 2.8 times greater than his entry-age salary due to merit increases alone. Similarly, an age-30 entrant will have a salary multiple of 1.9 at retirement, determined by dividing the age-65 factor by the age-30 factor (2.769 ÷ 1.487). The merit scale shows a continually decreasing rate of salary progression beginning at 4.5 percent at age 20 and declining to nearly zero by age 64.

---

[8] Another factor that is sometimes relevant is a "catch up" or "slow down" allowance, but this does not constitute a theoretical component to the long-run salary increase assumption.

TABLE 2–9

Merit Salary Scale

x	Scale	x	Scale	x	Scale
20	1.000	35	1.749	50	2.460
21	1.045	36	1.802	51	2.497
22	1.091	37	1.854	52	2.532
23	1.138	38	1.906	53	2.565
24	1.186	39	1.958	54	2.596
25	1.234	40	2.008	55	2.624
26	1.284	41	2.059	56	2.651
27	1.334	42	2.108	57	2.674
28	1.384	43	2.157	58	2.696
29	1.436	44	2.204	59	2.715
30	1.487	45	2.250	60	2.731
31	1.539	46	2.295	61	2.745
32	1.592	47	2.339	62	2.756
33	1.644	48	2.381	63	2.764
34	1.697	49	2.422	64	2.769

Productivity Component

The second factor that affects the salaries of the entire group of employees is labor's share of productivity gains. This factor has diminished in importance over the years, and it varies among industries. In the interest of simplicity, a productivity component of 1 percent per annum is assumed in connection with the numerical results presented in this book.[9]

Inflation Component

The third and perhaps the most powerful factor entering into the projection of an employee's future salary is inflation. This component, unlike the merit component, which generally increases salary at a decreasing rate, is more likely to increase the salary at a constant compound rate. This need not be the case, however, and empirical trends and/or subjective beliefs may suggest a gradually increasing or decreasing inflation rate over future years.

The inflation component used to project salaries in the material presented here is assumed to be 4 percent per year, a rate which may or may not be appropriate for a given plan. In light of current eco-

---

[9] There is some question whether or not any productivity gains will occur in the future for some groups of employees. In any event, the productivity factor for a given plan would be set with careful consideration being given to historical data and subjective attitudes towards the future.

nomic data, this rate may appear to be low, but since it is used to project long-run salary increases (20 to 40 years) it is less clear whether it is low or high. The cost effects of other rates of inflation are examined in Chapter 15.

Total Salary Increase

Table 2–10 shows the age-64 multiple and the corresponding compound rate of increase based on several entry ages, using the previously discussed merit scale, a 1 percent productivity component, and a 4 percent inflation component.[10] For entrants at ages 25 and 30, the salary projection factors to age 64 are about 15 and 10, respectively. This is approximately equal to a 7 percent compound rate of increase. These rates, while not intended to be appropriate for any particular plan, have been developed with consideration for their general appropriateness. They are higher, however, than the salary rates used for most pension plans, which have traditionally been in the vicinity of 3 to 5 percent.

TABLE 2–10

Salary Projections Inclusive of Merit, Productivity, and Inflation

Entry age y	Age-64 Multiple of Entry-Age Salary	Equivalent Compound Rate of Increase
20	23.70	0.075
25	15.04	0.072
30	9.78	0.069
35	6.52	0.067
40	4.45	0.064
45	3.11	0.062
50	2.23	0.059
55	1.64	0.056
60	1.23	0.054

It is not clear why the salary assumptions used for pension plans have tended to be unrealistically low. One reason often advanced is that a low salary scale, and a low interest assumption (yet to be

---

[10] Inflation and productivity will increase total payroll, while the merit component will have little effect on total payroll, as noted previously. Thus, the standard assumptions can be thought of as increasing total payroll by about 5 percent per year, while increasing a given participant's salary by about 7 percent per year.

discussed) will roughly cancel each other out. This subject is examined numerically at a later point, but it is worth noting here that the interest rate assumption has a stronger influence on pension costs than the salary assumption.

INTEREST ASSUMPTION

The interest assumption has a powerful effect on pension costs, since it is used to find the present value of dollars due 20, 40, and even 60 years into the future. Although it is common to find this assumption set at a constant compound rate, this is a special case of the more general assumption that would allow the rate of interest to vary over time. As with most actuarial assumptions, an element of sub-jectivity is involved in establishing the interest rate to be used in the valuation of pension costs and liabilities, but the interest rate and the previously discussed salary rate assumptions are probably the extreme cases in this respect.

The interest assumption is generally set at a level representing the return expected to be achieved on the plan's assets in future years, although it is not uncommon to find a rate being used that is ostensibly lower than the best-estimate expectations. In any event, the interest assumption, like the salary assumption, can be viewed as consisting of several components: (1) a pure rate of return, (2) a premium for investment risk, and (3) a premium for inflation.

Pure Rate

The pure rate of interest is one that would prevail if there were no current or anticipated inflation, and if the investment were 100 percent secure as to its principal and yield. It is generally agreed that the pure rate of interest is two to three percent. The pure rate used in this book is set at 2 percent.

Investment Risk

The second component making up the assumed interest rate is the investment risk inherent in the current and future portfolio of plan assets. A different investment risk, and hence risk premium, may be associated with each investment, although it is generally practicable to break investments down only into several broad categories for assignment of the risk premium; for example, equities, corporate bonds, and government bonds. The risk premium ideally would be tied to historical performance, current yields, and anticipated future investment returns of the plan. As a practical approach, a constant future risk premium is generally assumed rather than a more complicated approach that would inevitably lead to a graded risk premium over future years. In the pension cost illustrations presented later in this book, the risk premium is assumed to be 1 percent.

Inflation Component

A premium for the current and anticipated rate of inflation is the third component making up the interest rate assumption. This factor, it will be remembered, was present in the salary assumption also, and in this sense the salary and interest assumptions have a common basis. As noted earlier, the assumed rate of future inflation is likely to have a higher subjective element than most actuarial assumptions, since historical inflation rates tend not to be good predictors of future inflation rates. In some cases, it may be appropriate to use a graded inflation rate, beginning with the rate for the current year and grading downward or upward to some predetermined ultimate level. A constant inflation rate of 4 percent has been selected for the standard inflation assumption used in this book, as noted earlier under the discussion of salary increase components.

Total Interest Rate

The individual components of the interest rate assumption used in this book total 7 percent, consisting of a 2 percent pure rate of return, a 1 percent risk premium, and a 4 percent inflation premium.[11] Although it is not claimed that these values are necessarily appropriate for a given plan, they have been selected with an eye toward their general appropriateness. The 7 percent value, however, is two to three percentage points greater than the rate traditionally used in pension plans. A lower-than-best-estimate rate is often used in the interest of conservatism, since pension costs are inversely related to the rate assumed. ERISA will undoubtedly cause more attention to be given

---

[11] It is not clear that the full amount of the inflation assumption should be added to the interest rate assumption, but this is done for the numerical results presented in this book for the sake of simplicity.

to this assumption and other actuarial assumptions, since the law requires that the combined set of assumptions represent a best estimate, and it may be unduly complicated to achieve a best-estimate package using offsetting individual assumptions that are not in themselves best estimates.

Chapter 3

Basic Actuarial Functions

The purpose of this chapter is to introduce several important actuarial functions that are used in the development of pension costs throughout the remainder of the book. The discussion begins with the composite survival function and the interest function, perhaps the two most basic concepts in pension mathematics. Then annuities, which represent a combination of the interest and survival functions, are analyzed, and the basic benefit functions of a pension plan are discussed.

COMPOSITE SURVIVAL FUNCTION

The composite survival function gives the probability that an active plan participant survives in active service for a given period, based on all of the decremental rates to which the employee is exposed. Whereas the probability of surviving one year in a single-decrement environment is equal to the complement of the rate of decrement, the probability of surviving one year in a multiple-decrement environment is equal to the product of such complements for each applicable rate of decrement. Thus we have for an active participant age x:

$$p_x^{(T)} = (1 - q_x'^{(m)})(1 - q_x'^{(w)})(1 - q_x'^{(d)})(1 - q_x'^{(r)}), \qquad (3.1a)$$

or equivalently,

$$p_x^{(T)} = p_x'^{(m)} p_x'^{(w)} p_x'^{(d)} p_x'^{(r)}. \qquad (3.1b)$$

Another expression for the probability of surviving one year in the multiple-decrement case is

$$p_x^{(T)} = 1 - [q_x^{(m)} + q_x^{(w)} + q_x^{(d)} + q_x^{(r)}], \qquad (3.2a)$$

where the probabilities reflect competing decrements. For example,

29

the standard approximation for the mortality probability[1] would be

$$q_x^{(m)} \doteq q_x'^{(m)}(1 - \tfrac{1}{2}q_x'^{(w)})(1 - \tfrac{1}{2}q_x'^{(d)})(1 - \tfrac{1}{2}q_x'^{(r)}). \qquad (3.2b)$$

The probability of surviving in active service for n years is equal to the product of successive one-year composite survival probabilities:

$$_n p_x^{(T)} = \prod_{t=0}^{n-1} p_{x+t}^{(T)}. \qquad (3.2c)$$

Table 3–1 shows the probability of surviving to age 65 from each attained age under the standard rates of decrement as set out in the previous chapter. Since the termination decrement includes a 5-year select period, probabilities are given for the first five years of several entry ages. These probabilities illustrate that the chance of reaching retirement for the standard assumptions is quite low, even up through attained age 50, where the probability is 0.61. Since retirement-related pension cost estimates are in direct proportion to the survival probability (i.e., the lower the probability the lower are such estimates), it is clear that discounting for the various decrements reduces pension cost estimates significantly. Obviously, to the extent that a *benefit* is associated with each type of decrement (e.g., a vested termination benefit, a spouses's benefit, or a disability benefit), then the cost reduction associated with the decrement is mitigated. These relationships are analyzed in Chapters 14 and 15.

The calculation of survival probabilities in accordance with the above definitions can be quite arduous. The probabilities, however, are readily obtainable from a service table. A service table shows the number of employees out of an original group who survive to each future attained age. The initial number of employees is generally taken to be some large value, such as 100,000 or 1,000,000, and the notation for the survivors at age x is $l_x^{(T)}$.[2] The total number of employees leaving active service during the year is denoted by $d_x^{(T)}$ and defined as

$$d_x^{(T)} = l_x^{(T)} \cdot q_x^{(T)}. \qquad (3.3a)$$

These decrements to the active population, of course, are the sums of the separate decrements.

$$d_x^{(T)} = d_x^{(m)} + d_x^{(w)} + d_x^{(d)} + d_x^{(r)} \qquad (3.3b)$$

$$= l_x^{(T)}[q_x^{(m)} + q_x^{(w)} + q_x^{(d)} + q_x^{(r)}] \qquad (3.3c)$$

---

[1] See equation (2.2b).

[2] It is to be understood in this section that the symbol $l_x^{(T)}$ refers to the number of survivors at age x who entered the plan at age y. At a later point the more general symbol $l_{y,x}^{(T)}$ will be used, which makes the entry age variable explicit.

TABLE 3–1

Probability of Surviving in Service to Age 65, $_{65-x}p_x^{(T)}$

Entry Ages	y	$y+1$	$y+2$	$y+3$	$y+4$	x	Attained Ages
			Select Ages				
20	0.02	0.03	0.04	0.05	0.07	0.08	25
						0.09	26
						0.11	27
						0.13	28
						0.15	29
25	0.07	0.09	0.11	0.13	0.15	0.17	30
						0.19	31
						0.21	32
						0.23	33
						0.25	34
30	0.14	0.17	0.20	0.22	0.25	0.27	35
						0.29	36
						0.31	37
						0.33	38
						0.35	39
35	0.23	0.27	0.30	0.33	0.35	0.37	40
						0.40	41
						0.42	42
						0.44	43
						0.46	44
40	0.29	0.32	0.35	0.37	0.39	0.48	45
						0.51	46
						0.53	47
						0.56	48
						0.58	49
45	0.35	0.38	0.41	0.43	0.45	0.61	50
						0.64	51
						0.67	52
						0.71	53
						0.74	54
50	0.46	0.49	0.52	0.54	0.57	0.78	55
						0.79	56
						0.80	57
						0.81	58
						0.83	59
55	0.58	0.62	0.66	0.69	0.73	0.85	60
						0.87	61
						0.89	62
						0.92	63
						0.95	64
60	0.73	0.79	0.84	0.89	0.94	1.00	65

Table 3–2 illustrates the concept of a service table for 1,000,000 entrants at age 20. The probability of an entrant age-20 surviving in active service to age 65 is easily found from this table.

$$_{65-20}p_{20}^{(T)} = \frac{l_{65}^{(T)}}{l_{20}^{(T)}} = \frac{24,448}{1,000,000} = 0.0244. \tag{3.4a}$$

TABLE 3–2

Service Table

x	$l_x^{(T)}$	$d_x^{(m)}$	$d_x^{(w)}$	$d_x^{(d)}$	$d_x^{(r)}$	$d_x^{(T)}$
20. . . .	1,000,000	442	243,002	263	0	243,708
21. . . .	756,292	350	169,718	201	0	170,270
22. . . .	586,023	286	121,314	158	0	121,757
23. . . .	464,265	238	88,543	126	0	88,907
24. . . .	375,358	202	65,921	103	0	66,226
25. . . .	309,132	176	49,933	85	0	50,194
26. . . .	258,938	156	38,460	72	0	38,688
27. . . .	220,251	140	30,049	62	0	30,251
28. . . .	189,999	129	23,814	53	0	23,996
29. . . .	166,004	119	19,113	47	0	19,280
30. . . .	146,724	112	15,529	56	0	15,697
31. . . .	131,027	107	12,754	50	0	12,911
32. . . .	118,116	103	10,576	45	0	10,725
33. . . .	107,392	101	8,875	41	0	9,017
34. . . .	98,375	99	7,510	38	0	7,647
35. . . .	90,727	98	6,419	35	0	6,552
36. . . .	84,176	98	5,534	41	0	5,673
37. . . .	78,503	99	4,816	46	0	4,960
38. . . .	73,543	100	4,224	50	0	4,374
39. . . .	69,169	102	3,738	54	0	3,893
40. . . .	65,276	104	3,338	57	0	3,499
41. . . .	61,777	108	3,004	60	0	3,172
42. . . .	58,605	114	2,727	69	0	2,910
43. . . .	55,695	123	2,491	76	0	2,690
44. . . .	53,006	133	2,290	83	0	2,506
45. . . .	50,499	144	2,121	89	0	2,354
46. . . .	48,145	156	1,969	94	0	2,219
47. . . .	45,926	169	1,841	99	0	2,108
48. . . .	43,818	181	1,721	107	0	2,009
49. . . .	41,808	194	1,616	115	0	1,925
50. . . .	39,884	206	1,517	121	0	1,845
51. . . .	38,039	219	1,424	127	0	1,769
52. . . .	36,270	230	1,335	135	0	1,700
53. . . .	34,570	241	1,244	142	0	1,628
54. . . .	32,942	252	1,159	148	0	1,559
55. . . .	31,383	267	0	156	0	423
56. . . .	30,960	286	0	166	0	452
57. . . .	30,508	305	0	182	0	487
58. . . .	30,020	326	0	203	0	529
59. . . .	29,492	350	0	235	0	585
60. . . .	28,907	377	0	281	0	659
61. . . .	28,248	405	0	348	0	753
62. . . .	27,495	433	0	436	0	869
63. . . .	26,626	459	0	549	0	1,008
64. . . .	25,618	485	0	685	0	1,170
65. . . .	24,448	0	0	0	24,448	24,448

Similarly, the probability of an employee age 40 surviving to age 65 would be

$$_{25}p_{40}^{(T)} = \frac{l_{65}^{(T)}}{l_{40}^{(T)}} = \frac{24,448}{65,276} = 0.3745. \tag{3.4b}$$

Although service tables are an important source of computational efficiency, they are used only occasionally in the theory of pension mathematics presented in this book.

INTEREST FUNCTION

The interest function is used to discount a future payment to the present time. It plays a crucial role in determining pension costs, and like the survival function of the previous section, it reduces the value of pension costs. If i_t is the interest rate assumed for the tth year, the present value of one dollar due in n years is given by

$$\frac{1}{(1 + i_1)(1 + i_2) \cdots (1 + i_n)}, \tag{3.5a}$$

and if $i_1 = i_2 \cdots = i_n$, we have simply

$$\frac{1}{(1 + i)^n}. \tag{3.5b}$$

The following simplifying definition is used in connection with the present value function:

$$v = \frac{1}{(1 + i)}. \tag{3.6}$$

Thus, v^n represents the present value of one dollar due in n years at an annual compound rate of interest equal to i.

The interest function, v^t, begins at a value of unity for $t = 0$ and approaches zero as t approaches infinity, provided $i > 0$. Also v^t is inversely related to i, taking on the value of unity for $i = 0$ and approaching zero as i approaches infinity. Table 3-3 has been constructed to illustrate the significance of this interest factor. In addition to showing v^t for the standard interest assumption of 7 percent, the function is also given for 5 and 9 percent. Since the interest factor is associated with each potential future age of an entrant, a period of about 70 years for entrants around age 30, the interest discount function is tabulated at 5-year intervals for 70 years.

TABLE 3–3

Compound Interest Discount Function, v^t

	Interest Rate		
t	5%	7%	9%
0. . . .	1.0000	1.0000	1.0000
5. . . .	0.7835	0.7130	0.6499
10. . . .	0.6139	0.5083	0.4224
15. . . .	0.4810	0.3624	0.2745
20. . . .	0.3769	0.2584	0.1784
25. . . .	0.2953	0.1842	0.1160
30. . . .	0.2314	0.1314	0.0754
35. . . .	0.1813	0.0937	0.0490
40. . . .	0.1420	0.0668	0.0318
45. . . .	0.1113	0.0476	0.0207
50. . . .	0.0872	0.0339	0.0134
55. . . .	0.0683	0.0242	0.0087
60. . . .	0.0535	0.0173	0.0057
65. . . .	0.0419	0.0123	0.0037
70. . . .	0.0329	0.0088	0.0024

The significance of the interest rate function is illustrated by the fact that, for an age-30 entrant, v^{65-30} is 0.09 at a 7 percent rate of interest, 0.18 at 5 percent, and 0.05 at 9 percent. Moreover, since retirement-related cost estimates are directly related to this factor, and since the interest discount extends beyond age 65, the total effect of the interest assumption is even greater than the effect of v^{65-y} alone.

Figure 3–1 shows the survival function from age x to age 65 and the interest function over this same age interval for the age-30 entrant under standard assumptions. This graph indicates that the interest function, based on a 7 percent rate of interest, is more significant than the survival probability at all ages. This relationship may not hold for the general case, however. The product of the interest and survival probabilities is frequently encountered in pension mathematics, and since both functions are less than unity, their product is quite small over most attained ages, which in turn has a significant affect on pension costs.

SALARY FUNCTION

If a pension plan has benefits tied to a participant's salary and/or if the plan's contributions are tied to salary, it is necessary to develop salary-related notation and procedures for estimating future salary.

The current dollar salary for a participant age x is denoted by s_x.

FIGURE 3–1

Survival and Interest Functions from Age *x* to Age 65.

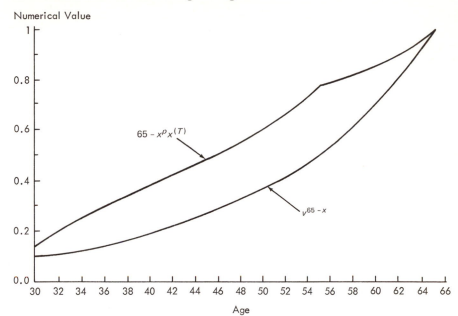

The *cumulative* dollar salary from his entry age *y* up to, but not including, age *x* is denoted by S_x.[3] Thus, for $x > y$ we have

$$S_x = \sum_{t=y}^{x-1} s_t. \qquad (3.7)$$

In order to estimate the employee's dollar salary at age *x*, based on his salary at age *y*, one would use the following:

$$S_x = s_y \frac{(SS)_x}{(SS)_y} (1 + I + P)^{x-y}, \qquad (3.8a)$$

where

$$s_y = \text{the entry-age dollar salary}$$
$$(SS)_x = \text{the merit salary scale at age } x$$
$$I = \text{the rate of inflation}$$
$$P = \text{the rate of productivity reflected in the}$$
$$\text{participant's salary increases.}$$

---

[3] It is to be understood throughout the remainder of this book that s_x and S_x are dependent on each participant's entry age *y*, despite the fact that *y* does not appear in the salary symbol. The author has used in other research the symbols $_{x-y}s_y$ and $_{x-y}S_y$ to denote these two functions, which have the virtue of making the entry age *y* explicit; however, it was believed that these symbols are unduly complex for the mathematics presented in this book.

In Chapter 8 the symbols $s_{y,x}$ and $S_{y,x}$ are used to make the entry age variable explicit, since the equations given at that point require a summation over all combinations of *x* and *y*.

An age-y entrant's salary at age x can also be defined in terms of his age-z salary ($y < z < x$)

$$s_x = s_z \frac{(SS)_x}{(SS)_z} (1 + I + P)^{x-z}. \tag{3.8b}$$

If all of the salary increase assumptions have been met from age y to age z, the employee's salary at age z would be equal to

$$s_z = s_y \frac{(SS)_z}{(SS)_y} (1 + I + P)^{z-y}. \tag{3.8c}$$

Substituting (3.8c) for s_z in (3.8b) reduces the latter to (3.8a), showing that s_x is identical whether derived from the entry age salary or the attained age salary, provided all assumptions have been met.

Table 3–4 shows the salary function per dollar of entry-age salary based on the merit scale given in the previous chapter, a 1 percent productivity factor, and a 4 percent inflation factor for decennial entry ages from 20 to 60. The age-64 salary for an age 20 entrant is 24 times greater than his entry-age salary. At the other extreme, an age-60 entrant's initial salary increases by 23 percent to his salary at age 64. Retirement-related cost estimates are directly proportional to an employee's final 5-year average salary under the standard benefit formula used to illustrate pension costs in this book; consequently, it is clear from Table 3–4 that the salary scale increases pension cost estimates significantly. This is in contrast to the interest rate and survival probability, both of which decrease pension cost estimates significantly, as noted in the previous two sections.

BENEFIT FUNCTION

The benefit function is used to determined the amount of benefits to be paid at retirement, vested termination, disablement, and death. This function, the interest function, and the survival function provide the basic components required to formulate pension costs, as shown in subsequent chapters. In this section consideration is given to the three basic benefit formulas found in defined benefit pension plans.

The symbol b_x is used to denote the annual benefit accrual during the year of age x to $x + 1$ for an age-y entrant. The *cumulative* benefit accrual, denoted by B_x, is the sum of each attained age accrual up to, but not including, age x. This function is called the *accrued benefit* function and is defined for $x > y$ as

$$B_x = \sum_{t=y}^{x-1} b_t. \tag{3.9}$$

TABLE 3–4

Salary Function per Dollar of Entry Age Salary, $s_x \div s_y$

	Entry Age				
x	20	30	40	50	60
20. . . .	1.000				
21. . . .	1.097				
22. . . .	1.203				
23. . . .	1.317				
24. . . .	1.441				
25. . . .	1.575				
26. . . .	1.720				
27. . . .	1.877				
28. . . .	2.045				
29. . . .	2.227				
30. . . .	2.423	1.000			
31. . . .	2.633	1.087			
32. . . .	2.858	1.180			
33. . . .	3.100	1.280			
34. . . .	3.360	1.387			
35. . . .	3.637	1.501			
36. . . .	3.933	1.624			
37. . . .	4.250	1.754			
38. . . .	4.587	1.893			
39. . . .	4.947	2.042			
40. . . .	5.329	2.200	1.000		
41. . . .	5.735	2.367	1.076		
42. . . .	6.167	2.545	1.157		
43. . . .	6.624	2.734	1.243		
44. . . .	7.108	2.934	1.334		
45. . . .	7.620	3.145	1.430		
46. . . .	8.161	3.369	1.531		
47. . . .	8.732	3.604	1.639		
48. . . .	9.334	3.853	1.752		
49. . . .	9.967	4.114	1.870		
50. . . .	10.633	4.389	1.995	1.000	
51. . . .	11.332	4.678	2.126	1.066	
52. . . .	12.065	4.980	2.264	1.135	
53. . . .	12.833	5.297	2.408	1.207	
54. . . .	13.637	5.629	2.559	1.282	
55. . . .	14.476	5.975	2.716	1.361	
56. . . .	15.352	6.337	2.881	1.444	
57. . . .	16.265	6.713	3.052	1.530	
58. . . .	17.214	7.105	3.230	1.619	
59. . . .	18.202	7.513	3.416	1.712	
60. . . .	19.226	7.936	3.608	1.808	1.000
61. . . .	20.289	8.374	3.807	1.908	1.055
62. . . .	21.388	8.828	4.013	2.011	1.112
63. . . .	22.525	9.298	4.227	2.118	1.172
64. . . .	23.699	9.782	4.447	2.229	1.233

Assumptions: Merit scale from Table 2.9, plus 1 percent productivity and 4 percent inflation.

The convention of using lower and upper case letters, with the upper case denoting a summation of lower case functional values, was used also in connection with the salary scale.[4]

Flat Benefit

Under a flat benefit formula b_x is equal to the annual benefit payable per year of service. These values are found to range from about \$50 to \$150 currently.[5] The attained age subscript on the benefit accrual is not necessary since the accrual is independent of the entry age and attained age. The cumulative benefit is a years-of-service multiple of the benefit accrual, that is,

$$B_x = (x - y) \cdot b_x. \tag{3.10}$$

Career Average

The career average benefit formula has the following definitions for the benefit accrual and the accrued benefit at age x:

$$b_x = k \cdot s_x; \tag{3.11a}$$

$$B_x = k \cdot S_x. \tag{3.11b}$$

where k denotes the proportion of attained age salary provided as an annual benefit accrual.

Clearly, the benefit functions under the career average benefit formula follow precisely the pattern of the attained age salary function and the cumulative salary function discussed and illustrated previously.

Final Average

The final average benefit formula is somewhat more complicated than the flat benefit or career average. Let n denote the number of years over which the participant's final years of salary are to be averaged and let k equal the proportion of that average provided per

---

[4] Again it is important to note that b_x and B_x are generally functions of the employee's age y. The author has used $_{x-y}b_y$ for b_x and $_{x-y}B_y$ for B_x in previous writings, but has abandoned these more complex symbols in this treatise in the interest of simplicity.

[5] It is more common to find the flat benefit formula expressed as the monthly benefit payable per year of service, for example, \$5 or \$10 per month per year of service. The \$50 annual amount noted above would equal \$4.17 on a monthly basis and the \$150 annual benefit amount becomes \$12.50 on this basis.

year of service. The projected retirement benefit, assuming retirement occurs at the beginning of age r, is defined as

$$B_r = k(r - y) \frac{1}{n} \sum_{t=r-n}^{r-1} S_t, \qquad (3.12a)$$

or more simply

$$B_r = k(r - y) \frac{1}{n} (S_r - S_{r-n}). \qquad (3.12b)$$

The attained age benefit accruals, and hence, the cumulative benefit accruals, can be defined in several ways under this benefit formula. One approach would be to defined B_x according to the benefit formula based on the participant's current salary average:

$$B_x = k(x - y) \frac{1}{n} (S_x - S_{x-n}), \qquad (3.13)$$

where n is the smaller of (1) the years specified in the benefit formula or (2) $x - y$. The corresponding benefit accrual at age x can be determined by the following basic relationship:

$$b_x = B_{x+1} - B_x. \qquad (3.14a)$$

Substituting (3.13) into (3.14a) and simplifying, we have:

$$b_x = k \frac{1}{n} (S_{x+1} - S_{x+1-n})$$

$$+ k \frac{1}{n} (x - y)[(S_{x+1} - S_{x+1-n}) - (S_x - S_{x-n})] \qquad (3.14b)$$

$$= k \frac{1}{n} (S_{x+1} - S_{x+1-n}) + k \frac{1}{n} (x - y)[s_x - s_{x-n}]. \qquad (3.14c)$$

The first term on the right side of (3.14b) is the portion of b_x earned in the current year based on the participants *current* n-year salary average, while the second term represents the portion of b_x associated with the increase in the n-year salary average base. Note that the increase in this salary base, which can be represented by $\frac{1}{n}(s_x - s_{x-n})$ as shown in (3.14c), is multiplied by the years of service to date. Since the benefit accrual during age x includes an implicit updating of the previous accruals, b_x may be a steeply increasing function of x. As shown later, a steeply increasing benefit accrual function produces an even steeper pension cost function under the accrued benefit cost method.[6] Since it may be desirable to reduce the slope of both of these functions, two modifications for accomplishing this are defined at this point.

The most significant of the two modifications is to define b_x as a pro rata share of the participant's retirement-age projected benefit, B_r:

$$^{CA}b_x = \frac{B_r}{(r-y)}, \qquad \text{for all } x. \tag{3.15a}$$

The accrued benefit can be expressed as

$$^{CA}B_x = \frac{B_r}{(r-y)}(x-y). \tag{3.15b}$$

These formulas are also applicable to modifying the benefit accruals under a career average benefit formula, but they are redundant for a flat benefit formula. Since this modification produces a benefit accrual equal to a constant (dollar) amount, it is known as the CA modification.

The second modification is to define b_x not as a constant dollar amount at each age but as a constant percentage of salary. The appropriate percentage is found by dividing the projected benefit, B_r, by the projected salary of the age-y entrant, S_r, and the benefit functions become

$$^{CS}b_x = \frac{B_r}{S_r} s_x \tag{3.16a}$$

$$^{CS}B_x = \frac{B_r}{S_r} S_x. \tag{3.16b}$$

This modification is redundant for the career average benefit formula, just as the CA modification is redundant for the flat benefit formula. Since this modification produces a benefit accrual equal to a constant percent of salary, it is designated by the initials CS.

Table 3–5 shows the benefit accruals and accrued benefits, expressed as a percentage of B_r, under the final five-year average benefit formula used in this book for both modifications as well as for the natural version. All of the data in this table are based on an age-30 entrant retiring at age 65. Note that the CS modification to the benefit function has only a minor effect on the attained age benefit accrual and accrued benefit. The CA modification, however, is seen to bring

---

[6] The accrued benefit cost method, which is the subject of Chapter 6, is a technique for developing a pension plan's annual dollar cost and liability.

TABLE 3–5

Benefit Accrual and Accrued Benefit Functions Expressed as a Percentage of the Projected Benefit

Age	$100 \dfrac{b_x}{B_r}$	$100 \dfrac{B_x}{B_r}$	$100 \dfrac{^{cs}b_x}{B_r}$	$100 \dfrac{^{cs}B_x}{B_r}$	$100 \dfrac{^{CA}b_x}{B_r}$	$100 \dfrac{^{CA}B_x}{B_r}$
30. . . . . 0.32	0.00	0.67	0.00	2.86	0.00
31. . . . . 0.35	0.32	0.73	0.67	2.86	2.86
32. . . . . 0.38	0.67	0.79	1.41	2.86	5.71
33. . . . . 0.41	1.06	0.86	2.20	2.86	8.57
34. . . . . 0.45	1.47	0.93	3.06	2.86	11.43
35. . . . . 0.58	1.92	1.01	4.00	2.86	14.29
36. . . . . 0.66	2.49	1.09	5.01	2.86	17.14
37. . . . . 0.75	3.15	1.18	6.10	2.86	20.00
38. . . . . 0.84	3.90	1.28	7.28	2.86	22.86
39. . . . . 0.95	4.74	1.38	8.56	2.86	25.71
40. . . . . 1.07	5.70	1.48	9.93	2.86	28.57
41. . . . . 1.19	6.76	1.59	11.42	2.86	31.43
42. . . . . 1.33	7.95	1.71	13.01	2.86	34.29
43. . . . . 1.47	9.28	1.84	14.73	2.86	37.14
44. . . . . 1.63	10.75	1.98	16.57	2.86	40.00
45. . . . . 1.80	12.39	2.12	18.54	2.86	42.86
46. . . . . 1.99	14.19	2.27	20.66	2.86	45.71
47. . . . . 2.18	16.18	2.43	22.93	2.86	48.57
48. . . . . 2.39	18.36	2.60	25.36	2.86	51.43
49. . . . . 2.62	20.75	2.77	27.96	2.86	54.29
50. . . . . 2.86	23.37	2.96	30.73	2.86	57.14
51. . . . . 3.11	26.23	3.15	33.68	2.86	60.00
52. . . . . 3.38	29.34	3.35	36.83	2.86	62.86
53. . . . . 3.66	32.72	3.57	40.19	2.86	65.71
54. . . . . 3.96	36.38	3.79	43.76	2.86	68.57
55. . . . . 4.28	40.34	4.03	47.55	2.86	71.43
56. . . . . 4.61	44.62	4.27	51.57	2.86	74.29
57. . . . . 4.96	49.23	4.52	55.84	2.86	77.14
58. . . . . 5.32	54.19	4.79	60.37	2.86	80.00
59. . . . . 5.70	59.51	5.06	65.15	2.86	82.86
60. . . . . 6.10	65.22	5.35	70.21	2.86	85.71
61. . . . . 6.51	71.32	5.64	75.56	2.86	88.57
62. . . . . 6.94	77.83	5.95	81.20	2.86	91.43
63. . . . . 7.38	84.77	6.26	87.15	2.86	94.29
64. . . . . 7.84	92.16	6.59	93.41	2.86	97.14
65. . . . . 0.00	100.00	0.00	100.00	0.00	100.00

about significant differences. As expected, this modification allocates a constant 2.86 percent, or $\frac{1}{35}$, of the projected benefit per year of service. The CA modification develops an accrued benefit equal to one-half of the projected benefit by age 48, while the CS modification shows a 25 percent benefit accrual at this age, and the unmodified accrued benefit shows an 18 percent benefit accrual. Thus, even though all of the accrued benefit functions begin at zero and attain B_r by age r, the

modifications, and particularly the CA modification, cause their intermediate values to be different.[7]

Since the CS and CA modifications to the natural attained age
benefit accrual will be important in later sections of this book, Figures
3–2 and 3–3 have been constructed to provide a graphical analysis
of the three basic types of benefit accrual and accrued benefit functions.

ANNUITY FUNCTIONS

Annuity functions represent a combination of the survival function
and the interest function. Most annuity functions are based on the
mortality-only survival function, and the material below reflects this
emphasis. However, a temporary, employment-based annuity, which
uses the composite survival function, plays a crucial role in pension
mathematics and this is also developed in this section.

Straight Life Annuity

When an employee reaches retirement age he begins to receive a
series of benefit payments, often at monthly intervals, but for convenience assumed here to be paid annually. If payments cease upon
death, the annuity is called a straight life annuity and its present value,
assuming an annual payment of one dollar, with the first payment due
at the beginning of age x, is given by

$$\ddot{a}_x = \sum_{t=0}^{\infty} {}_tp_x^{(m)}v^t. \tag{3.17}$$

The infinity sign is used as the upper limit of the summation strictly
for convenience since ${}_tp_x^{(m)}$ becomes zero beyond some advanced age.[8]

Clearly, the rate of interest in v^t and the mortality assumption
implicit in ${}_tp_x^{(m)}$ have an important bearing on the value of $\ddot{a}_x$. If $i = 0$,
(3.17) is equal to one plus the participant's curtate life expectancy
(based on whole years only), the latter denoted by e_x.

---

[7] The benefit accruals associated with ancillary benefits may differ from those used in connection with retirement benefits. This is especially the case in defining benefit accruals to be
used with an actuarial cost method (the mechanism used to allocate and/or fund pension costs).

[8] The standard approximation for the present value of an annuity payable m times a year is
to subtract $(m-1)/2m$ from the annually payable annuity. Since retirement benefits are paid
monthly, $\frac{11}{24}$ should be subtracted from the above annuity to approximate a monthly payment of $\frac{1}{12}$ of a dollar. As noted above, the annual-pay annuity is assumed throughout this
book in the interest of simplicity.

FIGURE 3–2

Attained Age Benefit Accrual Functions as a Percentage of the Projected Benefit

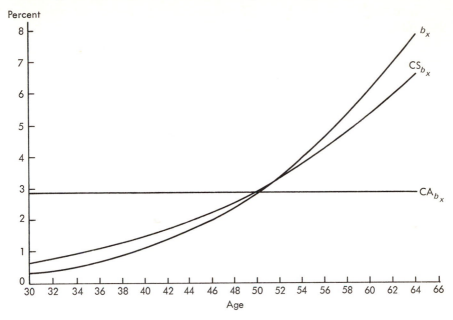

FIGURE 3–3

Attained Age Accrued Benefit Functions as a Percentage of the Projected Benefit

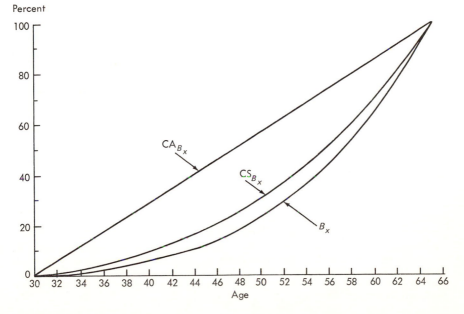

Period Certain Life Annuity

It is not uncommon to find an n-year period certain life annuity used as the basis for distributing a pension benefit. This type of annuity is a combination of an n-year period certain annuity plus an n-year deferred life annuity.

$$\begin{aligned}\ddot{a}_{\overline{x:\overline{n|}}} &= \ddot{a}_{\overline{n|}} + {}_np_x^{(m)}v^n\ddot{a}_{x+n} \\ &= \ddot{a}_{\overline{n|}} + {}_{n|}\ddot{a}_x.\end{aligned} \tag{3.18}$$

These equations introduce notations deserving comment. The bar over the subscript $x:\overline{n|}$ signifies that the annuity is paid until the last status fails, where the two statuses represent (1) the life of the plan member and (2) the n-year period. Thus the period certain life annuity is technically a last survivor annuity. An annuity discussed subsequently is $\ddot{a}_{x:\overline{n|}}$ without the bar. This annuity is known as an n-year temporary life annuity which pays until the *first* of the two statuses fails and is technically a joint annuity. Finally, (3.18) uses $\ddot{a}_{\overline{n|}}$ to indicate an n-year period certain annuity and ${}_{n|}\ddot{a}_x$ to indicate the present value of an n-year deferred life annuity applicable to a life age x.

Joint and Survivor Annuity

Another type of annuity is known as the joint and survivor annuity. The term "joint" suggests that the payment amount is based on more than one status, and the term "survivor" suggests that it pays at least some amount until the last status fails. A 50-percent joint and survivor annuity pays one dollar annually while both statuses are alive (usually husband and wife, but not necessarily restricted to couples), and reduces to 50 cents after the first death. Another version of this annuity is known as a *contingent* joint and survivor annuity. Under this form, the annuity reduces to 50 cents only if the plan member is the first to die. This type of joint and survivor annuity is frequently found in large corporate pension plans. The survivor's benefit might be any proportion, with one half, two thirds, and three fourths representing the choices usually available.

Let x denote the age of the plan member, y the age of his spouse and $100k$ the percentage of the annual pension continued in the event that the plan member predeceases his spouse. The $100k$ percent joint and survivor annuity may be represented mathematically as

$${}^k\ddot{a}_{\underset{1}{x}y} = \sum_{t=0}^{\infty} v^t[{}_tp_x^{(m)}\,{}_tp_y^{(m)} + {}_tp_x^{(m)}(1 - {}_tp_y^{(m)}) + k\,{}_tp_y^{(m)}(1 - {}_tp_x^{(m)})], \tag{3.19a}$$

where the 1 under the x subscript stipulates that k dollars are paid to y if x is the first to die. The bracketed expression represents a payment of \$1 if both x and y are alive at time t, a payment of \$1 if x is alive and y is not alive, and a payment of \$k$ if y is alive and x is not alive. This expression reduces to

$$k\ddot{a}_{\underset{1}{xy}} = \sum_{t=0}^{\infty} v^t [\, {}_t p_x^{(m)} + k\, {}_t p_y^{(m)} - k\, {}_t p_x^{(m)}\, {}_t p_y^{(m)}].\qquad(3.19b)$$

In this form, the bracketed term represents a payment of \$1 to x regardless of whether or not y is alive, a payment of \$k$ to y regardless of whether or not x is alive, and since this would result in a total payment of \$(1 + k)$ in the event both are alive in year t, \$k$ is subtracted if both persist to time t.

Refund Annuities

Pension plans that require employee contributions frequently provide a death benefit in retirement equal to the difference, if any, between the employee's accumulated contributions at his retirement date less the cumulative benefits received at his death. If the difference is paid in a lump sum, the annuity is termed a Modified Cash Refund Annuity, whereas if the difference is paid by continuing the benefit payments to a named beneficiary, the annuity is termed a Modified Installment Refund Annuity.

If C denotes the employee's accumulated contributions at retirement per dollar of retirement benefit, the present value at age r of the modified cash refund annuity may be denoted:

$$^{MCR}\ddot{a}_r = \sum_{t=0}^{\infty} v^t\, {}_t p_r^{(m)} [1 + v q_{r+t}^{(m)} \max\{(C - \tau - 1), 0\}].\quad(3.20)$$

This formulation assumes that the lump sum payment, if any, will be made at the end of the year of death.

If $\ddot{a}_{\overline{n}|}$ denotes the present value of an n-year annuity certain, the modified installment refund annuity may be expressed as

$$^{MIR}\ddot{a}_r = \ddot{a}_{\overline{n}|} + {}_{n'} p_r^{(m)} v^{n'} \ddot{a}_{r+n'}.\qquad(3.21)$$

where n' is the accumulated contributions divided by the annual pension benefit, that is, $n' = C \div B_r$.

Temporary Annuities

The temporary annuity, as will be shown in later chapters, plays a central role in pension costs. In this case we are dealing with an employment based annuity, subject to multiple decrements, rather than the typical retirement-related annuity which includes only a mortality decrement. As noted earlier, the temporary annuity has $x:\overline{n}|$ as its subscript, indicating that payments cease at the end of n years or at the time the status x fails if sooner. In addition, a superscript T is added to the annuity symbol to signify a multiple-decrement environment. Equation (3.22) sets forth the basic definition of this annuity.

$$\ddot{a}^T_{x:\overline{n}|} = \sum_{t=0}^{n-1} {}_t p^{(T)}_x v^t \tag{3.22}$$

The value of n is often set at $r - x$ in the context of pension mathematics, resulting in an annuity running from the participant's attained age x up to, but not including, his retirement age r.

The withdrawal decrement may have a unique effect on $\ddot{a}^T_{x:\overline{r-x}|}$, as shown in Table 3–6. Generally one would tend to think that the present value of a temporary annuity running to age 65 would become smaller as the employee becomes older. However, because of the withdrawal assumption the value of $\ddot{a}^T_{x:\overline{r-x}|}$ for most entry ages reaches a maximum at some age in between the employee's entry age and retirement age. This maximum for the data in Table 3–6 occurs at about age 40 and is equal to 8.7, with younger or older attained ages generating a smaller value. For example, at entry age 20, the 45-year annuity takes on a value of only 4.16.

The age-30 entrant's annuity values in Table 3–6 are equal to that of the age-20 entrant's at attained ages beyond the 5-year select period. The annuity values of the age-30 and age-40 entrants are never equal, however, because of the early retirement provision; that is, termination rates exist up to age 60 for the older entrant but end at age 55 for the younger entrants.

An important variation of $\ddot{a}^T_{x:\overline{r-x}|}$ is represented by ${}^s\ddot{a}^T_{x:\overline{r-x}|}$, the superscript s denoting that the annuity is salary-based. More formally, we have

$$ {}^s\ddot{a}^T_{x:\overline{r-x}|} = \sum_{t=x}^{r-1} \frac{S_t}{S_x} {}_{t-x} p^{(T)}_x v^{t-x}. \tag{3.23}$$

Formula (3.23) represents the present value of an employee's future salary from age x to age r, per unit of salary at age x.

TABLE 3–6

Present Value of a Temporary Employment-Based Life Annuity from Age *x* to 65, $\ddot{a}^{T}_{x:\overline{65-x}|}$

			Entry Ages		
x	*20*	*30*	*40*	*50*	*60*
20. . . .	4.16				
21. . . .	4.47				
22. . . .	4.79				
23. . . .	5.12				
24. . . .	5.46				
25. . . .	5.79				
26. . . .	6.12				
27. . . .	6.44				
28. . . .	6.75				
29. . . .	7.04				
30. . . .	7.31	6.44			
31. . . .	7.56	7.01			
32. . . .	7.79	7.48			
33. . . .	7.99	7.85			
34. . . .	8.17	8.13			
35. . . .	8.32	8.32			
36. . . .	8.44	8.44			
37. . . .	8.53	8.53			
38. . . .	8.60	8.60			
39. . . .	8.65	8.65			
40. . . .	8.68	8.68	7.90		
41. . . .	8.68	8.68	8.17		
42. . . .	8.66	8.66	8.32		
43. . . .	8.62	8.62	8.38		
44. . . .	8.57	8.57	8.36		
45. . . .	8.50	8.50	8.30		
46. . . .	8.42	8.42	8.19		
47. . . .	8.33	8.33	8.06		
48. . . .	8.22	8.22	7.92		
49. . . .	8.09	8.09	7.76		
50. . . .	7.96	7.96	7.59	7.34	
51. . . .	7.80	7.80	7.39	7.23	
52. . . .	7.63	7.63	7.17	7.05	
53. . . .	7.45	7.45	6.93	6.82	
54. . . .	7.24	7.24	6.65	6.56	
55. . . .	7.01	7.01	6.35	6.26	
56. . . .	6.52	6.52	6.01	5.90	
57. . . .	5.99	5.99	5.63	5.51	
58. . . .	5.43	5.43	5.20	5.06	
59. . . .	4.82	4.82	4.71	4.56	
60. . . .	4.17	4.17	4.17	4.00	3.89
61. . . .	3.47	3.47	3.47	3.37	3.34
62. . . .	2.72	2.72	2.72	2.67	2.66
63. . . .	1.90	1.90	1.90	1.88	1.88
64. . . .	1.00	1.00	1.00	1.00	1.00

Table 3–7 replicates Table 3–6 based on the annuity defined in (3.23). This annuity, as one would expect, develops larger attained age values than the straight employment-based annuity given in Table 3–6, since the attained age salary is assumed to increase according to the salary assumptions set out earlier. Whereas the straight employment-based annuity reaches a maximum around age 40, the salary-based annuity reaches a maximum at age 35 and takes on a value at this age of nearly 16, or just about double the maximum value of the straight employment-based annuity. By age 64, however, both annuity values are identical and are equal to 1. As was the case for the annuity values shown in Table 3–6, the values given in Table 3–7 for the same attained age, but for different entry ages, are affected to some extent by the select period of the withdrawal assumption and the elimination of withdrawal rates after the first early retirement qualification age.

FIGURE 3–4

Unit-Based and Salary-Based Temporary Annuities from Age *x* to Age 65

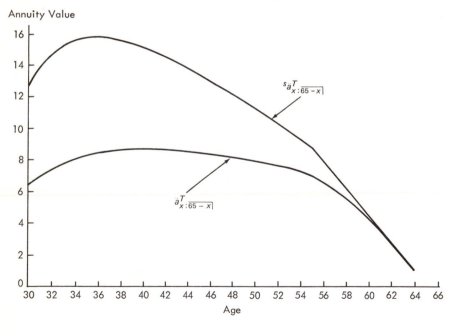

Figure 3–4 provides a graphical comparison of the annuities specified by equations (3.22) and (3.23) for the age-30 entrant under standard assumptions. This graph shows that these annuities can take on unique shapes from the employee's entry age to his retirement age.

TABLE 3–7

Present Value of a Temporary Employment-Based and Salary-Based Life Annuity from Age *x* to 65 ${}^{s}\ddot{a}^{T}_{x:65-x}$

			Entry Ages		
x	20	30	40	50	60
20....	7.28				
21....	8.10				
22....	8.94				
23....	9.80				
24....	10.64				
25....	11.46				
26....	12.23				
27....	12.95				
28....	13.60				
29....	14.18				
30....	14.66	12.66			
31....	15.07	13.81			
32....	15.38	14.70			
33....	15.60	15.31			
34....	15.74	15.66			
35....	15.79	15.79			
36....	15.78	15.78			
37....	15.69	15.69			
38....	15.55	15.55			
39....	15.35	15.35			
40....	15.10	15.10	13.43		
41....	14.81	14.81	13.68		
42....	14.49	14.49	13.68		
43....	14.14	14.14	13.50		
44....	13.76	13.76	13.21		
45....	13.37	13.37	12.83		
46....	12.96	12.96	12.40		
47....	12.54	12.54	11.95		
48....	12.11	12.11	11.49		
49....	11.67	11.67	11.02		
50....	11.22	11.22	10.53	10.13	
51....	10.75	10.75	10.04	9.77	
52....	10.28	10.28	9.52	9.32	
53....	9.80	9.80	9.00	8.83	
54....	9.29	9.29	8.45	8.30	
55....	8.78	8.78	7.88	7.74	
56....	7.95	7.95	7.29	7.14	
57....	7.13	7.13	6.67	6.50	
58....	6.29	6.29	6.02	5.84	
59....	5.45	5.45	5.33	5.14	
60....	4.60	4.60	4.60	4.41	4.28
61....	3.74	3.74	3.74	3.63	3.58
62....	2.85	2.85	2.85	2.80	2.79
63....	1.95	1.95	1.95	1.93	1.93
64....	1.00	1.00	1.00	1.00	1.00

Chapter 4

Pension Plan
Population Theory

BASIC CONCEPTS

This chapter deals with the population of pension plan members, which consists of various subpopulations. Active employees make up one of the most important subpopulations within the plan's membership, and this discussion is focused on them. Retired employees represent another subpopulation, and for present purposes, this group is assumed to consist only of members who entered the retired status directly from the service of the employer. This is in contrast to defining a retired member as any one of several types of benefit recipients. Vested terminated employees make up a third subpopulation, which can be further divided into those receiving benefits and those in the benefit deferral period. Disabled employees make up a fourth subpopulation in those plans providing disability benefits. Finally, beneficiaries—usually surviving spouses—make up a fifth subpopulation. The active group of employees is not only the most important subpopulation but also the source of members for the various other subpopulations.

Stationary Population

The discussion of pension plan populations begins at the most elementary level, namely, with the concept of a stationary population. A population is considered to be stationary when its size and its age distribution remain constant year after year. If the decrement rates associated with the population are constant, and if a constant number of new entrants flows into the population each year, a stationary

50

condition will exist after n years, where n equals the oldest age in the population less the youngest age.[1]

Understanding the concept of a stationary population can be facilitated by considering a simplified example. Assume that a population has four ages: y, $y + 1$, $y + 2$, and $y + 3$, and that the rates of decrement for each age are $\frac{1}{4}$, $\frac{1}{3}$, $\frac{1}{2}$, and 1, respectively, and that 100 new employees are hired each year, all at age y. The first few years of experience for a population exposed to these decremental factors is given in Table 4–1.

TABLE 4–1

Development of a Stationary Population

Elapsed time in years	Decrement Rates: Attained Ages:	← 1/4 → y	$y + 1$	← 1/3 → $y + 2$	← 1/2 → $y + 3$	← 1 → $y + 4$	Total size
0 · · · · · · ·	New entrants ⟶	100					100
1 · · · · · · ·	New entrants ⟶	100	75				175
2 · · · · · · ·	New entrants ⟶	100	75	50			225
3 · · · · · · ·	New entrants ⟶	100	75	50	25		250
4 · · · · · · ·	New entrants ⟶	100	75	50	25	0	250
5 · · · · · · ·	New entrants ⟶	100	75	50	25	0	250
·	·	·	·	·	·	·	·
·	·	·	·	·	·	·	·
Age distribution after 3 years:		40%	30%	20%	10%	0%	100%

It can be seen from Table 4–1 that after the first year, the original group of 100 employees hired at age y are age $y + 1$ and total only 75 in number. Since 100 new employees are hired at age y each year, the total population after one year is 175 members. This process continues for three years, after which the population attains a constant size of 250 members and its age distribution, as shown in percentage form at the bottom of Table 4–1, remains unchanged. Thus, as noted earlier, the population becomes stationary after n years, where n in this case is equal to three (i.e., the oldest age in the population, $y + 3$, less the youngest age, y).

---

[1] If the population is assumed to be continuous over each age interval, rather than descrete as is assumed in this chapter for simplicity, then n would be equal to the first age at which no survivors exist less the youngest age. In other words, one year would be added to the value of n for the continuous case.

In the context of a pension plan, it is important to note that the service distribution of a stationary population, as well as the age distribution, becomes constant after n years.[2] For example, Table 4–1 shows that 40 percent of the stationary population has zero years of service, 30 percent has one year of service, and so forth.

A pension plan population, unlike the example shown in Table 4–1, has multiple entry ages, and it is logical to inquire whether or not the concept of a stationary population applies in this case. To show that it does apply, one need only conceptualize a multiple entry age plan population as a series of single entry age populations, with each subpopulation representing a given entry age. Consequently, a multiple entry age active population will become stationary after m years, where m equals the largest retirement age-entry age spread among the various subpopulations.

Mature Population

The concept of a mature population is only slightly different from, and somewhat more general than, that of a stationary population. In fact, a stationary population is a special case of a mature population. Both concepts involve a constant year-to-year age and service distribution, but whereas the stationary population is one that always attains a constant size, this need not be the case for a mature population. If the increments to the population (newly hired employees) increase at a *constant rate*, the population will attain a constant percentage age and service distribution in precisely the same length of time as required for a population to become stationary. Moreover, the size of the mature population will grow at precisely the same *rate* as the growth in new entrants.

These facts are illustrated in Table 4–2 where each year the number of new entrants is doubled (i.e., a 100 percent growth rate). The decrement assumptions, however, remain the same as those used in Table 4–1. Once the population becomes mature, that is, after the third year, its membership size doubles each year thereafter, a rate of increase precisely equal to the rate of increase in new entrants. The age distribution, which is shown at the bottom of the table, is constant year after year, but considerably different from the age distribution developed in Table 4–1. This is the case for the service distribution also.

---

[2] This assumes, of course, that the distribution by age of new entrants is fixed.

TABLE 4-2

Development of a Mature Population

Elapsed Time in Years	Decrement Rates: Attained Ages:	←1/4→ y	 $y+1$	←1/3→ $y+2$	←1/2→ $y+3$	←1→ $y+4$	Total Size
0		100					100
1		200	75				275
2		400	150	50			600
3		800	300	100	25		1,225
4		1,600	600	200	50	0	2,450
5		3,200	1,200	400	100	0	4,900
6		6,400	2,400	800	200	0	9,800
7		12,800	4,800	1,600	400	0	19,600
.		.	.	.	.	.	.
.		.	.	.	.	.	.
Age distribution after 3 years:		65.3%	24.5%	8.2%	2.0%	0%	100%

Throughout the remainder of this book, reference will be made to a mature population, even in those cases where a stationary population applies, since it is the more general of the two concepts.

Undermature and Overmature Populations

A population is considered to be undermature if its age and service distribution has a larger proportion of younger, short-service employees than that of a mature population that faces the same decremental factors, is of the same size, and experiences the same entry age distribution. An overmature population is one that has a disproportionately large number of employees at older ages and with longer periods of service than that of a mature population based on the same decrement and entry age assumptions. Generally, industries that are growing in size are characterized by firms having undermature populations, while industries that are declining in size have firms with overmature populations.

An example of an undermature population is given in Table 4-3, where the number of new entrants increases by one hundred employees each year (i.e. a decreasing percentage growth rate). The membership distribution in the example, parenthetically expressed in percentage form, asymptotically approaches the same distribution as that for the stationary population discussed previously in Table 4-1. In fact, after 99 years of experience the population's age and service distribution is nearly identical to that of the corresponding stationary population.

TABLE 4–3

Development of an Undermature Population

Elapsed Time in Years	Decrement Rates: Attained Ages: y	←1/4→	←1/3→ $y + 1$	1/2 $y + 2$	←1→ $y + 3$	$y + 4$	Total Size
0	100 (100%)						100
1	200 (73%)		75 (27%)				275
2	300 (60%)		150 (30%)	50 (10%)			500
3	400 (53%)		225 (30%)	100 (13%)	25 (3%)	0	750
4	500 (50%)		300 (30%)	150 (15%)	50 (5%)	0	1,000
5	600 (48%)		375 (30%)	200 (16%)	75 (6%)	0	1,250
6	700 (47%)		450 (30%)	250 (17%)	100 (7%)	0	1,500
7	800 (46%)		525 (30%)	300 (17%)	125 (7%)	0	1,750
.	.		.	.	.	.	.
.	.		.	.	.	.	.
99	10,000 (40.4%)		7,425 (30%)	4,900 (19.8%)	2,425 (9.8%)	0	24,750
.	.		.	.	.	.	.
.	.		.	.	.	.	.
Asymptotic age distribution:	40%		30%	20%	10%	0%	100%

Finally, Table 4–4 illustrates the development of an overmature population, created by hiring 1,000 employees in the first year and 100 *fewer* employees each year thereafter. The degree to which the population is overmature is determinable by comparing its age and service distribution, parenthetically expressed in percentage form, to that of the stationary population based on the same decrement rates (given in the lower part of Table 4–4 for convenience).

TABLE 4–4

Development of an Overmature Population

Elapsed Time in Years	Decrement Rates: Attained Ages: y	←1/4→	←1/3→ $y + 1$	←1/2→ $y + 2$	←1→ $y + 3$	$y + 4$	Total Size
0	1,000 (100%)						1,000
1	900 (55%)		750 (45%)				1,650
2	800 (41%)		675 (34%)	500 (25%)			1,975
3	700 (35%)		600 (30%)	450 (22%)	250 (13%)		2,000
4	600 (34%)		525 (30%)	400 (23%)	225 (13%)	0	1,750
5	500 (33%)		450 (30%)	350 (23%)	200 (13%)	0	1,500
6	400 (32%)		375 (30%)	300 (24%)	175 (14%)	0	1,250
7	300 (30%)		300 (30%)	250 (25%)	150 (15%)	0	1,000
Age distribution for stationary population:	40%		30%	20%	10%	0%	100%

Size-Constrained Population

For purposes of illustration, the populations discussed so far have had their membership size as a derived or dependent variable and the number of newly hired employees as an independent variable. This is not a good assumption in dealing with pension plan populations, since the sponsoring firm determines the size of its employee group independent of the pension plan, causing the rate of new entrants to be the dependent variable. Switching the dependent and independent variables has significant implication for the resulting age and service distribution of the plan population.

The data in Table 4–5 show the results of a time-dependent plan population based on the same assumptions as before except for the membership size, which is assumed to be constant at 1,000 employees from the inception of the population onward. Although the data are presented in terms of numbers of employees, one need only shift the decimal point one position to the left to obtain the percentage distribution.

The age and service distribution of the constant-sized population is quite erratic at first, but becomes less so as time progresses. Although

TABLE 4–5

Development of a Size-Constrained Population

Elapsed Time in Years	Decrement Rates: Attained Ages:	←1/4→ y	←1/3→ y + 1	←1/2→ y + 2	←1→ y + 3	y + 4	Total Size
0		1,000*					1,000
1		250	750*				1,000
2		313	188	500*			1,000
3		391	234	125	250*		1,000
4		488*	293	156	63	0	1,000
5		360	366*	195	78	0	1,000
6		388	270	244*	98	0	1,000
7		407	291	180	122*	0	1,000
8		411*	305	194	90	0	1,000
9		391	308*	203	97	0	1,000
10		399	294	205*	102	0	1,000
11		402	299	196	103*	0	1,000
12		401*	302	200	98	0	1,000
13		398	301*	201	100	0	1,000
14		400	299	200*	101	0	1,000
15		400	300	199	100*	0	1,000
.		.		.	.	.	.
.		.	.	.	.	.	.
∞		400	300	200	100	0	1,000

* Indicates ripple: see text.

the age distribution in this example converges to that of the stationary population discussed in Table 4–1, the convergence is not a smooth one like that of the population studied in Table 4–3. In fact, a continually smaller and smaller ripple is seen to flow through the population during each successive year. This ripple, which begins with the initial group of 1,000 employees hired, is noted by asterisks in Table 4–5.

A size-constrained population will *generally* converge to its stationary counterpart created without a size constraint. The length of time required for the convergence is a function of the number of ages in the population and the rates of decrements at each of its ages. Naturally, the more attained ages, other things being equal, the longer it will take for the size-constrained population to come within a predetermined tolerance level of its stationary counterpart. Moreover, it turns out that the lower the age-specific rates of decrement, the longer it generally takes for a predetermined tolerance level to be reached. The latter generalization can be appreciated by considering the following extreme example.

Suppose the age-specific decrements are zero for each age up to the last age, at which point the decrement rate would be 100 percent. If a size constraint is imposed, the population will never converge to the uniform distribution that would result in the absence of the size constraint. In fact the population's age distribution will cycle indefinitely, with each n-year cycle consisting of n different distributions of 100 percent of the membership at each possible attained age, where n is the number of ages in the population. At the other extreme is the case where the rate of decrement is 100 percent at each age. The population under this assumption will be mature from its inception, since no employees will survive beyond age y and the entire labor force will be rehired at this age each year.

Up to this point, the discussion of a size-constrained population has dealt with a single entry age population. This is unrealistic for pension plan populations, since they conform to the more general multiple entry age, size-constrained population. It will be remembered that when the multiple entry age situation was discussed in the context of a stationary population without a size constraint, it was suggested that one conceptualize the population as consisting of a collection of single entry age populations. The situation is not nearly as simple when a size constraint is imposed. For example, it does not follow that each entry age subsector of the overall population will receive the same number of new entrants as the number of employees being decremented from it during the year. This is the case even if the hiring age distribution is held constant year after year, unless the population is mature. The ultimate effect is that the population tends to approach a mature status sooner than it takes the longest entry age sub-population to become mature under a size constraint. A numerical illustration of the convergence pattern of a multiple entry age population is given in the following section.

MODEL PLAN POPULATIONS

At later points in this book, pension costs are analyzed for individual participants and for various hypothetical pension plan populations. Naturally, an age and service distribution of plan members, a specific salary structure of active employees, and a benefit structure of nonactive plan members must be assumed when dealing with the plan as a whole. In the interest of generality, numerous plan populations, in varying states of maturity, are assumed for the numerical illustrations. Rather than choose the model populations arbitrarily, the experience of a single plan population is simulated over a period of fifty years. In order to simulate the various maturity statuses, the initial plan population in an undermature state is assumed to increase in size and then decrease over a 50-year period.[3]

The hiring age distribution and salary scale for new entrants during the 50-year simulation period is given in Table 4-6. The average hiring age is 28, and the hiring scale reflects one half of the standard merit increase from age 20 to each of the various entry ages. The total salary of active employees throughout the 50-year simulation increases according to the standard productivity and inflation rates specified earlier, that is, 1 percent and 4 percent, respectively. The increase in total salary, however, will be somewhat more than 5 percent because of the maturation that takes place in the population of active employees. The benefits of nonactive members, since there is no cost-of-living escalator incorporated in the plan, remain frozen at their terminating date.

---

[3] The initial undermature population itself is generated by a 25-year simulation. In order to avoid the rippling effect caused by hiring a large group of initial employees, the simulation assumed a zero sized labor force at the beginning and hired a progressively larger number of people each year. The rate of growth in this population was designed such that the rate in the last year (i.e., the first year of the model population) was equal to the rate of growth in the first year of the model population. Unlike the model population that develops various types of non-active members, the initial population consists only of active employees, consistent with the assumption that the pension plan is first begun at this point without provision for including the existing retired employees of the sponsoring firm.

TABLE 4–6

Hiring Age Distribution and Salary Scale

Entry Age	Hiring Distribution	Salary Scale
20	0.32	1.0000
25	0.26	1.1171
30	0.17	1.2437
35	0.10	1.3747
40	0.05	1.5042
45	0.04	1.6252
50	0.03	1.7301
55	0.02	1.8122
60	0.01	1.8655

Table 4–7 shows various statistics associated with the 50-year simulated plan population. The number of active employees, expressed as a percentage of the initial group, doubles during the first 25 years and then decreases to its original size over the succeeding 25 years. Thus, the population experiences (1) rapid growth, (2) gradual growth, (3) gradual decline, and (4) rapid decline during the 50-year period. Since the initial population of active employees is in an undermature state, the simulated population experiences various undermature, approximately mature, and overmature statuses. Several statistics associated with the corresponding *mature* population for the underlying decremental assumptions are given at the bottom of Table 4–7 for comparison.

The average age of active employees begins at age 35, increases to age 39.5 after 25 years and to age 46 by the end of the 50-year period. The average for the mature population is age 40.2, a value which is reached by the simulated population during its 29th year. The average service period of employees begins at 4.6 years, increases to 9.2 years after 25 years of simulation and to 16.0 years after 50 years. The average period of service for the mature population is 10.1 years, a value which is reached by the simulated population in its 30th year. These statistics show that even though the active population in its 30th year is not perfectly mature, its average age and service at this point are very nearly equal to that of the corresponding mature population. The speed with which the simulated population attains an approximately mature status is due, in part, to the assumption of multiple entry ages.

TABLE 4–7

Population Statistics

Year	Active Employees					Nonactive Employees as Percentage of Actives			
	Number as Percentage of Initial Size	Average Age	Average Service	Total Salary as Percentage of Initial	Average Salary as Percentage of Initial	Retired	Vested Terminated	Disabled	Surviving Spouses
0 . . .	100.0	34.9	4.6	100.0	100.0	0.0	0.0	0.0	0.0
1 . . .	107.8	35.0	4.8	113.6	105.3	0.3	0.7	0.0	0.0
2 . . .	115.4	35.1	4.9	128.1	111.0	0.7	1.4	0.0	0.0
3 . . .	122.6	35.3	5.1	143.6	117.1	1.0	2.0	0.1	0.0
4 . . .	129.4	35.5	5.2	160.0	123.6	1.3	2.7	0.1	0.0
5 . . .	136.0	35.7	5.4	177.4	130.5	1.6	3.4	0.1	0.0
6 . . .	142.2	35.9	5.6	195.9	137.7	1.9	4.1	0.1	0.0
7 . . .	148.2	36.1	5.8	215.4	145.4	2.2	4.8	0.1	0.0
8 . . .	153.8	36.3	6.0	236.0	153.5	2.6	5.5	0.2	0.1
9 . . .	159.0	36.5	6.2	257.7	162.1	2.9	6.3	0.2	0.1
10 . . .	164.0	36.7	6.4	280.6	171.1	3.2	7.1	0.2	0.1
11 . . .	168.6	37.0	6.6	304.5	180.6	3.6	7.9	0.3	0.1
12 . . .	173.0	37.2	6.8	329.7	190.6	4.0	8.8	0.3	0.1
13 . . .	177.0	37.4	7.0	356.0	201.2	4.3	9.7	0.4	0.1
14 . . .	180.6	37.6	7.2	383.5	212.3	4.7	10.6	0.4	0.2
15 . . .	184.0	37.7	7.4	412.2	224.0	5.1	11.6	0.4	0.2
16 . . .	187.0	37.9	7.6	442.1	236.3	5.5	12.6	0.5	0.2
17 . . .	189.8	38.1	7.7	473.1	249.3	6.0	13.6	0.5	0.2
18 . . .	192.2	38.3	7.9	505.4	263.0	6.4	14.7	0.6	0.3
19 . . .	194.2	38.5	8.1	538.9	277.4	6.9	15.8	0.7	0.3
20 . . .	196.0	38.7	8.3	573.5	292.6	7.4	16.9	0.7	0.3
21 . . .	197.4	38.8	8.5	609.2	308.5	7.8	18.0	0.8	0.4
22 . . .	198.6	39.0	8.7	646.0	325.3	8.4	19.2	0.9	0.4
23 . . .	199.4	39.2	8.8	683.9	343.0	8.9	20.4	0.9	0.5
24 . . .	199.8	39.3	9.0	722.8	361.7	9.4	21.6	1.0	0.5
25 . . .	200.0	39.5	9.2	762.6	381.3	10.0	22.9	1.1	0.6
26 . . .	199.8	39.7	9.4	803.3	402.0	10.6	24.1	1.2	0.6
27 . . .	199.4	39.8	9.5	844.7	423.7	11.2	25.4	1.2	0.7
28 . . .	198.6	40.0	9.7	886.8	446.6	11.8	26.8	1.3	0.8
29 . . .	197.4	40.1	9.9	929.5	470.8	12.4	28.2	1.4	0.8
30 . . .	196.0	40.3	10.1	972.6	496.2	13.1	29.6	1.5	0.9
31 . . .	194.2	40.4	10.2	1015.9	523.0	13.8	31.1	1.6	1.0
32 . . .	192.2	40.6	10.4	1059.4	551.3	14.6	32.6	1.7	1.1
33 . . .	189.8	40.8	10.6	1102.7	581.1	15.3	34.1	1.8	1.1
34 . . .	187.0	40.9	10.8	1145.8	612.6	16.1	35.8	1.9	1.2
35 . . .	184.0	41.1	10.9	1188.3	645.8	17.0	37.5	2.1	1.3
36 . . .	180.6	41.3	11.1	1230.0	680.9	17.9	39.2	2.2	1.4
37 . . .	177.0	41.4	11.3	1270.5	718.0	18.8	41.1	2.3	1.5
38 . . .	173.0	41.6	11.5	1309.7	757.2	19.8	43.0	2.4	1.7
39 . . .	168.6	41.8	11.7	1347.1	798.8	20.9	45.1	2.6	1.8
40 . . .	164.0	42.0	12.0	1382.3	842.9	22.0	47.3	2.7	1.9
41 . . .	159.0	42.3	12.2	1414.9	889.6	23.2	49.7	2.9	2.1
42 . . .	153.8	42.5	12.4	1444.4	939.4	24.5	52.2	3.0	2.2
43 . . .	148.2	42.8	12.7	1470.3	992.3	25.9	54.9	3.2	2.4
44 . . .	142.2	43.1	13.0	1492.0	1048.9	27.4	57.9	3.4	2.5
45 . . .	136.0	43.4	13.4	1509.0	1109.5	29.1	61.2	3.6	2.7
46 . . .	129.4	43.7	13.8	1520.4	1174.6	30.9	64.9	3.9	3.0
47 . . .	122.6	44.2	14.2	1525.5	1244.7	33.0	69.0	4.2	3.2
48 . . .	115.4	44.6	14.7	1523.7	1320.8	35.3	73.7	4.5	3.5
49 . . .	107.8	45.2	15.3	1513.8	1403.8	38.1	79.1	4.8	3.8
50 . . .	100.0	45.9	16.0	1495.0	1495.0	41.2	85.4	5.2	4.2
Mature population:		40.2	10.1			22.2	46.1	2.7	2.3

Table 4–7 also shows the total and average salary of active employees expressed as percentages of their respective values at the outset of the 50-year period. The ratio for total salaries increases to exactly double the ratio for average salaries after 25 years, a relationship consistent with the increase in the number of active employees. After 50 years, however, the total salary percentage is identical to the average salary percentage, since the population has returned to its initial size by this time. The rate of growth in average salary is approximately 5.5 percent during the first 25 years, and approximately 5.6 percent during the last 25 years. These values exceed 5 percent (i.e., 1 percent productivity and 4 percent inflation) because of the maturation of the population and its interaction with the merit salary scale.

The last four columns of Table 4–7 show the number of nonactive plan members as a percentage of active employees. There are no nonactives at the outset of the simulation, by definition, but by the end of 25 years, retired employees total 10 percent, vested termination employees (in both a pre- and post-retirement status) total 23 percent, disabled employees total 1.1 percent and surviving spouses total a mere 0.6 percent of active employees. After 50 years, retired employees total 41 percent of active employees, a considerably overmature state in comparison to 22 percent for the mature population (see the bottom of Table 4–7). The corresponding number of vested terminated employees after 50 years is 85 percent, as compared to 46 percent for the mature population. The largest number of disabled employees and surviving spouses totals only 5.2 and 4.2 percent respectively, even for the extremely overmature population at the end of the 50-year period.

The active population during the 25th year of the simulation is used to illustrate the cost impact of various plan benefits in Chapter 14 and of various actuarial assumptions in Chapter 15. The 25th year population was selected for these cost illustrations since it has characteristics similar to many plans in practice. All 50 plan populations shown in Table 4–7, however, are used as the basis for a financial comparison of actuarial cost methods in Chapter 16. Chapter 17 illustrates various pension cost forecasts, again using 50 hypothetical plan populations, but in this case the plan populations are different from those in Table 4–7. The initial plan population is assumed to be the population of active employees existing in the 16th year of the simulated population shown in Table 4–7, and the populations during the first 10 years are identical to those shown in Table 4–7 from the 16th to 25th year. The succeeding 40 years of populations, however, are based on a zero growth rate. A constant-sized population is used

TABLE 4–8

Population Statistics

Year	Active Employees					Nonactive Employees as Percentage of Actives			
	Number as Percentage of Initial Size	Average Age	Average Service	Total Salary as Percentage of Initial	Average Salary as Percentage of Initial	Retired	Vested Terminated	Disabled	Surviving Spouses
1 . . .	100.0	37.9	7.6	100.0	100.0	5.5	12.6	0.5	0.2
2 . . .	101.5	38.1	7.7	107.0	105.5	6.0	13.6	0.5	0.2
3 . . .	102.7	38.3	7.9	114.3	111.3	6.4	14.7	0.6	0.3
4 . . .	103.8	38.5	8.1	121.9	117.4	6.9	15.8	0.7	0.3
5 . . .	104.8	38.7	8.3	129.7	123.8	7.4	16.9	0.7	0.3
6 . . .	105.6	38.8	8.5	137.8	130.5	7.8	18.0	0.8	0.4
7 . . .	106.2	39.0	8.7	146.1	137.7	8.4	19.2	0.9	0.4
8 . . .	106.6	39.2	8.8	154.7	145.1	8.9	20.4	0.9	0.5
9 . . .	106.8	39.3	9.0	163.5	153.0	9.4	21.6	1.0	0.5
10 . . .	106.9	39.5	9.2	172.5	161.3	10.0	22.9	1.1	0.6
11 . . .	106.9	39.6	9.4	181.8	170.0	10.5	24.1	1.2	0.6
12 . . .	106.9	39.8	9.5	191.5	179.1	11.1	25.4	1.2	0.7
13 . . .	106.9	39.9	9.7	201.7	188.6	11.7	26.6	1.3	0.8
14 . . .	106.9	40.0	9.8	212.3	198.6	12.3	27.8	1.4	0.8
15 . . .	106.9	40.1	9.9	223.4	209.0	12.8	29.0	1.5	0.9
16 . . .	106.9	40.2	10.0	235.0	219.8	13.4	30.2	1.6	1.0
17 . . .	106.9	40.2	10.0	247.2	231.2	14.0	31.3	1.7	1.0
18 . . .	106.9	40.3	10.1	259.9	243.0	14.5	32.4	1.7	1.1
19 . . .	106.9	40.3	10.2	273.2	255.5	15.1	33.5	1.8	1.2
20 . . .	106.9	40.3	10.2	287.0	268.4	15.6	34.5	1.9	1.2
21 . . .	106.9	40.3	10.3	301.6	282.0	16.2	35.4	2.0	1.3
22 . . .	106.9	40.4	10.3	316.8	296.2	16.7	36.4	2.0	1.4
23 . . .	106.9	40.4	10.3	332.7	311.1	17.2	37.2	2.1	1.4
24 . . .	106.9	40.4	10.3	349.4	326.7	17.7	38.1	2.2	1.5
25 . . .	106.9	40.4	10.3	366.8	343.1	18.1	38.8	2.2	1.6
26 . . .	106.9	40.4	10.3	385.1	360.2	18.6	39.6	2.3	1.6
27 . . .	106.9	40.3	10.3	404.3	378.1	19.0	40.3	2.3	1.7
28 . . .	106.9	40.3	10.3	424.4	396.9	19.4	40.9	2.4	1.8
29 . . .	106.9	40.3	10.3	445.4	416.6	19.8	41.5	2.4	1.8
30 . . .	106.9	40.3	10.3	467.5	437.2	20.1	42.0	2.5	1.9
31 . . .	106.9	40.3	10.2	490.7	458.9	20.4	42.6	2.5	1.9
32 . . .	106.9	40.3	10.2	515.0	481.6	20.7	43.0	2.6	2.0
33 . . .	106.9	40.2	10.2	540.5	505.5	21.0	43.5	2.6	2.0
34 . . .	106.9	40.2	10.2	567.3	530.5	21.3	43.8	2.6	2.1
35 . . .	106.9	40.2	10.2	595.4	556.8	21.5	44.2	2.6	2.1
36 . . .	106.9	40.2	10.2	625.0	584.5	21.7	44.5	2.7	2.1
37 . . .	106.9	40.2	10.1	656.0	613.5	21.8	44.8	2.7	2.2
38 . . .	106.9	40.2	10.1	688.6	644.0	22.0	45.1	2.7	2.2
39 . . .	106.9	40.2	10.1	722.8	676.0	22.1	45.3	2.7	2.2
40 . . .	106.9	40.1	10.1	758.8	709.6	22.2	45.5	2.7	2.2
41 . . .	106.9	40.1	10.1	796.6	745.0	22.3	45.6	2.7	2.2
42 . . .	106.9	40.1	10.1	836.3	782.1	22.4	45.8	2.7	2.3
43 . . .	106.9	40.1	10.1	878.0	821.1	22.4	45.9	2.7	2.3
44 . . .	106.9	40.1	10.1	921.8	862.1	22.5	46.0	2.7	2.3
45 . . .	106.9	40.1	10.1	967.9	905.2	22.5	46.1	2.7	2.3
46 . . .	106.9	40.1	10.1	1016.3	950.4	22.5	46.2	2.7	2.3
47 . . .	106.9	40.1	10.1	1067.1	998.0	22.5	46.2	2.7	2.3
48 . . .	106.9	40.1	10.1	1120.5	1047.9	22.5	46.2	2.7	2.3
49 . . .	106.9	40.1	10.1	1176.6	1100.4	22.5	46.3	2.7	2.3
50 . . .	106.9	40.1	10.1	1235.6	1155.5	22.5	46.3	2.7	2.3

for these analyses in order to reduce the effect of a sharply changing maturity status. The characteristics of this population are given in Table 4–8. It is interesting to observe that the population's average age and service are quite stable beyond the point at which the population is assumed to be constant in size. Also, in comparing the number of nonactives in Tables 4–8 to those in Table 4–7, one will note that there are considerably fewer of these members than was the case for the previous population, which was assumed to decrease in size during its final 25 years of experience.

Chapter 5

Basic Pension
Cost Concepts

The purpose of this chapter is to define certain basic pension cost concepts that are essential to understanding the more specific pension cost models studied in later chapters. The discussion begins by defining the liability associated with future benefits under the plan, and then moves to the termination-of-plan and continuation-of-plan liabilities, both of which may be used as yardsticks for measuring the adequacy of plan assets. The actuarial liability and the supplemental liability are also defined in this chapter, as are the related concepts of the plan's normal cost and supplemental cost.

PENSION PLAN LIABILITY MEASURES

Present Value of Future Benefits

The liability associated with the future benefits of all *existing* plan members is known as the present value of future benefits (PVFB). Future benefits refer to benefits accrued to date plus all benefits expected to accrue throughout the remainder of each employee's working career. Theoretically, if a plan has assets equal to its PVFB liability, there would be sufficient funds to pay all of the accrued and future benefits to each *existing* plan member, provided that all actuarial assumptions are precisely experienced by the plan over future years, and that no plan changes are made. The plan's PVFB liability is not a funding target liability, but rather, a liability used in determining a plan's annual costs and other liability measures.

Mathematics.   The calculation of the PVFB liability for active employees includes, at a minimum, future retirement benefits and future vested termination benefits; future disability benefits, surviving spouse benefits, and death benefits will also be included in a particular pension plan's liability if the plan includes these benefit provisions. At this point, only the present value of future retirement benefits is mathematically defined, but the same underlying concepts apply to the present value of future benefits attributable to each ancillary benefit, as will be shown in Chapters 10 and 11.

Notationally, the PVFB function for an employee currently age x, having entered the plan at age y and retiring at age r, is

$$(\text{PVFB})_x = B_r \,_{r-x}p_x^{(T)} v^{r-x} \ddot{a}_r \qquad (x < r), \tag{5.1a}$$

where

B_r = the pension benefit at retirement for the age-y entrant

$_{r-x}p_x^{(T)}$ = the probability that the employee age x survives in employment to age r

v^{r-x} = the interest discount from age x to r

$\ddot{a}_r$ = the present value, at age r, of a life annuity due in the amount of one dollar payable at the beginning of the age.

After retirement this function is equal to

$$(\text{PVFB})_x = B_r \ddot{a}_x \qquad (x \geqslant r). \tag{5.1b}$$

The PVFB liability for the plan as a whole is equal to the sum of each plan participant's PVFB liability.

The PVFB function for active employees increases with age from entry age y to retirement age r, since both $_{r-x}p_x^{(T)}$ and v^{r-x} approach unity as x approaches r. Beyond age r, however, the PVFB function decreases, since $\ddot{a}_x$ is a decreasing function of attained age. The PVFB function for a given individual at a specific attained age has a direct relationship to the projected benefit, and an inverse relationship to the interest rate and various rates of decrement.

The first column of Table 5–1 shows the $(\text{PVFB})_x$ function at various attained ages for an age-30 entrant under standard assumptions, expressed as a percentage of the $(\text{PVFB})_{65}$ value. The second column shows this function as a percentage of attained age salary during the participant's pre-retirement ages. The results of assuming a 5 percent and a 9 percent rate of interest, instead of the standard 7 percent assumption, are given in columns three and four, and the results of assuming withdrawal rates equal to 50 percent and 150 percent of the standard withdrawal assumption are given in the last two columns.

The (PVFB)$_x$ function is quite small for the majority of the participant's working life and does not reach 50 percent of the age-65 value until about 10 years prior to retirement. After retirement the (PVFB)$_x$ function declines relatively slowly and reaches the 50 percent value after about 20 years into retirement. These data illustrate that the PVFB liability takes on its largest values for active employees near retirement and for retired employees during their age-65 life expectancy period (i.e., for about 15 years or so after retirement).

TABLE 5–1

Attained Age and Sensitivity Analysis of the (PVFB)$_x$ Function for an Age-30 Entrant

Age	$100 \dfrac{(PVFB)_x}{(PVFB)_{65}}$	$\dfrac{(PVFB)_x}{s_x}$	$i = 0.05$	$i = 0.09$	$0.5q_x^{(w)}$	$1.5q_x^{(w)}$
30....	1.32	55.80	220.53	46.57	226.17	42.54
35....	3.54	99.96	200.67	51.08	162.05	60.94
40....	6.90	132.99	182.61	56.04	137.76	72.08
45....	12.51	168.61	166.17	61.48	121.98	81.65
50....	22.22	214.58	151.21	67.44	109.95	90.79
55....	39.60	280.95	137.59	73.98	100.00	100.00
60....	60.30	322.10	125.21	81.16	100.00	100.00
65....	100.00	412.30	113.94	89.03	100.00	100.00
70....	86.69	0.00	111.74	90.49	100.00	100.00
75....	73.79	0.00	109.69	91.94	100.00	100.00
80....	61.07	0.00	107.83	93.32	100.00	100.00
85....	50.48	0.00	106.25	94.54	100.00	100.00
90....	41.78	0.00	104.90	95.64	100.00	100.00
95....	34.10	0.00	103.67	96.67	100.00	100.00
100....	26.98	0.00	102.52	97.67	100.00	100.00
105....	19.62	0.00	101.33	98.75	100.00	100.00
110....	10.95	0.00	100.00	100.00	100.00	100.00

(PVFB)$_x$ Function under Alternative Assumptions as a Percentage of (PVFB)$_x$ under Standard Assumptions

A change in the interest rate has its largest effect on the (PVFB)$_x$ function at the youngest age, with the effect of such changes diminishing as x approaches the end of the human life span. The same is true for changes in the rates of termination, but in this case there is no effect beyond the age for which the employee first qualifies for early retirement. Table 5–1 shows that a change in the interest rate has a fairly significant effect on the (PVFB)$_x$ function at those ages surrounding the participant's retirement date, while the termination rate assumption has no influence beyond age 55. Thus, a given percentage change in the interest rate will change the plan's overall present value of future benefits more than an equal percentage change in the termination assumptions. These relationships for the plan as a whole are investigated in Chapter 15.

Termination-of-Plan Liability

The termination-of-plan liability (TPL) is the present value of all accrued benefits. It is calculated using two factors importantly different from those used in the determination of the PVFB liability for active employees, although for nonactive plan members the two liabilities are equal in value. One factor that distinguishes the TPL from the PVFB liability for active employees is the use of the *accrued* benefit rather than the projected benefit. This is a logical difference in calculating the TPL liability since, in the event that the plan were to terminate, an employee would not have earned his projected benefit. The second important difference is that the present value calculation under the TPL includes a mortality decrement only, rather than including all decremental factors as was the case for the PVFB liability. The reason for using solely the mortality decrement is that only death prevents the participant from eventually receiving retirement payments if the plan were to terminate in the current year with adequate assets. This is in contrast to the PVFB liability, where the chances of receiving the projected benefit are reduced by the withdrawal and disability contingencies as well as the mortality contingency.

The termination-of-plan liability for an employee age x, who entered the plan at age y, is given by

$$(\text{TPL})_x = B_{x\ r-x}p_x'^{(m)}v^{r-x}\ddot{a}_r, \tag{5.2}$$

where B_x is the age-y entrant's accrued benefits at age x in the event that the plan were to terminate at that age, $_{r-x}p_x'^{(m)}$ is the probability (in a single-decrement environment) of living from age x to age r, and the other components are as defined previously. Although $_{r-x}p_x'^{(m)} > {}_{r-x}p_x^{(T)}$, the accrued benefit B_x generally will be considerably smaller than the projected benefit B_r for most attained ages; hence, the TPL generally will be *smaller* than the PVFB liability. As noted above, these two liabilities are equal for employees at and beyond age r.

The termination-of-plan liability for the entire plan is equal to the sum of each individual's TPL. The *vested* TPL is found by summing the TPL associated with vested accrued benefits only, which includes the benefits of nonactive employees. Under current law, however, all employees are deemed to be fully vested in their accrued benefits if the plan should be terminated, and this is the basis used in subsequent portions of this book when referring to the TPL.

The termination-of-plan liability offers a yardstick for measuring the adequacy of plan assets. Clearly, if all actuarial assumptions were to be realized over future years (and for the TPL this involves only the mortality rate and interest rate assumptions) a plan holding funds equal to the TPL would be able to pay all of the benefits that have accrued to date on behalf of active employees plus all benefits due to nonactive plan members.

Continuation-of-Plan Liability

The fact is that most pension plans are not going to terminate within the foreseeable future, and hence, the TPL may not represent the most meaningful liability measure. In this case, the continuation-of-plan liability (CPL) may be more useful.

The continuation-of-plan liability is the present value of all accrued benefits, where the accrued benefits are defined as being equal to a *pro rata* share of the participant's projected benefit B_r, the prorating being based on the employee's service to date versus his total potential service. The CPL, therefore, is calculated by using accrued benefits that have an element of future salary increase built into them for plans having a salary-based benefit formula. Moreover, the present value of the accrued benefits under the CPL is determined by using *all* of the decremental factors, unlike the TPL, for which only the mortality decrement is used. The CPL for an active employee age x, having entered the plan at age y and retiring at age r, is given by

$$(\text{CPL})_x = B_r \frac{(x - y)}{(r - y)} \,_{r-x}p_x^{(T)} v^{r-x} \ddot{a}_r, \tag{5.3a}$$

or simply,

$$(\text{CPL})_x = \frac{(x - y)}{(r - y)} (\text{PVFB})_x \tag{5.3b}$$

Thus, the CPL represents a pro rata share of the PVFB function, prorated according to the employee's years of service to date relative to his potential years of service. The CPL for nonactive employees is precisely equal to the PVFB liability (and the TPL) for these plan members as defined earlier. Finally, as before, the total CPL for the plan is equal to the sum of each individual plan participant's continuation-of-plan liability.

Table 5–2 shows a comparison of the TPL and CPL as a percentage of the PVFB liability for the age-30 entrant under the standard assumptions. Both the TPL and the CPL percentages are zero at the employee's entry age and equal to unity at and beyond age 65. The

CPL percentage in this example exceeds the TPL percentage at each attained age, but this relationship may not always hold. For example, under a flat benefit formula, the accrued benefits at age x are identical for both the TPL and the CPL, while the survival probability, $_{r-x}p_x^{(T)}$, used in the continuation-of-plan liability will be *less* than the probability used in the termination-of-plan liability. In this case, the CPL will be less than the TPL, or just the opposite of that shown in Table 5–2. On the other hand, an early retirement provision could reverse this relationship. Although no definite relationship exists between these two liabilities, it is generally true that the CPL is the larger for a final average salary plan, while the TPL is the larger for a flat benefit plan. These two measures are studied for a final average salary plan in Chapter 16.

TABLE 5–2

(TPL)$_x$ and (CPL)$_x$ as a Percentage of the (PVFB)$_x$ Liability

Age	$100 \dfrac{(TPL)_x}{(PVFB)_x}$	$100 \dfrac{(CPL)_x}{(PVFB)_x}$
30.	0.00	0.00
32.	2.80	5.71
34.	4.86	11.43
36.	7.04	17.14
38.	9.64	22.86
40.	12.53	28.57
42.	15.76	34.29
44.	19.36	40.00
46.	23.33	45.71
48.	27.67	51.43
50.	32.35	57.14
52.	37.35	62.86
54.	42.64	68.57
56.	49.96	74.29
58.	59.99	80.00
60.	71.13	85.71
62.	83.02	91.43
64.	94.72	97.14
65.	100.00	100.00

Figure 5–1 has been constructed to show the relationship among the (PVFB)$_x$, (TPL)$_x$, and (CPL)$_x$ for the age-30 entrant until his assumed death at age 110 under standard assumptions. Prior to retirement, the three functions take on a predictable pattern, but it should be noted that one must measure the vertical distance between the lines in order to ascertain the differences among these functions

FIGURE 5–1

Attained Age Liability Functions as a Percentage of the Age-65 Values

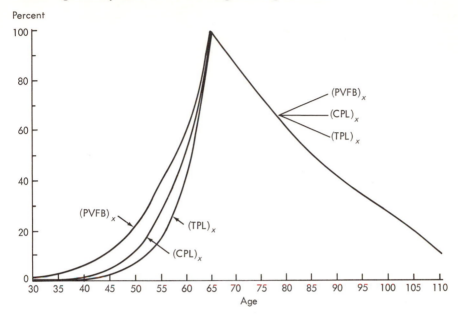

at each attained age. As noted earlier, the three liability measures are identical after retirement. Figure 5–1 portrays the observation made earlier that the bulk of an employee's liability is associated with ages near retirement.

ACTUARIAL COST METHOD CONCEPTS

Normal Cost

The normal cost for a particular participant, or for the plan as a whole, is defined quite specifically by the particular actuarial cost method under consideration. Although subsequent chapters take up the various actuarial cost methods in considerable detail, it is nevertheless worthwhile to present the general normal cost concept at this point.

In general, the normal cost is designed to amortize $(PVFB)_y$ over the employee's working lifetime, the pattern of amortization payments being specified by the particular actuarial cost method. Thus, prospectively, the present value of a participant's normal costs at age y

is equal to his $(PVFB)_y$ at that age. Retrospectively, the normal costs will accumulate by age r to the participant's $(PVFB)_r$.[1] Alternatively, the actuarial accumulation of the normal costs up to age x ($y < x < r$) plus the present value of *future* normal costs at that age is equal to $(PVFB)_x$.

The age-specific normal costs need not be constant over all ages and in theory, at least, they may take on any positive or negative value at certain ages. The only theoretical restriction on the age-specific normal cost values is that their present value (or accumulated value) satisfy the above relationships. Since an infinite number of normal cost patterns could be calculated such that these conditions hold, there exists an infinite number of possible actuarial cost methods, only a few of which are formally recognized and discussed in this book.

Actuarial Liability

The actuarial liability (AL) associated with a given participant is equal to the portion of $(PVFB)_y$ theoretically amortized by age x, exclusive of the normal cost then due. At the employee's entry age none of $(PVFB)_y$ will have been amortized; hence, the actuarial liability is zero. At the employee's retirement age all of $(PVFB)_y$ will have been amortized, but note that $(PVFB)_y$ will have increased to $(PVFB)_r$ by this age. During the intermediate ages, the portion of $(PVFB)_y$ amortized may be expressed in several ways.

Prospectively, the actuarial liability at age x ($y < x < r$) is equal to the present value of future benefits at that age less the present value of future normal costs yet to be made.[2]

$$(AL)_x = (PVFB)_x - (PVFNC)_x. \tag{5.4}$$

If we let $(NC)_t$ denote the normal cost at age t under a given actuarial cost method; then the present value of future normal costs is represented by

$$(PVFNC)_x = \sum_{t=x}^{r-1} (NC)_t \, {}_{t-x}p_x^{(T)} v^{t-x}. \tag{5.5}$$

---

[1] In actual fact the past normal costs of a plan may not accumulate to the value of $(PVFB)_r$ at age r because of the granting of past service credits for years prior to the plan establishment, plan changes, and/or actuarial gains or losses. Mathematically, however, the relationship holds.

[2] It might be helpful to consider the PVFB as a participant's gross liability with his actuarial liability representing a net liability (i.e., the gross liability less the intangible asset known as the present value of future normal costs). In addition, the actuarial liability is often called the accrued liability. The term accrued liability should be used only with the TPL or CPL, since these liabilities measure the value of accrued benefits under the plan.

Since $(PVFB)_y$ will have increased to $(PVFB)_x$ by age x, equation (5.4) shows that $(AL)_x$ is the portion of $(PVFB)_x$ not yet amortized by age x. The actuarial liability in retirement is simply equal to the $(PVFB)_x$ at each age $(x \geq r)$, as was the case for the TPL and CPL for retired plan participants.

The actuarial liability of an active employee can also be defined retrospectively, in which case it is equal to the accumulated value of past normal costs (AVPNC).[3] Thus, $(AL)_x$, a value which *excludes* the normal cost due at the beginning of the current age x, is given by

$$(AL)_x = (AVPNC)_x = \sum_{t=y}^{x-1} (NC)_t (1 + i)^{x-t} \frac{1}{x-t p_t^{(T)}}. \qquad (5.6a)$$

The second factor in the summation, $(1 + i)^{x-t}$, increases each value of $(NC)_t$ with interest from age y to age x, while the third factor increases the normal cost at each age according to the benefit of survivorship in employment.

The benefit of interest is a fairly straightforward concept, but the benefit of survivorship may not be at first glance. In order to explore the latter, we write equation (5.6a) with $x-t p_t^{(T)}$ replaced by its more basic form: $l_x^{(T)} \div l_t^{(T)}$.[4]

$$(AL)_x = \sum_{t=y}^{x-1} (NC)_t (1 + i)^{x-t} \frac{l_t^{(T)}}{l_x^{(T)}} \qquad (5.6b)$$

In this form we see that for each age t, a normal cost is generated on behalf of all of the hypothetical employees at this age, yet the total accumulation at age x is shared only by the lesser number of those who survive in service to this age; hence, they receive the benefit of survivorship in service.

A more general definition of the actuarial liability, appropriate both before and after retirement, is given by

$$(AL)_x = \sum_{t=y}^{x-1} [(NC)_t - B_t](1 + i)^{x-t} \frac{1}{x-t p_t^{(T)}}. \qquad (5.7)$$

In this formulation the annual pension benefit, B_t, would be zero prior to retirement and equal to B_r after retirement. Conversely, $(NC)_t$ would be positive prior to retirement and zero after retirement.

---

[3] As noted under the discussion of normal costs, the actual normal costs of a plan may not conform to the theoretical normal costs for various reasons (see footnote 1). The above discussion is assuming the theoretical, rather than the actual, normal costs for a given employee.

[4] $l_x^{(T)}$ is the number of survivors out of an arbitrary number of employees beginning at some entry age y and who are exposed to the various decrements from y to x. See Chapter 3, Table 3–2, for an example of the $l_x^{(T)}$ function.

It will be shown in subsequent chapters that the normal cost pattern for an employee during his working career will vary according to the actuarial cost method being used, with some methods developing a larger cost at younger ages and a smaller cost at older ages than other methods. Since the value of $(PVFNC)_x$ used in (5.4) or the value of $(AVPNC)_x$ in (5.6a) is a function of the actuarial cost method, the actuarial liability up to age r must also be a function of the actuarial cost method. Some actuarial cost methods develop a larger actuarial liability at ages between y and r than other methods.

Supplemental Liability

The retrospective (using actual normal cost values) and prospective valuation approaches to determining a plan participant's actuarial liability will be equal, provided that several rigid conditions are met. In a more typical situation, however, one or more of these conditions will be violated, and in turn, there will be a discrepancy between the two calculations of the actuarial liability. This discrepancy, called the plan's supplemental liability, is brought about by several factors.

One major source of a supplemental liability is the granting of pension credits for service rendered prior to the establishment of the plan; that is, for ages during which normal costs, quite logically, were not determined. In this case the prospectively determined actuarial liability takes on a positive value while the retrospectively determined actuarial liability is clearly zero, the difference representing the supplemental liability at the point of plan establishment. This liability is often referred to as the *past service liability* of the plan.

Another source of supplemental liability is the liberalization of plan benefits, since this causes an increase in the prospectively determined actuarial liability without a commensurate increase in the accumulation of past normal costs. A third source is the changing of an actuarial assumption. Such a change affects only the prospectively determined actuarial liability, leaving the accumulation of past normal costs unaffected, and a supplemental liability (positive or negative) results. Finally, year-to-year deviations of the plan's experience from that anticipated by the actuarial assumptions generates a positive or negative discrepancy between the prospectively valued actuarial liability and the accumulation of past normal costs. This particular discrepancy is known more generally as an actuarial gain or loss, but it clearly falls within the more formal definition of a supplemental liability.

In theory, the supplemental liability for an individual age x is equal to the actuarial liability valued prospectively less the actuarial liability valued retrospectively (using actual past normal cost values). Thus, letting $(SL)_x$ denote the supplemental liability, we have

$$(SL)_x = \begin{array}{c}\text{Prospective}\\\text{Actuarial}\\\text{Liability}\end{array} - \begin{array}{c}\text{Retrospective}\\\text{Actuarial}\\\text{Liability}\end{array} \qquad (5.8a)$$

$$= [(PVFB)_x - (PVFNC)_x] - (AVPNC)_x, \qquad (5.8b)$$

where $(AVPNC)_x$ represents the accumulated value of past normal costs at age x.[5] If we restrict the true actuarial liability to its prospective definition, then (5.8a) may be written as

$$(SL)_x = (AL)_x - (AVPNC)_x. \qquad (5.8c)$$

The above shows that the supplemental liability is a residual item, making up the difference between the PVFB liability at age x and the accumulated value of (actual) past normal costs and the present value of future normal costs. The above equations are applicable to both active and nonactive plan members, with $(PVFNC)_x$ equal to zero for nonactives.

The supplemental liability *increment* (SLI) during age x, a value determined at the beginning of age $x + 1$, can be found by the following formula:[6]

$$(SLI)_x = (AL)_{x+1} - \frac{(SL)_x(1 + i)}{p_x^{(T)}} - (AVPNC)_{x+1}. \qquad (5.9)$$

In words, the actuarial liability at age $x + 1$ less the actuarial accumulations of any supplemental liability at the previous age, should be precisely offset by the actuarial accumulation of past normal costs at age $x + 1$. If the offset is not exact, then a positive or negative supplemental liability increment will have been created during age x.

Supplemental Cost

The supplemental cost of a plan participant is designed to amortize the associated supplemental liability. In this sense, the supplemental

---

[5] The accumulated value of past normal costs is based on the actual experience of the plan, rather than the actuarial assumptions from which the present value of future normal costs is determined.

[6] This equation is not used in practice, and is of only theoretical significance. Also, if this equation were to be made applicable to the plan as a whole, the benefit of survivorship in service, generated by $p_x^{(T)}$, would be eliminated from the formulation, i.e. $(SLI)_{t+1} = (AL)_{t+1} - (SL)_t(1 + i) - (PVFNC)_{t+1}$, where t is the year under consideration and each symbol denotes the value for the entire plan.

cost is like the normal cost which is designed to amortize $(PVFB)_y$ over the period from age y to r, but which may fail to do so because one or more of the conditions given in the previous section has not been met. The failure of the normal cost to amortize $(PVFB)_y$ creates a supplemental liability, which in turn generates a supplemental cost.

The supplemental cost can be a one-time cost equal in value to the supplemental liability created during a given year, or it can extend over a period of years. If the latter approach is used, the precise pattern of supplemental costs may be level, or it may be geared to the corresponding normal cost pattern of the actuarial cost method in use, as will be shown at a subsequent point.

The accumulated value of past supplemental costs (AVPSC) plus the present value of future supplemental costs (PVFSC) is at all times equal to the supplemental liability:

$$(SL)_x = (AVPSC)_x + (PVFSC)_x. \tag{5.10a}$$

Substituting this definition of $(SL)_x$ into equation (5.8b) and re-arranging we have

$$\begin{aligned}(PVFB)_x &= (AVPNC)_x + (AVPSC)_x \\ &\quad + (PVFNC)_x + (PVFSC)_x.\end{aligned} \tag{5.10b}$$

Thus, the PVFB liability is equal at all times to the accumulated value of past normal and supplemental costs plus the present value of future normal and supplemental costs.

Unfunded Liability

The unfunded liability of a plan is the difference between a given liability measure and the plan's assets. The unfunded *accrued* liability is an expression denoting the difference between the plan's TPL or the CPL and its assets.[7] Thus, we have

$$^{TPL}(UL)_t = (TPL)_t - (Assets)_t \tag{5.11a}$$

$$^{CPL}(UL)_t = (CPL)_t - (Assets)_t \tag{5.11b}$$

where each symbol represents the appropriate value for the plan as a whole at time t.

The unfunded *actuarial* liability, on the other hand, is an expression

---

[7] The market value of assets should be used in (5.11a), while actuary's book should be used in (5.11b) and (5.11c). Actuary's book is generally equal to the amortized book value of bonds and some average market value (e.g., five-year average) of equity investments.

denoting the difference between the plan's actuarial liability and its assets:

$$^{AL}(UL)_t = (AL)_t - (Assets)_t. \tag{5.11c}$$

Actuarial Gains and Losses

An important year-to-year source of supplemental liability increments (or decrements) is actuarial losses (or gains). The supplemental liability created during year t from actuarial deviations is equal to the *actual* unfunded liability at $t + 1$ less the *expected* unfunded liability at this point:

$$^{AD}(SLI)_t = {}^{AL}(UL)_{t+1} - E^{AL}(UL)_{t+1}, \tag{5.12}$$

where

$^{AD}(SLI)_t$ = supplemental liability increment (positive or negative) from actuarial deviations during year t

$E^{AL}(UL)_{t+1}$ = expected unfunded actuarial liability at $t + 1$.

In order to operationalize equation (5.12), an expression must be developed for $E^{AL}(UL)_{t+1}$. This will be done by developing expressions for the expected actuarial liability at $t + 1$ and the expected plan assets at this point, the difference of which is equal to the $E^{AL}(UL)_{t+1}$.

The expected actuarial liability at $t + 1$ is given by

$$E(AL)_{t+1} = [(AL)_t + (NC)_t - B_t](1 + i), \tag{5.13}$$

where $(NC)_t$ is the total normal cost of the plan and B_t is the total benefits paid from the plan, both assumed to occur at the beginning of the year.[8] If the actual actuarial liability at $t + 1$ is not equal to $E(AL)_{t+1}$ as defined above, then a liability-based actuarial deviation will have occurred during year t.

The expected assets at $t + 1$ may be written as

$$E(Assets)_{t+1} = [(Assets)_t + (Cont)_t - B_t](1 + i), \tag{5.14}$$

where $(Cont)_t$ is the total plan contributions (normal and supplemental cost) at time t.[9] If actual assets are different from $E(Assets)_{t+1}$, an asset-based actuarial deviation will have occurred during year t.

---

[8] If benefits are paid monthly, the above equation must be adjusted to reflect expected benefit payments and interest thereon. The same applies to (5.14).

[9] If contributions are not paid at the beginning of the year, as is assumed in (5.14), the equation must be modified to reflect the corresponding loss in interest.

The *expected* unfunded actuarial liability at $t + 1$, equal to the difference between the expected actuarial liability and expected assets, is

$$E^{AL}(UL)_{t+1} = E(AL)_{t+1} - E(Assets)_{t+1}, \qquad (5.15a)$$

and substituting (5.13) and (5.14), we have

$$E^{AL}(UL)_{t+1} = [(AL)_t + (NC)_t - (Assets)_t - (Cont)_t](1 + i). \quad (5.15b)$$

Finally, substituting $E^{AL}(UL)_{t+1}$ into (5.12) yields an operational expression for determining the net actuarial gain or loss during year t:

$$
\begin{aligned}
^{AD}(SLI)_t &= \;^{AL}(UL)_{t+1} - [(AL)_t + (NC)_t - (Assets)_t \\
&\quad - (Cont)_t](1 + i)
\end{aligned}
\qquad (5.16a)
$$

$$= \;^{AL}(UL)_{t+1} - [^{AL}(UL)_t + (NC)_t - (Cont)_t](1 + i). \quad (5.16b)$$

In words, (5.16b) shows that there will be no supplemental liability increment if the unfunded actuarial liability, $^{AL}(UL)_t$, plus the net change in the unfunded actuarial liability, $[(NC)_t - (Cont)_t]$, accumulated with interest, is equal to the actuarial unfunded liability at the end of the year.

Observe from (5.16b) that if $(NC)_t = (Cont)_t$, and if $^{AD}(SLI)_t$ were zero for the year, then $(UL)_{t+1} = (UL)_t(1 + i)$. In this case contributions equal to the normal cost *plus* the present value of the interest on the unfunded actuarial liability will keep the unfunded actuarial liability constant from year to year, that is,

$$(Cont)_t = (NC)_t + vi(UL)_t \qquad (5.17a)$$

$$= (NC)_t + d(UL)_t, \qquad (5.17b)$$

where

$$d = vi = \text{rate of discount.}$$

Chapter 6

Accrued Benefit
Cost Method

The accrued benefit actuarial cost method denotes a family of specific actuarial cost methods which are the subject of this chapter. Chapter 7 considers another family of actuarial cost methods known generally as the projected benefit cost method. Generalizations of these methods appear in Chapter 9 and indicate the comprehensiveness of these families.

ACCRUED BENEFIT COST METHOD
WITH SUPPLEMENTAL LIABILITY[1]

The accrued benefit cost method, ABCM, *with* supplemental liability is a method that explicitly considers the benefits that accrue (or are assumed to accrue) in the current year, and the cumulative benefits that have accrued (or are assumed to have accrued) to date. The cost of benefits accruing in the current year represents the normal cost of the method, while the value of all benefits accrued to date represents the actuarial liability. This is a somewhat different explanation of a cost method's normal cost and actuarial liability than that presented in Chapter 5. At that point the normal cost was described as the annual amount necessary to amortize $(PVFB)_y$ from age y to age r, and the actuarial liability was described as the cumulative portion of $(PVFB)_y$ amortized at each age. The equivalence of these seemingly different descriptions is shown at a later point in this chapter.

---

[1] This method is technically known as the Individual Accrued Benefit Cost Method With Supplemental Liability to distinguish it from the so-called Aggregate Accrued Benefit Cost Method With Supplemental Liability, which is studied in Chapter 8.

Normal Cost

In Chapter 3 we defined a participant's benefit accrual at age x, and denoted this quantity by b_x. Two modifications to the natural benefit accrual were also introduced. The CA modification transformed b_x into a pro rata share of the projected benefit, while the CS modification transformed b_x into a value equal to a constant percentage of salary at each age. The benefit accruals under these two modifications are denoted by $^{CA}b_x$ and $^{CS}b_x$, respectively.

As noted above, the normal cost under the ABCM represents the cost of the benefit accruing in the current year. If the natural benefit accruals are assumed, we have

$$(\text{NC})_x = b_x \,_{r-x}p_x^{(T)}v^{r-x}\ddot{a}_r \tag{6.1}$$

where

$$_{r-x}p_x^{(T)} = \text{probability of surviving in service from age } x \text{ to age } r$$

$$v^{r-x} = \text{interest discount from age } x \text{ to age } r$$

$$\ddot{a}_r = \text{life annuity valued at age } r.$$

The normal cost under the two modified accrued benefit cost methods, the ^{CA}ABCM and the ^{CS}ABCM, is found by substituting $^{CA}b_x$ and $^{CS}b_x$, respectively, into equation (6.1) for b_x, where

$$^{CA}b_x = \frac{B_r}{(r-y)} = \text{benefit accrual under the } ^{CA}\text{ABCM} \tag{3.15a}$$

$$^{CS}b_x = \frac{B_r}{S_r}s_x = \text{benefit accrual under the } ^{CS}\text{ABCM.} \tag{3.16a}$$

At the employee's entry age the following inequality holds:

$$b_y \leqslant \,^{CS}b_y \leqslant \,^{CA}b_y, \tag{6.2a}$$

while during his last year of employment, age $r-1$, the inequality is reversed:

$$b_{r-1} \geqslant \,^{CS}b_{r-1} \geqslant \,^{CA}b_{r-1}. \tag{6.2b}$$

These relationships among the benefit accruals show that the normal cost under the natural benefit accruals will be the lowest of the three approaches in the early years of the employee's career and just the opposite in the later years. The precise normal cost relationship among the three versions of the accrued benefit cost methods can be seen for an age-30 entrant under the standard assumptions in Table 3.5, where b_x, $^{CS}b_x$, and $^{CA}b_x$ are compared at each attained age.

Equation (6.1) shows that the normal cost under the accrued benefit cost method is an increasing function of attained age up to age r, since $_{r-x}p_x^{(T)}$ and v^{r-x} both approach unity as x approaches r. The increase generated by these two factors, however, is augmented by the increase in the benefit accrual, unless the ^{CA}ABCM is used, for which the benefit accrual is constant.

It was stated in Chapter 5 that the normal cost of an actuarial cost method amortizes $(PVFB)_y$ from age y to age r. This implies that the present value of future normal costs for a new participant at his entry age y must be equal to $(PVFB)_y$. Notationally, this relationship may be expressed as

$$(PVFB)_y = \sum_{t=y}^{r-1} (NC)_t \, _{t-y}p_y^{(T)} v^{t-y}. \tag{6.3a}$$

This relationship holds under the accrued benefit cost methods, as well as all other methods, and the proof is as follows. First we write the left side of (6.3a) in its basic form and substitute (6.1) for $(NC)_t$.

$$B_r \, _{r-y}p_y^{(T)} v^{r-y} \ddot{a}_r = \sum_{t=y}^{r-1} (b_t \, _{r-t}p_t^{(T)} v^{r-t} \ddot{a}_r)_{t-y}p_y^{(T)} v^{t-y}. \tag{6.3b}$$

The product of $_{r-t}p_t^{(T)}$ and $_{t-y}p_y^{(T)}$ is $_{r-y}p_y^{(T)}$ and the product of v^{r-t} and v^{t-y} is v^{r-y}. Thus, (6.3b) reduces to the defined relationship

$$B_r = \sum_{t=y}^{r-1} b_t. \tag{6.3c}$$

The same result obtains under the ^{CA}ABCM and the ^{CS}ABCM. Consequently, the normal cost under the accrued benefit cost method does indeed amortize $(PVFB)_y$ over the period from age y to age r.

A numerical example of the components making up the ABCM normal cost, based on an age-30 entrant under standard assumptions, is shown in Table 6–1. In order to avoid the restrictive use of dollar amounts, the benefit accruals in the first column are expressed as a percentage of the participant's attained age salary, as is the normal cost given in the right-hand column of Table 6–1. The calculations are given for the ABCM and for both modifications.

The results given in Table 6–1 point out quite clearly the magnitude by which the ABCM normal cost increases with attained age, being equal to less than 0.2 percent of salary at age 30, and increasing to nearly 20 percent of salary by age 60. This dramatic increase is brought about by the fact that b_x, $_{r-x}p_x^{(T)}$, and v^{r-x} all increase substantially with increasing values of x and, of course, their product increases even more significantly.

TABLE 6–1

Normal Cost Calculations under Various Accrued Benefit Cost Methods

Cost Method	x	$\dfrac{100}{s_x} b_x$	$_{65-x}p_x^{(T)}$	v^{65-x}	$\ddot{a}_{65}$	$\dfrac{100}{s_x}(NC)_x$
ABCM	30	1.500	0.141	0.094	9.130	0.180
	40	2.250	0.375	0.184	9.130	1.418
	50	3.021	0.613	0.362	9.130	6.128
	60	3.570	0.846	0.713	9.130	19.653
CSABCM	30	3.128	0.141	0.094	9.130	0.376
	40	3.128	0.375	0.184	9.130	1.971
	50	3.128	0.613	0.362	9.130	6.344
	60	3.128	0.846	0.713	9.130	17.219
CAABCM	30	13.265	0.141	0.094	9.130	1.594
	40	6.031	0.375	0.184	9.130	3.800
	50	3.022	0.613	0.362	9.130	6.131
	60	1.672	0.846	0.713	9.130	9.203

Based on the standard assumptions for an age-30 entrant.

FIGURE 6–1

Normal Cost as a Percentage of Salary under Various Accrued Benefit Cost Methods

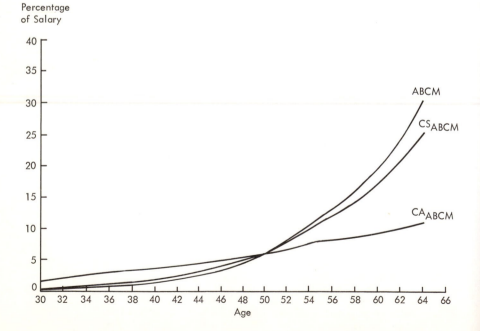

The attained age normal cost of each of the accrued benefit cost methods is plotted in Figure 6–1. The ^{CS}ABCM normal cost is only slightly higher at the younger ages and slightly lower at the older ages than the normal cost under the ABCM. The ^{CA}ABCM, however, produces a considerably flatter normal cost pattern than the other two versions of the accrued benefit cost method. The normal cost under all three cost methods is nearly identical at age 50 for the age-30 entrant under the standard assumptions, as depicted in Figure 6–1.

Actuarial Liability

The actuarial liability under each version of the accrued benefit cost method is equal to the present value of the actual (or assumed) benefits accrued up to, but not including, age x.[2] Under the ABCM, we have

$$(AL)_x = B_x \, {}_{r-x}p_x^{(T)} v^{r-x} \ddot{a}_r \qquad (6.4)$$

where

$$B_x = \sum_{t=y}^{x-1} b_t = \text{benefits accrued up to age } x. \qquad (3.9)$$

The actuarial liability under the modified accrued benefit cost methods is found by substituting $^{CA}B_x$ or $^{CS}B_x$ for B_x in equation (6.4), where

$$^{CA}B_x = \frac{B_r}{(r-y)}(x-y) \qquad (3.15b)$$

$$^{CS}B_x = \frac{B_r}{S_r} S_x. \qquad (3.16b)$$

It can be shown for the typical case that the following holds:

$$B_x \leqslant {}^{CS}B_x \leqslant {}^{CA}B_x. \qquad (6.5)$$

At age y, of course, each accrued benefit is zero, while at age r each accrued benefit is equal to B_r. The natural accrued benefit will be the lowest at the intermediate ages while the CA accrued benefit will be the largest. The relationship among the accrued benefits also indicates the relative size of the actuarial liability under each version of the

---

[2] The term accrued liability in place of actuarial liability would be appropriate for the ABCM, since this method focuses on benefits accrued to date. The distinction between the two terms, however, becomes significant under the modified accrued benefit cost methods because of the artificial benefits assumed to accrue, and the distinction will take on even greater significance under the projected benefit cost methods.

accrued benefit cost method. The precise relationship among the three versions can be seen for the age-30 entrant under standard assumptions in Table 3.5, where B_x, $^{CS}B_x$, and $^{CA}B_x$ are given for each attained age.

Equation (6.4) shows that the actuarial liability at age x is a multiple of the normal cost at that age. This multiple, for each variation of the ABCM, is as follows:

$$\frac{(AL)_x}{(NC)_x} = \frac{B_x}{b_x} \qquad \text{for the ABCM;}$$

$$= x - y \qquad \text{for the } ^{CA}\text{ABCM;} \qquad (6.6)$$

$$= \frac{S_x}{s_x} \qquad \text{for the } ^{CS}\text{ABCM.}$$

The actuarial liability associated with nonactive employees, being equal to the $(PVFB)_x$ function for $x \geq r$, is identical under all actuarial cost methods and under other liability measures such as the TPL and the CPL.

It was stated in Chapter 5 that the actuarial liability for a given cost method is equal to the portion of $(PVFB)_y$ amortized by age x. This relationship was expressed prospectively as

$$(AL)_x = (PVFB)_x - (PVFNC)_x. \qquad (5.4)$$

To show that this definition holds for the accrued benefit cost method, we write $(PVFB)_x$ and $(PVFNC)_x$ in their basic form, using the natural benefit accruals to illustrate the point:

$$(AL)_x = B_r {}_{r-x}p_x^{(T)}v^{r-x}\ddot{a}_r - \sum_{t=x}^{r-1}[b_t {}_{r-t}p_t^{(T)}v^{r-t}\ddot{a}_r]_{t-x}p_x^{(T)}v^{t-x}. \qquad (6.7a)$$

In equation (6.7a) the bracketed term represents the ABCM normal cost. The right-most term can be written as

$$\left(\sum_{t=x}^{r-1}b_t\right)_{r-x}p_x^{(T)}v^{r-x}\ddot{a}_r, \qquad (6.7b)$$

and since

$$B_r - \sum_{t=x}^{r-1}b_t = B_x, \qquad (6.7c)$$

equation (6.7a) simplifies to

$$(AL)_x = B_x {}_{r-x}p_x^{(T)}v^{r-x}\ddot{a}_r. \qquad (6.7d)$$

The same result obtains under the ^{CS}ABCM and the ^{CA}ABCM.

Another definition of the actuarial liability given in Chapter 5, which holds under certain rigid conditions, is the retrospective approach:

$$(AL)_x = (AVPNC)_x. \qquad (5.6a)$$

Again, using the natural benefit accruals we have

$$(AL)_x = \sum_{t=y}^{x-1} (NC)_t (1 + i)^{x-t} \frac{1}{x-t p_t^{(T)}} \qquad (6.8a)$$

$$= \sum_{t=y}^{x-1} [b_{t\ r-t} p_t^{(T)} v^{r-t} \ddot{a}_r](1 + i)^{x-t} \frac{1}{x-t p_t^{(T)}} \qquad (6.8b)$$

$$= \left(\sum_{t=y}^{x-1} b_t \right)_{r-x} p_x^{(T)} v^{r-x} \ddot{a}_r \qquad (6.8c)$$

$$= B_{x\ r-x} p_x^{(T)} v^{r-x} \ddot{a}_r. \qquad (6.8d)$$

The same result, of course, can be shown for the ^{CS}ABCM and the ^{CA}ABCM.

Table 6–2 shows the results of determining the actuarial liability for the age-30 entrant under the same assumptions as the normal cost calculations of Table 6–1. Observe that Table 6–2 differs from Table 6–1 only in that B_x replaces b_x, and in both cases the benefit functions are expressed as a percentage of the participant's attained age salary.

TABLE 6–2

Actuarial Liability Calculations under Various Accrued Benefit Cost Methods

Cost Method	x	$\frac{100}{S_x} B_x$	$_{65-x} p_x^{(T)}$	v^{65-x}	$\ddot{a}_{65}$	$\frac{100}{S_x} (AL)_x$
ABCM	30	0.000	0.141	0.094	9.130	0.000
	40	12.021	0.375	0.184	9.130	7.574
	50	24.724	0.613	0.362	9.130	50.151
	60	38.155	0.846	0.713	9.130	210.063
^{CA}ABCM	30	0.000	0.141	0.094	9.130	0.000
	40	20.969	0.375	0.184	9.130	13.211
	50	32.505	0.613	0.362	9.130	65.935
	60	41.078	0.846	0.713	9.130	226.156
^{CS}ABCM	30	0.000	0.141	0.094	9.130	0.000
	40	60.307	0.375	0.184	9.130	37.996
	50	60.449	0.613	0.362	9.130	122.619
	60	50.147	0.846	0.713	9.130	276.086

Based on the standard assumptions for an age-30 entrant.

FIGURE 6–2

Actuarial Liability as a Percentage of Salary under Various Accrued Benefit Cost Methods

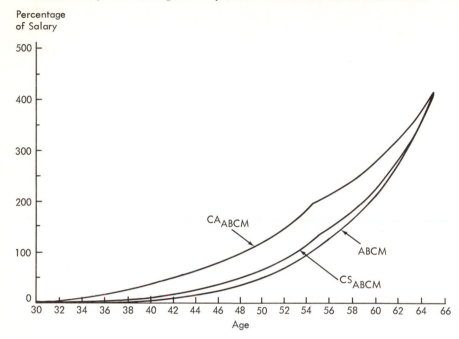

The accrued benefit function at age *x excludes* the benefit accrual at that age, thus the actuarial liability at the entry age is zero, as indicated in Table 6–2. Beyond the entry age, however, the accrued benefits increase significantly, as does the actuarial liability under each variation of the accrued benefit cost method. At age 60 the actuarial liability under the ABCM is seen to be about double the salary at that age, and for the ^{CA}ABCM the actuarial liability at age 60 is nearly three times the salary at that age.

Figure 6–2 shows the attained age pattern of the actuarial liability under each version of the accrued benefit cost method. The actuarial liability under the ^{CA}ABCM is seen to be significantly larger than the actuarial liability of the other two cost methods at the intermediate ages from 30 to 65. Thus, we see that the actuarial liability under the various accrued benefit cost methods is affected significantly by the pattern of costs under each method.

Summary

It was stated in Chapter 5 that the $(PVFB)_x$ function was used in determining the normal cost and actuarial liability under a given actuarial cost method. This is less obvious under the various accrued benefit cost methods than it is under the projected benefit cost methods yet to be discussed. Nevertheless, there is a well-defined relationship between this important function and the normal cost and actuarial liability values under each version of the accrued benefit cost method. This relationship is summarized below.

	Actuarial Cost Method		
	ABCM	^{CS}ABCM	^{CA}ABCM
Normal cost	$\dfrac{b_x}{B_r}(PVFB)_x$	$\dfrac{s_x}{S_r}(PVFB)_x$	$\dfrac{1}{r-y}(PVFB)_x$
Actuarial liability	$\dfrac{B_x}{B_r}(PVFB)_x$	$\dfrac{S_x}{S_r}(PVFB)_x$	$\dfrac{x-y}{r-y}(PVFB)_x$

In general the normal cost and actuarial liability under each version of the accrued benefit cost method are equal to a specified portion of the attained age PVFB function. The proportion for the normal cost is equal to the ratio of the benefits that accrue (or are assumed to accrue) in the current year to the projected retirement age benefit, while for the actuarial liability, the proportion is equal to the ratio of the benefits accrued (or assumed to have accrued) to date to the projected benefit at retirement. These ratios under the CS and CA versions simplify to salary ratios and years-of-service ratios, respectively. Note that the ^{CA}ABCM actuarial liability is equal to a prorata share of $(PVFB)_x$, and it will be remembered that this is the definition of the continuation-of-plan liability (CPL) as set forth in Chapter 5. Finally, the above relationships allow the size of the normal cost and actuarial liability values under the accrued benefit cost methods to be found by simply comparing the different coefficients of the $(PVFB)_x$ function.

Supplemental Liability

A general definition of the supplemental liability for an individual plan participant was set forth in Chapter 5, and is given below for convenience.

$$(SL)_x = (PVFB)_x - [(PVFNC)_x + (AVPNC)_x]. \quad (5.8b)$$

However, under the ABCM, or any of its modifications, it was shown that the present value of future benefits less the present value of future normal costs is equal to the present value of *accrued* benefits (PVAB). Thus, equation (5.8b) can be written as

$$(SL)_x = (PVAB)_x - (AVPNC)_x. \qquad (6.9)$$

which shows that the supplemental liability is equal to the difference between the present value of accrued benefits (the actuarial liability in this case) and the accumulated value of past normal costs. At the inception of the plan, the supplemental liability (past service liability) is identical to the actuarial liability, since $(AVPNC)_x$ is obviously zero at this point. The actuarial liability beyond this point will exceed the supplemental liability, the difference between the two depending on the experience under the plan. The yearly increment in the supplemental liability may be determined by using equation (5.9).

The supplemental liability of a plan is seldom, if ever, broken down on a participant-by-participant basis. Moreover, the *true* supplemental liability is seldom recorded for a given plan simply because there is little use in keeping track of the various components of the true supplemental liability once they have been fully funded. For example, the initial supplemental liability value is generally dropped from further consideration once it becomes fully funded, as is each subsequent increment or decrement once it becomes fully funded.

Supplemental Cost

The supplemental cost, it will be remembered, is designed to amortize the supplemental liability over a given period according to a specified pattern. If the supplemental liability increment during age x were to be amortized in perpetuity, the annual supplemental cost would be equal to the interest on this increment. If the supplemental liability increment is amortized over n years, then the annual supplemental cost associated with the age-x increment is found by dividing the increment by $\ddot{a}_{\overline{n}|}$.

ACCRUED BENEFIT COST METHOD WITHOUT
SUPPLEMENTAL LIABILITY[3]

The accrued benefit cost method without supplemental liability is a method which does not develop an initial supplemental liability at

---

[3] The "without" supplemental liability phraseology may suggest that there is no supplemental liability when indeed there is. The difference is that the "with" supplemental liability version deals with this liability explicitly, while the "without" version deals with it implicitly and integrates the supplemental cost into the plan's annual cost.

the plan's inception based on the benefits accrued (or assumed to have accrued) to date.[4] Instead, this method allocates the past service benefit accruals over the participant's future working life by an appropriate increase in the attained age benefit accrual. If the conventional ABCM is used, the increment to the benefit accrual, assuming the plan starts at age z, is

$$\frac{B_z}{B_r - B_z} b_x \qquad (z \leqslant x < r). \qquad (6.10)$$

This increment is equal to the past service benefit, B_z, divided by the future service benefits, $B_r - B_z$, times the attained age benefit accrual. If this increment is summed over all x from z to r, its value is B_z which is the past service benefit that must be allocated over this period. The total benefit accrual under the conventional ABCM without supplemental liability is equal to

$$b_x^T = b_x + \frac{B_z}{B_r - B_z} b_x = \frac{B_r}{B_r - B_z} b_x \qquad (z \leqslant x < r). \quad (6.11)$$

This relationship shows that the attained age benefit accrual is increased by the amount that the projected benefit, B_r, exceeds the future service benefit, $B_r - B_z$. This increase in the attained age benefit accrual is a logical consequence of allocating the past service accrual, B_z, over future years. The accrued benefit at age x is equal to the sum of the attained age benefit accruals from age z up to age x. Thus, the total accrued benefit is

$$B_x^T = \frac{B_r}{B_r - B_z} [B_x - B_z] = \frac{B_x - B_z}{B_r - B_z} B_r. \qquad (6.12)$$

Equation (6.12) shows that the total accrued benefit under the ABCM without supplemental liability is equal to a fraction of the projected benefit, B_r, where the fraction is determined by the ratio of future service benefits from age z to x to the total future service benefits from age z to r.

The annual cost and actuarial liability under the ABCM without supplemental liability is found by substituting b_x^T and B_x^T for b_x and B_x, respectively, in equations (6.1) and (6.4)

The increment to the attained age benefit accrual under the ^{CA}ABCM must be sufficient to allocate the accrued benefit at age z

---

[4] The "without" supplemental liability approach generally refers to the way the past service liability is dealt with, vis-a-vis the way the supplemental liability increments (or decrements) that occur after the plan is in operation are dealt with. This need not be the case, however.

on a constant basis from age z to age r. This increment is equal to

$$\frac{\text{Accrued benefit at age } z}{\text{Years from age } z \text{ to retirement}} = \frac{\dfrac{B_r}{r-y}(z-y)}{r-z} \tag{6.13}$$

The total attained age benefit accrual then becomes

$$^{CA}b_x^T = \frac{B_r}{r-y} + \frac{\dfrac{B_r}{r-y}(z-y)}{r-z} = \frac{B_r}{r-z}. \tag{6.14a}$$

This result shows that the attained age benefit accrual is found by prorating the projected retirement age benefit, B_r, over the years from z to r, instead of over the ages from y to r as is the case under the ^{CA}ABCM with supplemental liability. The total accrued benefit at age x is

$$^{CA}B_x^T = \frac{B_r}{r-z}(x-z) = \frac{x-z}{r-z}B_r. \tag{6.14b}$$

Again the accrued benefit is equal to a fraction of the projected benefit, but in this case the fraction is the ratio of years from age z to x to the years from age z to r. The annual cost and actuarial liability under the ^{CA}ABCM without supplemental liability is found by substituting $^{CA}b_x^T$ and $^{CA}B_x^T$, respectively, for b_x and B_x in equations (6.1) and (6.4).

Finally, the benefit accrual and accrued benefit under the ^{CS}ABCM without supplemental liability are given as follows:

$$^{CS}b_x^T = \frac{B_r}{S_r - S_z}s_x \tag{6.15a}$$

$$^{CS}B_x^T = \frac{S_x - S_z}{S_r - S_z}B_r. \tag{6.15b}$$

Equation (6.15a) shows that the benefit accrual is defined in such a way so as to allocate B_r as a constant percentage of salary from age z to r, while (6.15b) shows that the accrued benefit is a fraction of B_r represented by the ratio of salary from age x to z to the salary from age r to z. These benefit functions are substituted into equations (6.1) and (6.4) in order to obtain the annual cost and actuarial liability under the ^{CS}ABCM without supplemental liability.

In summary the accrued benefit cost method without supplemental liability, assuming the plan starts at age z, has an annual cost designed to amortize $(PVFB)_z$ from age z to age r, and its actuarial liability at age x $(x > z)$ is the portion of $(PVFB)_z$ amortized to date. The supplemental liability (positive or negative) created from (1) actuarial deviations, (2) plan amendments, or (3) changes in actuarial assumptions may still be dealt with explicitly, even though the approach is referred to as being "without" supplemental liability. Finally, if only the initial past service liability is dealt with by the implicit approach described above, it should be clear that the "without" and "with" supplemental liability versions of the ABCM are identical for new employees and for the plan as a whole once all of the initial employees are no longer in active service.

EMPLOYEE CONTRIBUTIONS

There is no change in the total cost or liability associated with retirement benefits if the plan requires employee contributions, but the normal cost payable by the employer and the employer's associated actuarial liability at each attained age is reduced. The employer's normal cost under any one of the three accrued benefit cost methods would be reduced in direct proportion to the employee's contribution. If the employee contributes $100C$ percent of his attained age salary, the normal cost payable by the employer would be reduced by $C \cdot s_x$.

The actuarial liability faced by the employer would be equal to the previously defined actuarial liability less the present value of future employee contributions (PVFC), an intangible asset of the plan:

$$(PVFC)_x = C \cdot s_x \cdot {}^s\ddot{a}^T_{x:\overline{r-x}|}. \tag{6.16}$$

It is assumed in this section that the employee is not entitled to a refund of his contributions upon death or termination. This unrealistic assumption is relaxed in Chapter 10, where the subject of ancillary benefits is discussed.

PLAN TERMINATION COST METHOD[5]

A method closely akin to the accrued benefit cost method, and for this reason included at this point, is the plan termination cost method (PTCM). This method has as its distinguishing characteristic an

---

[5] This method was first developed by Dan M. McGill and Howard E. Winklevoss in "A Quantitative Analysis of Actuarial Cost Method for Pension Plans," *Proceedings of the Conference of Actuaries in Public Practice*, vol. 23 (1974) pp. 212–43.

actuarial liability which is precisely equal to the termination-of-plan liability (TPL) as set forth in Chapter 5.[6] The normal cost under this method is dependent upon the progression of year-to-year values of the participant's TPL. Thus, the normal cost at age x is equal to the difference between the present value of the TPL at age $x + 1$ less the TPL at age x:

$$(NC)_x = p_x^{(T)} v (TPL)_{x+1} - (TPL)_x. \qquad (6.17a)$$

Upon substituting the components making up the TPL, equation (6.17a) becomes

$$(NC)_x = p_x^{(T)} v B_{x+1} {}_{r-x-1}p_{x+1}'^{(m)} v^{r-x-1} \ddot{a}_r - B_x {}_{r-x}p_x'^{(m)} v^{r-x} \ddot{a}_r. \qquad (6.17b)$$

Observe the use of the mortality-only survival function in this formulation. Equation (6.17b) reduces to

$$(NC)_x = [B_{x+1} p_x^{(T)} {}_{r-x-1}p_{x+1}'^{(m)} - B_x {}_{r-x}p_x'^{(m)}] v^{r-x} \ddot{a}_r. \qquad (6.17c)$$

Noting that $p_x^{(T)} = p_x'^{(m)} p_x'^{(w)} p_x'^{(d)} p_x'^{(r)}$, we may write equation (6.17c) as

$$(NC)_x = [B_{x+1} p_x'^{(w)} p_x'^{(d)} p_x'^{(r)} - B_x]_{r-x}p_x'^{(m)} v^{r-x} \ddot{a}_r. \qquad (6.17d)$$

Although B_{x+1} exceeds B_x, it is possible for this excess to be more than offset by the product of the withdrawal, disability, and retirement rates, especially for young employees. If this were to occur, $(NC)_x$ as given by (6.17d) could take on negative values over some ages beyond age y.

The normal cost under the PTCM for the age-30 entrant is shown along with the normal cost under the ABCM in Figure 6–3. A comparison of the actuarial liability under each cost method is given in Figure 6–4. The normal cost of the PTCM takes on a non-uniform shape relative to the normal cost of the ABCM, starting out higher, ending up lower, and crossing over the ABCM normal cost four times during the 35-year period. The actuarial liability, on the other hand, is uniformly lower than the ABCM actuarial liability beyond age 30 and up to age 65.

---

[6] We observed earlier that the actuarial liability of the ^{CA}ABCM is equal to the Continuation-of-Plan Liability (CPL).

FIGURE 6–3

Normal Cost Functions under the ABCM and PTCM

Percentage
of Salary

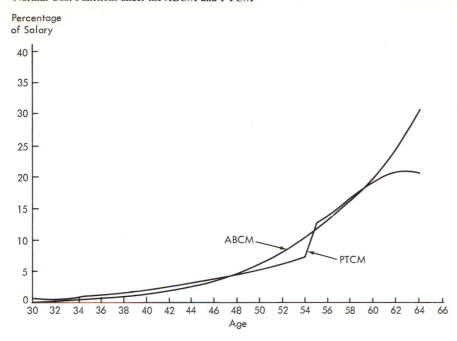

FIGURE 6–4

Actuarial Liability Functions under the ABCM and PTCM

Percentage
of Salary

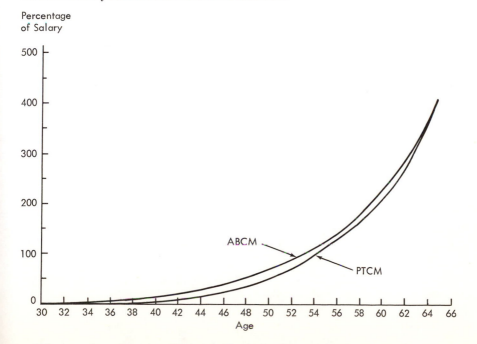

Chapter 7

Projected Benefit Cost Method

The accrued benefit actuarial cost method, as noted in the previous chapter, makes the *benefit accrual* associated with employment during age x the independent variable and the corresponding normal cost the dependent variable. In contrast to this procedure, the projected benefit actuarial cost method makes the *normal cost* associated with employment during age x the independent variable, and the corresponding benefit accural under this method, which must be derived from the normal cost function, is the dependent variable. The switching of the independent and dependent variables under these two cost methods has significant financial implications for pension plans.

This chapter considers the mathematics of the projected benefit cost method. Numerical results useful in comparing costs under variations of this method, and for comparing such costs with those of the accrued benefit cost method, are also given.

PROJECTED BENEFIT COST METHOD WITH SUPPLEMENTAL LIABILITY[1]

Normal Cost

The projected benefit cost method (with supplemental liability) develops a normal cost that remains constant, either as a dollar amount or as a percentage of salary, throughout the individual's period of

---

[1] This method is technically known as the Individual Projected Benefit Cost Method With Supplemental Liability to distinguish it from the so-called Aggregate Projected Benefit Cost Method With Supplemental Liability which is studied in Chapter 8. It is sometimes referred to as the Entry Age Normal cost method.

credited service, provided that there are no benefit increases or other plan revisions that would affect the cost, that there are no changes in the actuarial assumptions, and that there are no actuarial gains or losses. The symbol ^{CA}PBCM is used when the method is designed to generate a normal cost equal to a constant dollar amount, whereas ^{CS}PBCM is used to denote the method when the normal cost equals a constant percentage of the participant's attained age salary. It is important to note that these superscripts are used also with the ABCM, but in that case they denote the pattern of *benefit* accruals, whereas here they denote the pattern of *cost* accruals.

In order to derive the ^{CA}PBCM normal cost for a particular plan participant at his entry age, we equate the present value of future normal costs to the present value of projected benefit, hence the name of the method. The equation of value may be written

$$^{CA}(NC)_x \; \ddot{a}^T_{y:\overline{r-y|}} = (PVFB)_y, \qquad (7.1a)$$

where

$\qquad ^{CA}(NC)_x$ = normal cost at age x under the ^{CA}PBCM with supplemental liability, a constant value for all x ($y \leqslant x < r$)

$\qquad \ddot{a}^T_{y:\overline{r-y|}}$ = present value of a temporary, employment-based annuity running from age y to age r

$\qquad (PVFB)_y = B_r \,_{r-y}p_y^{(T)}v^{r-y}\ddot{a}_r$ = present value of future benefits at age y.

Solving equation (7.1a) for the level annual normal cost, one obtains

$$^{CA}(NC)_x = \frac{(PVFB)_y}{\ddot{a}^T_{y:\overline{r-y|}}}. \qquad (7.1b)$$

The normal cost in this form is clearly designed to amortize $(PVFB)_y$ over the age-y entrant's working career.

Equation (7.1b) is not as easily analyzed for changes in the rates of decrement and interest rate as was the normal cost under the accrued benefit cost methods, since both the numerator and denominator are affected by such changes. Nevertheless, like the ABCM, the $^{CA}(NC)_x$ is inversely related to these parameters, and directly related to the projected benefit, the latter found only in the numerator of (7.1b). If salary is an increasing function of age, the normal cost under this version of the PBCM represents an ever-decreasing percentage of the participant's salary.

The normal cost under the ^{CS}PBCM, as stated earlier, represents a constant portion of the employee's attained age salary. In order to ascertain the constant proportion, K, one must first equate the present value of the participant's future salary (time K) to the present value of his projected benefit. Thus, we have

$$K \cdot s_y \cdot {}^s\ddot{a}^T_{y:\overline{r-y}|} = (\text{PVFB})_y, \qquad (7.2a)$$

where

$${}^s\ddot{a}^T_{y:\overline{r-y}|} = \text{the present value of the age-}y\text{ entrant's}$$
$$\text{salary per unit of entry age salary}$$

$$s_y = \text{the entry age salary.}$$

Solving for K we have

$$K = \frac{(\text{PVFB})_y}{s_y \cdot {}^s\ddot{a}^T_{y:\overline{r-y}|}} \qquad (7.2b)$$

and

$$^{CS}(\text{NC})_x = K \cdot s_x \qquad (7.2c)$$

If salary is an increasing function of age, the normal cost under this version of the PBCM represents an ever-increasing dollar amount.

It is not necessary to construct a table in order to calculate the normal cost under the PBCM, as was the case under the ABCM in the previous chapter, simply because the normal cost values are determined once and for all at the employee's entry age. It turns out that $(\text{PVFB})_{30}$ under the standard assumptions is equal to 55.795 percent of the age-30 salary, and $\ddot{a}^T_{30:\overline{65-30}|}$ is equal to 6.440. Thus, the constant dollar amount (CA) normal cost is 8.6633 percent of the age-30 salary, a value which decreases as a percentage of s_x with advancing age as indicated in Table 7–1.

In contrast, the value of $^s\ddot{a}^T_{30:\overline{65-30}|}$ is 12.656, and dividing this value into $(\text{PVFB})_{30}$ (again expressed as a percentage of the entry-age salary) yields a normal cost under the ^{CS}PBCM of 4.4087 percent of

TABLE 7–1

Normal Cost as a Percentage of Attained Age Salary under Various Actuarial Cost Methods $\left(\dfrac{100}{s_x} \cdot (\text{NC})_x\right)$

x	*ABCM*	$^{CS}ABCM$	$^{CA}ABCM$	$^{CS}PBCM$	$^{CA}PBCM$
30. . . .	0.1803	0.3759	1.5941	4.4087	8.6633
40. . . .	1.4176	1.9705	3.7996	4.4087	3.9384
50. . . .	6.1284	6.3443	6.1309	4.4087	1.9739
60. . . .	19.6526	17.2194	9.2029	4.4087	1.0916

salary. This percentage remains constant throughout the employee's working career. The results are summarized in Table 7–1, where the normal cost under all three versions of the ABCM are given for comparative purposes.

Although the ^{CA}PBCM normal cost is nearly double the ^{CS}PBCM normal cost at the entry age, it is less than one-fourth of the ^{CS}PBCM normal cost by age 60. Figure 7–1 shows the attained age cost pattern of all five actuarial cost methods for the age-30 entrant, where it can be seen that a significant difference exists among the various actuarial cost methods. The normal cost pattern for the plan as a whole under each of the cost methods shown in Figure 7–1, plus several other actuarial cost methods yet to be discussed, are given in Chapter 16.

FIGURE 7–1

Normal Cost as a Percentage of Salary under Various Actuarial Cost Methods

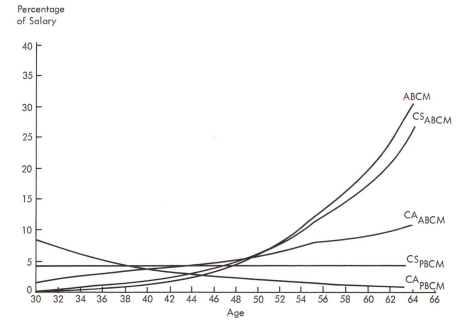

Actuarial Liability

The actuarial liability, as noted in previous chapters, is equal to the present value of future benefits at age x less the present value of future normal costs. This leads to the following equation for the actuarial liability under the ^{CA}PBCM:

$$^{CA}(AL)_x = (PVFB)_x - {}^{CA}(NC)_x \ddot{a}^T_{x:\overline{r-x}|}. \tag{7.3a}$$

An expression for the ^{CS}PBCM actuarial liability is

$$^{CS}(AL)_x = (PVFB)_x - K \cdot s_x \cdot {}^s\ddot{a}^T_{x:\overline{r-x}|}. \tag{7.3b}$$

The actuarial liability under each version of the PBCM can be expressed as a fraction of $(PVFB)_x$, as was the case for the actuarial liability under each version of the ABCM. The derivation of this result under the ^{CA}PBCM version is given below. Substituting equation (7.1b) for $^{CA}(NC)_x$ in (7.3a), we have

$$^{CA}(AL)_x = (PVFB)_x - \frac{(PVFB)_y}{\ddot{a}^T_{y:\overline{r-y}|}}\, \ddot{a}^T_{x:\overline{r-x}|}. \tag{7.4a}$$

Replacing $(PVFB)_y$ by $_{x-y}p_y^{(T)}v^{x-y}(PVFB)_x$, and factoring out $(PVFB)_x$, one obtains

$$^{CA}(AL)_x = (PVFB)_x \left[1 - \frac{_{x-y}p_y^{(T)}v^{x-y}\ddot{a}^T_{x:\overline{r-x}|}}{\ddot{a}^T_{y:\overline{r-y}|}} \right]. \tag{7.4b}$$

Establishing a common denominator, (7.4b) becomes

$$^{CA}(AL)_x = (PVFB)_x \frac{\ddot{a}^T_{y:\overline{r-y}|} - {}_{x-y}p_y^{(T)}v^{x-y}\ddot{a}^T_{x:\overline{r-x}|}}{\ddot{a}^T_{y:\overline{r-y}|}}. \tag{7.4c}$$

The numerator represents a temporary employment based annuity running from age y to age x, that is, a temporary annuity from y to r minus a deferred temporary annuity payable from x to r. Thus, we have the following expression for the ^{CA}PBCM actuarial liability:

$$^{CA}(AL)_x = \frac{\ddot{a}^T_{y:\overline{x-y}|}}{\ddot{a}^T_{y:\overline{r-y}|}}(PVFB)_x. \tag{7.4d}$$

The corresponding expression for the ^{CS}PBCM actuarial liability is

$$^{CS}(AL)_x = \frac{{}^s\ddot{a}^T_{y:\overline{x-y}|}}{{}^s\ddot{a}^T_{y:\overline{r-y}|}}(PVFB)_x. \tag{7.4e}$$

The coefficients to the $(PVFB)_x$ function are zero at age y and unity at age r. If salary is a non-decreasing function of age, it can be shown that the following inequalities hold:

$$\frac{B_x}{B_r} \leqslant \frac{S_x}{S_r} \leqslant \frac{x-y}{r-y} \leqslant \frac{{}^s\ddot{a}^T_{y:\overline{x-y}|}}{{}^s\ddot{a}^T_{y:\overline{r-y}|}} \leqslant \frac{\ddot{a}^T_{y:\overline{x-y}|}}{\ddot{a}^T_{y:\overline{r-y}|}}. \tag{7.5a}$$

These inequalities indicate the relative size of the actuarial liability of each actuarial cost method, since the above are all coefficients to the $(PVFB)_x$ function in determining each method's actuarial liability. If we let the initials of each cost method represent the corresponding actuarial liability, we have the following ranking of the actuarial liability under each cost method:

$$\text{ABCM} \leqslant {}^{\text{CS}}\text{ABCM} \leqslant {}^{\text{CA}}\text{ABCM} \leqslant {}^{\text{CS}}\text{PBCM} \leqslant {}^{\text{CA}}\text{PBCM}. \qquad (7.5b)$$

Table 7–2 sets forth the calculation of the actuarial liability for an age-30 entrant under standard assumptions. Dollar values are avoided by expressing each component of the actuarial liability calculation as a percentage of the participant's attained age salary and the actuarial liability is likewise so expressed. It is clear, from the basic definition of the normal cost under the PBCM, that the actuarial liability at the entry age is zero, as shown in Table 7–2. However, the $(PVFB)_x$ function increases with x while the present value of future normal costs decreases, causing their difference (the actuarial liability) to increase substantially as a percentage of salary, reaching a value of 300 percent by age 60. As would be expected the present value of future normal costs decreases faster with increasing age under the ${}^{\text{CA}}\text{PBCM}$ than under the ${}^{\text{CS}}\text{PBCM}$, which in turn causes the ${}^{\text{CA}}\text{PBCM}$ actuarial liability to be significantly larger at the intermediate ages between y and r. The actuarial liability at age r is equal to $(PVFB)_r$ under both cost methods (and all others for that matter) since the present value of future normal costs is obviously zero at this age.

TABLE 7–2

Actuarial Liability Calculations under Various Projected Benefit Cost Methods

x	$\dfrac{100}{S_x}(PVFB)_x$	$-\left(\dfrac{100}{S_x}{}^{\text{CA}}(NC)_x\right)\cdot(\ddot{a}^T_{x:\overline{r-x}\,}) =$	$\dfrac{100}{S_x}{}^{\text{CA}}(AL)_x$
30	55.7950	8.6633	6.4404	0.0000
40	132.9856	3.9384	8.6758	98.8163
50	214.5829	1.9739	7.9554	198.8800
60	322.1006	1.0916	4.1720	317.5462

x	$\dfrac{100}{S_x}(PVFB)_x$	$-(100K)\cdot({}^s\ddot{a}^T_{x:\overline{r-x}\,}) =$	$\dfrac{100}{S_x}{}^{\text{CS}}(AL)_x$
30	55.7950	4.4087	12.6557	0.0000
40	132.9856	4.4087	15.0978	66.4239
50	214.5829	4.4087	11.2162	165.1338
60	322.1006	4.4087	4.6022	301.8109

Table 7–3 compares the actuarial liability of the accrued benefit cost methods studied in the previous chapter to those of the projected benefit cost methods. These data depict the magnitude by which each

TABLE 7–3

Actuarial Liability as a Percentage of Attained Age Salary under Various Actuarial Cost Methods

x	$ABCM$	$^{CS}ABCM$	$^{CA}ABCM$	$^{CS}PBCM$	$^{CA}PBCM$
30. . . .	0.0000	0.0000	0.0000	0.0000	0.0000
40. . . .	7.5739	13.2113	37.9959	66.4239	98.8163
50. . . .	50.1515	65.9346	122.6188	165.1338	198.8800
60. . . .	210.0625	226.1565	276.0862	301.8109	317.5462

cost method's actuarial liability exceeds or is exceeded by the actuarial liability of the other methods, the basic relationship among the actuarial liabilities having been set out in (7.5b). The ^{CA}PBCM actuarial liability, to take the extreme example, exceeds the ABCM actuarial liability at age 40 by a factor of 13, and at age 50 by a factor of 4. Although each of the ABCM modifications lessens this differential, it is safe to conclude that a significant difference exists between the actuarial liabilities of these five actuarial cost methods at ages beyond the employee's entry age and prior to his retirement age. Figure 7–2

FIGURE 7–2

Actuarial Liability as a Percentage of Salary under Various Actuarial Cost Methods

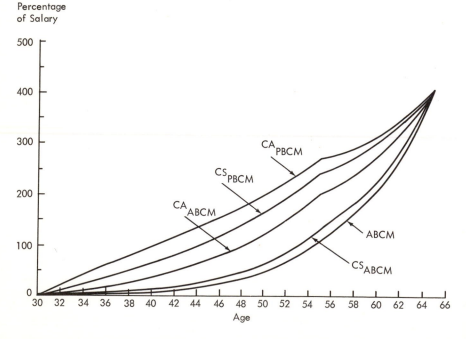

shows these relationships among the various actuarial cost methods for the age-30 entrant. A comparison of the liability among cost methods for the plan as a whole is given in Chapter 16.

Supplemental Liability

The supplemental liability at the inception of the plan under the projected benefit actuarial cost methods, like that of the accrued benefit cost methods, is equal to the actuarial liability at that point. The supplemental liability at age x, assuming the plan started at age z, is equal to the age-z supplemental liability updated for the benefit of survivorship and interest. If the actuarial liability at the plan's inception is expressed as a fraction of the $(PVFB)_z$ function, such as in equations (7.4d) and (7.4e), the updating process changes $(PVFB)_z$ in these equations to $(PVFB)_x$, leaving the annuity ratio unaffected. Consequently, a participant's supplemental liability due to plan establishment is easily found for all subsequent ages once the coefficients in (7.4d) and (7.4e) are determined.

The supplemental liability generated from other sources, namely, actuarial deviations, plan changes, or changes in actuarial assumptions, is determined, once again, by comparing the prospectively determined actuarial liability for the current year to the accumulated value of past normal costs plus the accumulated value of previously determined supplemental liabilities.

Supplemental Cost

The supplemental cost associated with either the initial supplemental liability or subsequent supplemental liabilities is found by establishing an amortization procedure. If the supplemental liability is to be amortized over n years, the supplemental cost during the n years is equal to the supplemental liability increment divided by $\ddot{a}_{\overline{n}|}$. If the supplemental liability were to be determined for each participant, a procedure seldom followed, a supplemental cost would have to be made for n years irrespective of the future status of the participant. The more common approach is to determine the total supplemental liability increment for the plan and to amortize this amount over n years. This approach avoids the need of keeping track of individual supplemental costs for current and previously employed participants.

PROJECTED BENEFIT COST METHOD WITHOUT
SUPPLEMENTAL LIABILITY[2]

The projected benefit cost method without supplemental liability, like its ABCM counterpart, is an approach which does not develop an initial supplemental liability at the inception of the plan. This is accomplished, assuming the plan is started at age z, by amortizing $(PVFB)_z$ from age z to age r. The annual cost (AC), which includes an implicit normal cost and supplemental cost, under each version of the PBCM, for $z \leqslant x < r$, is written as

$$^{CA}(AC)_x = \frac{(PVFB)_z}{\ddot{a}^T_{z:\overline{r-z}|}} \tag{7.6a}$$

$$^{CS}(AC)_x = K \cdot s_x = \frac{(PVFB)_z}{s_z \cdot {}^s\ddot{a}^T_{z:\overline{r-z}|}} s_x. \tag{7.6b}$$

The corresponding actuarial liabilities are determined in the usual fashion, that is, $(PVFB)_x - (PVFNC)_x$, using the above values in calculating the present value of future normal costs. The actuarial liability may also be expressed as a ratio of temporary annuities times the $(PVFB)_x$ function:

$$^{CA}(AL)_x = \frac{\ddot{a}^T_{z:\overline{x-z}|}}{\ddot{a}^T_{z:\overline{r-z}|}} (PVFB)_x \tag{7.7a}$$

$$^{CS}(AL)_x = \frac{{}^s\ddot{a}^T_{z:\overline{x-z}|}}{{}^s\ddot{a}^T_{z:\overline{r-z}|}} (PVFB)_x. \tag{7.7b}$$

The annual cost under the PBCM without supplemental liability may be derived by taking the normal cost of the PBCM *with* supplemental liability and adding to this the cost of amortizing the initial supplemental liability over the participant's remaining working career. If the plan commences at age z, we know from equation (7.4d) that the actuarial liability at the outset of the plan, or the initial supplemental liability, may be expressed as

$$^{CA}(AL)_z = {}^{CA}(SL)_z = \frac{\ddot{a}^T_{y:\overline{z-y}|}}{\ddot{a}^T_{y:\overline{r-y}|}} (PVFB)_z. \tag{7.8a}$$

If this quantity is amortized from age z to age r by $\ddot{a}^T_{z:\overline{r-z}|}$, adding it

---

[2] This method is sometimes referred to as the Individual Level Premium Method.

to the normal cost under the "with supplemental liability" approach, yields the following cost.

$$^{CA}(AC)_x = \frac{(PVFB)_y}{\ddot{a}^T_{y:\overline{r-y}|}} + \frac{\ddot{a}^T_{y:\overline{z-y}|}(PVFB)_z}{\ddot{a}^T_{y:\overline{r-y}|}\ddot{a}^T_{z:\overline{r-z}|}} \qquad (7.8b)$$

Establishing a common denominator, we have

$$^{CA}(AC)_x = \frac{(PVFB)_y\ddot{a}^T_{z:\overline{r-z}|} + \ddot{a}^T_{y:\overline{z-y}|}(PVFB)_z}{\ddot{a}^T_{y:\overline{r-y}|}\ddot{a}^T_{z:\overline{r-z}|}}. \qquad (7.8c)$$

Equation (7.8c) can be rewritten in the following manner:

$$^{CA}(AC)_x = \frac{(PVFB)_z}{\ddot{a}^T_{z:\overline{r-z}|}}\left[\frac{_{z-y}p_y^{(T)}v^{z-y}\ddot{a}^T_{z:\overline{r-z}|} + \ddot{a}^T_{y:\overline{z-y}|}}{\ddot{a}^T_{y:\overline{r-y}|}}\right] = \frac{(PVFB)_z}{\ddot{a}^T_{z:\overline{r-z}|}}. \qquad (7.8d)$$

The bracketed term is equal to unity, since the numerator is the sum of a deferred temporary employment-based annuity from age z to r, plus a temporary annuity from age y to z. Thus we see that the total cost for a participant under the PBCM with supplemental liability, when the initial supplemental liability is amortized over the participant's future years of employment, is equivalent to the annual cost under the PBCM without supplemental liability, that is, the initial $(PVFB)_z$ is amortized over the period from z to r. These results hold also for the ^{CS}PBCM.

It should be clear that the actuarial liability under this method can likewise be determined by adding to the "with supplemental liability" actuarial liability the proportion of (7.8a) amortized by age x.

The "without supplemental liability" method may be restricted to amortizing the initial supplemental liability or the approach may include the amortizing of the supplemental liability increments (or decrements) that occur beyond the plan's inception.

An approach to determining the annual cost at age x under either the ^{CA}PBCM or the ^{CS}PBCM, assuming all supplemental liability increments and decrements are to be factored into the annual cost, is illustrated for the ^{CA}PBCM in the equation:

$$^{CA}(AC)_x = \frac{(PVFB)_x - [(AVPNC)_x + (AVPSL)_x]}{\ddot{a}^T_{x:\overline{r-x}|}}, \qquad (7.9)$$

where

$(AVPNC)_x$ = accumulated value of past normal costs

$(AVPSL)_x$ = accumulated value of past supplemental liability increments (or decrements).

If no supplement liability were to exist for the employee, it can be shown that the annual cost in (7.9) is identical to the entry age cost given by equation (7.1b) for the ^{CA}PBCM. On the other hand, if the plan is started at age z, and assuming no other supplemental liability is created, the annual cost given by (7.9) becomes equal to the annual cost given by (7.6a), that is, where the initial supplemental liability is amortized over the ages z to r. The important point, however, is that equation (7.9), and its analogue for the ^{CS}PBCM, can be used to amortize implicitly the year-to-year (positive or negative) supplemental liability increments over the expected future working lifetime of the plan participant.

Unless the "without supplemental liability" is extended to the supplemental liability created after the plan's inception, the PBCM with and without supplemental liability are identical for new employees and for the plan as a whole once all of the active employees at the plan's inception are no longer in active service.

PROJECTED BENEFIT COST METHOD WITH PARTIAL SUPPLEMENTAL LIABILITY[3]

The PBCM with partial supplemental liability is an approach under which the initial (past service) supplemental liability is defined to be equal to the present value of accrued benefits, that is, the actuarial liability under the ABCM. The normal cost at each future age is defined in terms of the future benefit only, while the actuarial liability is equal to the present value of the past service benefits plus the actuarial liability associated with future service benefits. The normal cost under the ^{CA}PBCM with partial supplemental liability, assuming the plan is started at age z, would be

$$^{CA}(NC)_x = \frac{(B_r - B_z)_{r-z}p_z^{(T)}v^{r-z}\ddot{a}_r}{\ddot{a}_{z:\overline{r-z}|}^T}, \tag{7.10}$$

while the actuarial liability would be

$$^{CA}(AL)_x = B_{z\ r-x}p_x^{(T)}v^{r-x}\ddot{a}_r + (B_r - B_z)_{r-x}p_x^{(T)}v^{r-x}\ddot{a}_r \\ - {}^{CA}(NC)_x\ddot{a}_{x:\overline{r-x}|}^T \tag{7.11a}$$

$$= (PVFB)_x - {}^{CA}(NC)_x\ddot{a}_{x:\overline{r-x}|}^T. \tag{7.11b}$$

The actuarial liability equation is identical in form to the equation applicable under the "with" or "without" supplemental liability ver-

---

[3] This method is sometimes referred to as the Attained Age Normal Method.

sion of the ^{CA}PBCM, the difference among the three being the value of $^{CA}(NC)_x$.

The results in this section apply equally well to the ^{CS}PBCM with partial supplemental liability.

EMPLOYEE CONTRIBUTIONS

As noted in the previous chapter, employee contributions affect the cost and actuarial liability faced by the employer, but they have no effect on the total cost or the true actuarial liability of the plan participant. The employer's normal cost under either version of the projected benefit cost method is found by amortizing the difference between $(PVFB)_y$ and $(PVFC)_y$, the latter denoting the present value of future contributions from the employee. Thus $(PVFC)_y$ would be subtracted from the numerator of equations (7.1b) and (7.2b). Note that for the ^{CS}PBCM, the normal cost percentage payable by the employer becomes equal to $100(K - C)$, where $100C$ is the contribution percentage.

The employer-related actuarial liability, under the assumption of employee contributions, is found by subtracting $(PVFC)_x$ from equations (7.3a) and (7.3b) which give the actuarial liability under the ^{CA}PBCM and the ^{CS}PBCM, respectively.

The above discussion is based on the presumption that employees are not entitled to a refund of their contributions at termination or death. This assumption is relaxed in Chapter 10.

Chapter 8

Aggregate Cost Methods

All of the actuarial cost methods discussed up to this point have been "individual" methods in that they are applied to each plan member individually. In this chapter the aggregate form of each cost method so far discussed is given. The term "aggregate" indicates that the formulas for deriving the plan's costs and liabilities use *all* plan members as opposed to applying to each member separately.[1]

AGGREGATE ACCRUED BENEFIT COST METHOD WITH SUPPLEMENTAL LIABILITY

The aggregate version of the accrued benefit cost methods with supplemental liability is not a commonly used method, but a mathematical definition is possible. The normal cost at time t under the conventional ABCM for the entire plan is given as follows:

$$(\text{NC})_t = \sum l_{y,x} b_{y,x} \left[\frac{\sum l_{y,x} (\text{PVFB})_{y,x}}{\sum l_{y,x} B_{y,r}} \right], \qquad (8.1)$$

where

$\sum$ = summation over all y, x ($y < r$; $y < x < r$) combinations

$l_{y,x}$ = number of active participants at age x who entered the plan at age y

$b_{y,x}$ = benefit accrual at age x for an entrant at age y

---

[1] There is massive confusion over the meaning of the term "aggregate" when used with an actuarial cost method. In particular, some pension practitioners use the term to refer to the aggregation of the plan's liabilities as opposed to separating out a supplemental liability. As noted in previous chapters, this procedure is properly referred to as an actuarial cost method "without" supplemental liability.

$B_{y,x}$ = accrued benefit at age x for an entrant at age y

$(PVFB)_{y,x}$ = present value of future benefits at age x for an entrant at age y.

Observe that if there were only one active employee, or equivalently, if all active employees had the same attained age and entry age, then (8.1) simplifies to the individual ABCM as given by equation (6.1). The corresponding equation for the ^{CA}ABCM is given below.

$$^{CA}(NC)_t = \sum l_{y,x} \left[\frac{\sum l_{y,x}(PVFB)_{y,x}}{\sum l_{y,x}(r-y)} \right]. \tag{8.2}$$

The above illustrates the basic principle behind an aggregate actuarial cost method; namely, the division operation is made for the plan as a whole instead of for each individual participant. The difference between the individual and aggregate versions of the ^{CA}ABCM (with supplemental liability) is more easily seen by expressing the individual approach as a uniform cost per plan participant:

$$^{CA}(NC)_t = \sum l_{y,x} \frac{(PVFB)_{y,x}}{(r-y)}. \tag{8.3}$$

Equation (8.3) shows that the ratio $(PVFB)_{y,x} \div (r-y)$ is weighted by the number of participants at each x, y combination, while equation (8.2) shows that the aggregate method weights the numerator and denominator of this ratio separately by the number of participants at each y, x combination.

The normal cost of the plan under the CS version of the accrued benefit cost method is represented in the following manner.

$$^{CS}(NC)_t = \sum l_{y,x} s_{y,x} \left[\frac{\sum l_{y,x}(PVFB)_{y,x}}{\sum l_{y,x} S_{y,r}} \right], \tag{8.4}$$

where

$s_{y,x}$ = salary at age x for an age-y entrant

$S_{y,r}$ = cumulative salary from age y to r.[2]

This is in contrast to the individual ^{CS}ABCM normal cost of the plan:

$$^{CS}(NC)_t = \sum l_{y,x} \frac{(PVFB)_{y,x}}{S_{y,r}} s_{y,x}. \tag{8.5}$$

---

[2] It was understood that the salary functions used previously, that is, s_x and S_x, were based on a given entry age y. Since we are dealing with multiple entry ages in this chapter, the y variable is added to the symbol for clarity.

The actuarial liability under the aggregate accrued benefit cost methods, as well as under the aggregate projected benefit cost methods, is defined by the actuarial liability under each method's individual counterpart.

AGGREGATE ACCRUED BENEFIT COST METHOD WITHOUT SUPPLEMENTAL LIABILITY

The annual cost under the aggregate ABCM without supplemental liability is designed to amortize the initial plan supplemental liability over the future working years of the plan participants. If we assume the plan is initiated at age z, the annual cost under the conventional ABCM without supplemental liability is

$$(AC)_t = \sum l_{y,x} b_{y,x} \left[\frac{\sum l_{y,x}(PVFB)_{y,x}}{\sum l_{y,x}(B_{y,r} - B_{y,z})} \right]. \tag{8.6}$$

Again, if there were only one employee, or if all employees had the same attained age and entry age, equation (8.6) simplifies to its individual counterpart, for which the benefit accrual is given by equation (6.11). As new employees enter the plan in future years, the value of B_z would be zero. Eventually, after all of the employees in the initial group retire, equation (8.6) will equal equation (8.1).

Similarly, the annual cost equation for the ^{CA}ABCM and the ^{CS}ABCM without supplemental liability are given by equations (8.7) and (8.8).

$$^{CA}(AC)_t = \sum l_{y,x} \left[\frac{\sum l_{y,x}(PVFB)_{y,x}}{\sum l_{y,x}(r - z)} \right]. \tag{8.7}$$

$$^{CS}(AC)_t = \sum l_{y,x} s_{y,x} \left[\frac{\sum l_{y,x}(PVFB)_{y,x}}{\sum l_{y,x}(S_{y,r} - S_{y,z})} \right]. \tag{8.8}$$

The actuarial liability under the aggregate accrued benefit cost methods without supplemental is defined by their individual counterparts.

AGGREGATE PROJECTED BENEFIT COST METHOD WITH SUPPLEMENTAL LIABILITY[3]

The aggregate PBCM with supplemental liability has an actuarial liability defined by its individual counterpart, and a normal cost defined as follows:

---

[3] This method is sometimes referred to as the Frozen Initial Liability Method.

$$^{CA}(NC)_t = \sum l_{y,\,x} \left[\frac{\sum l_{y,\,x}(PVFB)_y}{\sum l_{y,\,x}\ddot{a}^T_{y:\overline{r-y}|}} \right].\tag{8.9}$$

This formulation, consistent with the principle stated earlier for an aggregate method, is a weighted average of all participants' entry-age present value of future benefits divided by a weighted average of their entry-age annuity values running from age y to r, the result being multiplied by the number of active participants. Equation (8.9) would be calculated each year to arrive at a new normal cost that takes into account new entrants.

Observe that the following relationship is valid under the individual ^{CA}PBCM with supplemental liability:

$$^{CA}(NC)_x = \frac{(PVFB)_y}{\ddot{a}^T_{y:\overline{r-y}|}} = \frac{(PVFB)_x - (AL)_x}{\ddot{a}^T_{x:\overline{r-x}|}}.\tag{8.10}$$

Moreover, the actuarial liability is equal to

$$^{CA}(AL)_x = (AVPNC)_x + (AVPSC)_x + (USL)_x,\tag{8.11}$$

where $(USL)_x$ is equal to the unamortized supplemental liability. In the context of funding, (8.11) may be written as

$$^{CA}(AL)_x = (Assets)_x + (USL)_x.\tag{8.12}$$

Substituting (8.12) into (8.10), we have

$$^{CA}(NC)_x = \frac{(PVFB)_x - (Assets)_x - (USL)_x}{\ddot{a}^T_{x:\overline{r-x}|}}.\tag{8.13}$$

Observe that this is applicable to both active and nonactive employees, with $^{CA}(NC)_x$ zero for nonactives.

Applying these principles to the aggregate PBCM with supplemental liability, we have

$$^{CA}(NC)_t = \sum l_{y,\,x} \left[\frac{\overset{all}{\sum} l_{y,\,x}(PVFB)_y - (Assets)_t - (USL)_t}{\sum l_{y,\,x}\ddot{a}^T_{x:\overline{r-x}|}} \right],\tag{8.14}$$

where

$$\overset{all}{\sum} = \text{summation over all active and nonactive employees}$$

$(Assets)_t = $ total plan assets during year t.

$(USL)_t = $ total plan unfunded (unamortized) supplemental liability during year t.

This version is nearly always used in a funding context; however, by replacing assets in equation (8.14) by the sum of the accumulated value of past normal costs (AVPNC) and past supplemental costs (AVPSC), one may obtain an expression applicable to pension costing only, irrespective of the funding aspects of the plan.

A component of (8.14) that provides this method with an interesting twist is the unfunded supplemental liability (USL). In order for equation (8.14) to be exclusive of any amortization of supplemental liability, the unfunded supplemental liability must be determined annually, and defined by the actuarial liability under the individual ^{CA}PBCM less the assets of the plan. If this procedure is followed, the normal cost derived from (8.14) is nearly identical to the normal cost under the individual ^{CA}PBCM, the only difference being attributable to the numerical variation caused by the averaging process inherent in (8.14).

The more typical use of the aggregate projected benefit cost method is to calculate an unfunded supplemental liability (1) at the inception of the plan, (2) when an actuarial assumption of significance is changed, or (3) when a plan amendment is made. The normal cost developed by (8.14) during the intervening years (that is, between the times that the unfunded supplemental liability is recalculated) will include a supplemental cost payment (positive or negative) to the extent that a supplemental liability (positive or negative) is created during these years.

The normal cost under the aggregate ^{CS}PBCM is

$$^{CS}(NC)_t = \sum l_{y,x} s_{y,x} \left[\frac{\sum\limits^{all} l_{y,x}(PVFB)_y - (Assets)_t - (USL)_t}{\sum l_{y,x} s_{y,x}\, {}^{s}\ddot{a}^{T}_{x:\overline{r-x}|}} \right]. \quad (8.15)$$

AGGREGATE PROJECTED BENEFIT COST METHOD WITHOUT SUPPLEMENTAL LIABILITY[4]

The aggregate PBCM without supplemental liability is a method which includes in its annual cost an implicit normal cost and a supplemental cost, the latter designed to amortize the associated implicit supplemental liability of the plan. The annual cost under the aggregate ^{CA}PBCM is found by eliminating the USL term in equation (8.14), while the corresponding ^{CS}PBCM is found by eliminating this term in equation (8.15). As with the other aggregate cost methods, the actuarial liability would be determined by the individual projected benefit cost method.

---

[4] This method is sometimes referred to as the Aggregate Method.

AGGREGATE PROJECTED BENEFIT COST METHOD WITH
PARTIAL SUPPLEMENTAL LIABILITY

It will be remembered that the individual PBCM with partial supplemental liability defined the supplemental liability at the plan's inception equal to the present value of accrued benefits for past service at that point. This same principle is applicable to the aggregate version of the PBCM. In particular, the USL in equations (8.14) and (8.15) would be a quantity having its initial value equal to the present value of accrued benefits at the plan's inception and its current value equal to the unfunded portion of this liability. Since the actuarial liability under the ABCM is smaller than the actuarial liability under the PBCM, the numerator of equations (8.14) and (8.15) would be larger under the "partial supplemental liability" approach than under the "full supplemental liability" approach. The corresponding supplemental costs, however, would have just the opposite relationship due to the difference in the initial supplemental liability at the outset of the plan.

EMPLOYEE CONTRIBUTIONS

If the plan provides for employee contributions, the present value of future employee contributions must be deducted from the prospective liability of the plan in the previously discussed equations. If $100C$ is the percentage of salary that each employee contributes, then the present value of future contributions is

$$(\text{PVFC})_t = \sum l_{y,\,x} C s_{y,\,x} {}^s\ddot{a}^T_{x:\overline{r-x}|}. \tag{8.16}$$

As in the previous two chapters, there is the underlying assumption that employee contributions are not refunded at termination or death, an assumption eliminated in Chapter 10.

Chapter 9

Generalized Actuarial Cost Methods

Three generalized actuarial cost methods are developed in this chapter, for which each specific actuarial cost method studied up to this point represents a special case. The first is called the generalized accrued benefit cost method; the second, the generalized projected benefit cost method; and the third, the generalized aggregate projected benefit cost method.

GENERALIZED ACCRUED BENEFIT COST METHOD[1]

The generalized accrued benefit cost method is one having a normal cost equal to the present value of the benefit accrual assumed to occur during age x. The only theoretical constraint placed on the attained age benefit accrual is that the sum of such accruals from age y to age r equals B_r. If we let b'_x denote the assumed benefit accrual, the normal cost under the generalized ABCM is

$$(\text{NC})_x = b'_x\,_{r-x}p_x^{(T)}v^{r-x}\ddot{a}_r, \tag{9.1}$$

and the actuarial liability is

$$(\text{AL})_x = B'_x\,_{r-x}p_x^{(T)}v^{r-x}\ddot{a}_r, \tag{9.2}$$

where B'_x represents the sum of the benefit accruals used in (9.1) from the employee's entry age y up to (but not including) his attained age x.

The conventional accrued benefit cost method is obtained from the generalized ABCM by letting b'_x and B'_x take on the benefit accrual

---

[1] An approach similar to the one developed here is given in S. L. Cooper and J. C. Hickman, "A Family of Accrued Benefit Actuarial Cost Methods," *Transactions of the Society of Actuaries,* vol. 19, 1967.

and accrued benefit, respectively, as determined by applying the plan's benefit formula to the employee at his current age. Similarly, the ^{CA}ABCM and ^{CS}ABCM are determined by letting the benefit accrual and accrued benefit equal the corresponding factors as defined under each modification. The pattern of benefit accruals for each of these versions of the ABCM were studied in Chapter 6.

It is not evident what pattern of benefit accruals is required in order to make the generalized ABCM equal to the ^{CA}PBCM or the ^{CS}PBCM. This pattern is found, however, by solving (9.1) for b'_x and substituting the desired normal cost for $(NC)_x$:

$$b'_x = \frac{(NC)_x}{_{r-x}p_x^{(T)}v^{r-x}\ddot{a}_r}.\tag{9.3}$$

Substituting the normal cost under the ^{CA}PBCM from equation (7.1b) for $(NC)_x$ in (9.3), one obtains upon simplification

$$b'_x = \frac{B_r\,_{x-y}p_y^{(T)}v^{x-y}}{\ddot{a}^T_{y:\overline{r-y}|}}\tag{9.4}$$

When x is equal to y, equation (9.4) takes on the value of $B_r \div \ddot{a}^T_{y:\overline{r-y}|}$, since the other two factors in the numerator of (9.4) are both equal to unity. As x increases, $_{x-y}p_y^{(T)}$ and v^{x-y} both become progressively smaller and their product is likely to decrease rather significantly, implying that the portion of B_r allocated to each attained age is a sharply decreasing function. This is in contrast to the portion of B_r actually earned at each attained age in accordance with the benefit formula of the plan which is generally a constant or an increasing function of x.

Thus, we see that the hypothetical benefit accrual which is required under the generalized ABCM to produce the normal cost of the ^{CA}PBCM decreases with advancing age. Since the benefit allocation (or benefit accrual) under the ^{CA}PBCM exceeds the benefit under the ABCM in the early years of the employee's career, the sum of these accruals (or the accrued benefit) is similarly greater than the accrued benefit of the ABCM. Thus, it is easy to see why the actuarial liability, which, under the generalized ABCM is equal to the present value of the accrued benefit, is greater for the ^{CA}PBCM than for the ABCM.

The benefit allocations under the ^{CS}PBCM are likewise found by substituting the ^{CS}PBCM normal cost from equation (7.2c) into the equation (9.3). After simplifying, we have

$$b'_x = \frac{s_x B_r\,_{x-y}p_y^{(T)}v^{x-y}}{{}^s\!s_y\,\ddot{a}^T_{y:\overline{r-y}|}}.\tag{9.5}$$

Although s_x is generally an increasing function of age, its increase is likely to be offset by the decrease in the interest function. Consequently, b'_x is again seen to be a decreasing function of age, although the decrease would not be as steep as that for the ^{CA}PBCM.

As noted earlier, the only constraint placed on the attained age value of b'_x is that the sum of such accruals from age y to age r equals the projected benefit. Thus, it is easy to see that an infinite number of actuarial cost methods exist, since this condition can be met by an infinite number of attained age patterns of b'_x.

TABLE 9–1

Percentage of Projected Retirement Benefit Allocated to Each Age under Various Actuarial Cost Methods

Age	ABCM	^{CS}ABCM	^{CA}ABCM	^{CS}PBCM	^{CA}PBCM
30	0.32	0.67	2.86	7.90	15.53
31	0.35	0.73	2.86	6.67	12.06
32	0.38	0.79	2.86	5.81	9.68
33	0.41	0.86	2.86	5.20	7.99
34	0.45	0.93	2.86	4.75	6.73
35	0.58	1.01	2.86	4.41	5.77
36	0.66	1.09	2.86	4.14	5.01
37	0.75	1.18	2.86	3.90	4.36
38	0.84	1.28	2.86	3.68	3.82
39	0.95	1.38	2.86	3.49	3.36
40	1.07	1.48	2.86	3.32	2.96
41	1.19	1.59	2.86	3.16	2.62
42	1.33	1.71	2.86	3.01	2.32
43	1.47	1.84	2.86	2.87	2.06
44	1.63	1.98	2.86	2.74	1.83
45	1.80	2.12	2.86	2.61	1.63
46	1.99	2.27	2.86	2.50	1.46
47	2.18	2.43	2.86	2.38	1.30
48	2.39	2.60	2.86	2.27	1.16
49	2.62	2.77	2.86	2.16	1.03
50	2.86	2.96	2.86	2.05	0.92
51	3.11	3.15	2.86	1.95	0.82
52	3.38	3.35	2.86	1.85	0.73
53	3.66	3.57	2.86	1.75	0.65
54	3.96	3.79	2.86	1.66	0.58
55	4.28	4.03	2.86	1.57	0.52
56	4.61	4.27	2.86	1.53	0.48
57	4.96	4.52	2.86	1.50	0.44
58	5.32	4.79	2.86	1.46	0.40
59	5.70	5.06	2.86	1.41	0.37
60	6.10	5.35	2.86	1.37	0.34
61	6.51	5.64	2.86	1.32	0.31
62	6.94	5.95	2.86	1.26	0.28
63	7.38	6.26	2.86	1.21	0.25
64	7.84	6.59	2.86	1.14	0.23

It is interesting to consider two extreme cases for this benefit accrual pattern. Suppose that b'_x were zero for all ages except one, at which age it took on the value of B_r. If the single age were the employee's entry age y, the entire projected benefit would be accounted for at that point. The normal cost, of course, would equal $(PVFB)_y$ and the actuarial liability at each age thereafter would equal $(PVFB)_x$. This procedure is known as initial funding in the context of pension plan funding.

If the single age for which b'_x is equal to B_r is the participant's retirement age, then the normal cost would be equal to $(PVFB)_r$ for this single age. The actuarial liability also would be zero up to this age, and would equal $(PVFB)_x$ thereafter (for $x > r$). In the context of pension funding, this procedure is known as terminal funding.

The percentages of the participant's projected retirement benefit allocated to each age under the three accrual benefit and two projected benefit actuarial cost methods are given in Table 9–1 and graphed in Figure 9–1 for an age-30 entrant under standard assumptions. The attained age accruals under the ^{CA}ABCM are constant, as would be expected, while those of the ABCM and ^{CS}ABCM are steeply increasing functions, and those of the two projected benefit cost methods are steeply decreasing functions. Since the normal cost at age x under

FIGURE 9–1

Percentage of Projected Retirement Benefit Allocated to Each Age under Various Actuarial Cost Methods

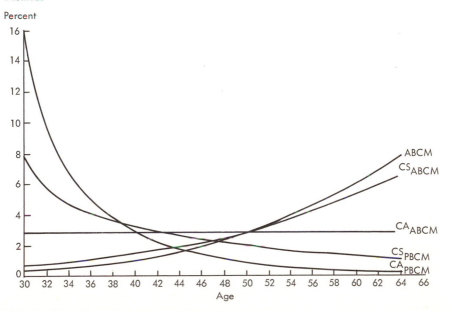

any one of the actuarial cost methods given in Table 9–1 can be found
by multiplying the benefit percentage by the value of the expression

$$B_{r\ r-x}p_x^{(T)}v^{r-x}\ddot{a}_r,\tag{9.6}$$

the data in Table 9–1 show the relative size of each method's normal
cost. For example, at age 30 the ^{CS}ABCM normal cost is seen to be
about double the ABCM normal cost.

The actuarial liability of the generalized ABCM, it will be remembered, is found by taking the present value of all benefit allocations
up to age x. In terms of the percentages given in Table 9–1, the accrued

TABLE 9–2

Cumulative Percentage of Projected Retirement Benefit Allocated to Each Age under Various Actuarial Cost Methods

Age	ABCM	^{CS}ABCM	^{CA}ABCM	^{CS}PBCM	^{CA}PBCM
30	0.00	0.00	0.00	0.00	0.00
31	0.32	0.67	2.86	7.90	15.53
32	0.67	1.41	5.71	14.57	27.58
33	1.06	2.20	8.57	20.38	37.26
34	1.47	3.06	11.43	25.58	45.25
35	1.92	4.00	14.29	30.34	51.99
36	2.49	5.01	17.14	34.75	57.76
37	3.15	6.10	20.00	38.88	62.76
38	3.90	7.28	22.86	42.78	67.13
39	4.74	8.56	25.71	46.46	70.95
40	5.70	9.93	28.57	49.95	74.31
41	6.76	11.42	31.43	53.26	77.27
42	7.95	13.01	34.29	56.42	79.89
43	9.28	14.73	37.14	59.43	82.21
44	10.75	16.57	40.00	62.30	84.27
45	12.39	18.54	42.86	65.04	86.11
46	14.19	20.66	45.71	67.65	87.74
47	16.18	22.93	48.57	70.15	89.20
48	18.36	25.36	51.43	72.53	90.49
49	20.75	27.96	54.29	74.80	91.65
50	23.37	30.73	57.14	76.96	92.68
51	26.23	33.68	60.00	79.01	93.60
52	29.34	36.83	62.86	80.96	94.42
53	32.72	40.19	65.71	82.81	95.15
54	36.38	43.76	68.57	84.57	95.80
55	40.34	47.55	71.43	86.23	96.38
56	44.62	51.57	74.29	87.80	96.90
57	49.23	55.84	77.14	89.33	97.37
58	54.19	60.37	80.00	90.83	97.81
59	59.51	65.15	82.86	92.29	98.22
60	65.22	70.21	85.71	93.70	98.59
61	71.32	75.56	88.57	95.07	98.92
62	77.83	81.20	91.43	96.39	99.23
64	92.16	93.41	97.14	98.86	99.77
65	100.00	100.00	100.00	100.00	100.00

liability can be determined by multiplying the sum of the benefit allocations up to, but not including, age x by expression (9.6).

Table 9–2 has been constructed to show the cumulative percentages given in Table 9–1 which, in turn, show the relationships among the actuarial liabilities under the various actuarial cost methods. These results are also graphed in Figure 9–2. The projected benefit cost methods have cumulative benefit allocations that are far greater than those of the other cost methods. For example, one-half of the projected benefit is allocated by age 35 under the ^{CA}PBCM and by age 40 under the ^{CS}PBCM. This is in sharp contrast to the ABCM, which allocates one-half of B_r by age 57. Although not shown in Table 9–2, the benefit allocations under the initial funding procedure discussed earlier would be 100 percent at age 30, while those of the terminal benefit cost method would be 100 percent at age 65.

FIGURE 9–2

Cumulative Percentage of Projected Retirement Benefit Allocated to Each Age under Various Actuarial Cost Methods

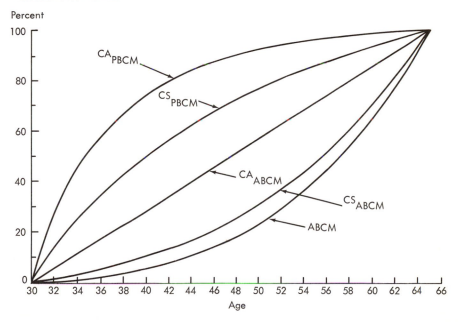

GENERALIZED PROJECTED BENEFIT COST METHOD

The normal cost under the generalized projected benefit cost method is given by

$$(NC)_x = k_x[(PVFB)_x - (AL)'_x]. \tag{9.7}$$

In this equation, k_x is some value between zero and unity, and $(AL)'_x$ is the retrospective definition of the plan's actuarial liability; that is, the accumulation of the actual past normal costs from previous years (exclusive of the normal cost currently payable). If k_x were equal to unity for all values of x, the entire pension benefit is costed at the employee's entry age y. In this case, the one-time normal cost at age y is equal to $(PVFB)_y$ and the actuarial liability takes on the value of $(PVFB)_x$ for each age. This procedure, as noted previously, is known as initial funding.

If k_x were zero for all x up to age r, and unity at age r, the normal cost is $(PVFB)_r$ at age r. This procedure is identical to terminal funding as described earlier.

The normal cost under all of the individual actuarial cost methods studied so far can be determined by the appropriate choice of k_x at each attained age. An expression for the value of k_x in terms of any conventional actuarial cost method can be determined by solving (9.7) for k_x:

$$k_x = \frac{(NC)_x}{(PVFB)_x - (AL)'_x}. \tag{9.8}$$

In the general case, k_x can theoretically take on *any* pattern from age y to age $r - 1$, provided it attains unity at one attained age. The latter condition is necessary in order to have the entire pension costed by the employee's retirement date. Thus, the generalized projected benefit cost method shows, once again, that there exists an infinite number of actuarial cost methods.

The values of $100k_x$ for each of the individual actuarial cost methods studied (except the plan termination cost method) are given in Table 9-3 for an age-30 entrant under the standard assumptions. Note that the first row of Table 9-3 is identical to the first row of Table 9-1. This occurs because the actuarial liability is zero at this age, and the ratio of $(NC)_y$ to $(PVFB)_y$ gives the proportion of B_r allocated at age y.

As would be expected, there is a striking difference at the younger ages between k_x as determined under the accrued benefit cost methods, and k_x derived for the projected benefit cost methods. For example, $100k_{30}$ is three percent or less for the accrued benefit cost methods, but 8 and 16 percent for the two projected benefit cost methods. The value of $100k_x$ approaches 100 percent at age 64 under all methods. The merging pattern of k_x does not imply that the normal cost values are nearly identical at older ages, since in each case the $100k_x$ value is applied against $[(PVFB)_x - (AL)'_x]$, and $(AL)'_x$ differs significantly among the actuarial cost methods at these ages.

TABLE 9–3

The Value of 100k_x under the Generalized Projected Benefit Actuarial Cost Method that Corresponds to the Normal Cost of Various Actuarial Cost Methods

Age	ABCM	$^{CS}ABCM$	$^{CA}ABCM$	$^{CS}PBCM$	$^{CA}PBCM$
30	0.32	0.67	2.86	7.90	15.53
31	0.35	0.74	2.94	7.24	14.27
32	0.38	0.81	3.03	6.80	13.37
33	0.42	0.88	3.13	6.53	12.73
34	0.45	0.96	3.23	6.39	12.30
35	0.59	1.05	3.33	6.33	12.02
36	0.68	1.15	3.45	6.34	11.85
37	0.77	1.26	3.57	6.37	11.72
38	0.88	1.38	3.70	6.43	11.62
39	1.00	1.50	3.85	6.52	11.56
40	1.13	1.65	4.00	6.62	11.53
41	1.28	1.80	4.17	6.75	11.52
42	1.44	1.97	4.35	6.90	11.55
43	1.63	2.16	4.55	7.07	11.59
44	1.83	2.37	4.76	7.27	11.66
45	2.06	2.60	5.00	7.48	11.76
46	2.32	2.86	5.26	7.71	11.87
47	2.60	3.15	5.56	7.97	12.01
48	2.93	3.48	5.88	8.26	12.17
49	3.30	3.85	6.25	8.57	12.36
50	3.73	4.27	6.67	8.92	12.57
51	4.21	4.75	7.14	9.30	12.82
52	4.78	5.31	7.69	9.73	13.10
53	5.44	5.97	8.33	10.21	13.43
54	6.23	6.74	9.09	10.76	13.81
55	7.17	7.67	10.00	11.39	14.27
56	8.33	8.81	11.11	12.57	15.34
57	9.77	10.24	12.50	14.03	16.69
58	11.62	12.08	14.29	15.89	18.43
59	14.09	14.52	16.67	18.34	20.74
60	17.54	17.95	20.00	21.73	23.97
61	22.71	23.08	25.00	26.75	28.79
62	31.31	31.63	33.33	35.03	36.78
63	48.50	48.73	50.00	51.39	52.65
64	100.00	100.00	100.00	100.00	100.00

GENERALIZED AGGREGATE PROJECTED BENEFIT COST METHOD[2]

The total normal cost during year t under the generalized aggregate projected benefit cost method, i.e. the contribution for the entire plan rather than for one participant, is expressed as follows:

$$(NC)_t = k_t \left[\sum_{}^{all} (PVFB)_{y,x} - \sum(AL)'_t \right], \qquad (9.9)$$

---

[2] An approach similar to the one developed here is given in C. L. Trowbridge, "The Unfunded Present Value Family of Pension Funding Methods," *Transactions of the Society of Actuaries*, vol. 15, 1963.

where

$$\sum^{all} (PVFB)_{y,\,x} = \text{present value of future benefit for all active and nonactive plan participants}$$

$$\sum (AL)'_x = \text{actuarial liability of the plan, the prime denoting a special definition for this equation.}$$

Once again, the actuarial liability in (9.9), which is exclusive of the current year's normal cost, is determined retroactively using the actual normal cost values. Since we are dealing with the aggregate of plan membership, the actuarial liability in theory is found by the following formula:

$$\sum (AL)'_t = \left[\sum (AL)'_{t-1} + (NC)_{t-1} - \sum B_{t-1}\right](1 + i), \quad (9.10)$$

where

$$(NC)_{t-1} = \text{total normal cost at time } t - 1$$

$$\sum B_{t-1} = \text{total benefit payments during time } t - 1$$

$$i = \text{the interest rate reflecting the investment experience of the plan, or the investment experience recognized if an averaging process is used.}$$

Thus, the total actuarial liability at time t is equal to the previous year's actuarial liability plus the previous year's normal cost (both as defined in this section) less the benefits paid out at that time (assumed to be paid at the beginning of the year), all of which is accumulated with one year's investment experience. In the context of funding, where the generalized projected benefit cost method would be used, the actuarial liability is replaced by the assets of the plan. Thus we have

$$(NC)_t = k_t \left[\sum^{all} (PVFB)_{y,\,x} - (Assets)_t\right]. \quad (9.11)$$

BENEFIT OF INTEREST AND SURVIVORSHIP IN SERVICE

The purpose of this section is to discuss and illustrate numerically the importance of the benefit of interest and survivorship to pension costs. It will be remembered that, if the actuarial assumptions of the plan are exactly realized, the actuarial liability for an individual at age x may be determined retroactively by accumulating the past normal costs according to the benefits of interest and survivorship.[3]

---

[3] We assume in this section that there are no benefits payable prior to retirement. If ancillary benefits are provided, the retroactively determined actuarial liability must reflect such benefit payments.

For example, the actuarial liability associated with an individual at the beginning of age $y + 1$ (but prior to the current year's normal cost) may be expressed in terms of the normal cost made at the beginning of age y:

$$(AL)_{y+1} = \frac{(NC)_y(1 + i)}{p_y^{(T)}}. \tag{9.12}$$

The benefit of interest in equation (9.12) is represented notationally by $(1 + i)$. This component increases the actuarial liability. The benefit of survivorship, on the other hand, is represented in (9.12) by the survival probability. Since the latter is less than one, it is clear that the actuarial liability associated with an individual is larger than it would be without the benefit of survivorship.

The benefit of survivorship can be seen more clearly by noting that $p_y^{(T)} = l_{y+1}^{(T)} \div l_y^{(T)}$, and substituting this into equation (9.12) we have

$$(AL)_{y+1} = \frac{(NC)_y l_y^{(T)}(1 + i)}{l_{y+1}^{(T)}}. \tag{9.13}$$

In this form, the actuarial liability at the beginning of age $y + 1$ may be interpreted as the normal cost at the beginning of age y times a hypothetical number of persons at that age, accumulated with one year's interest, and shared by all survivors at age $y + 1$. Thus, the survivors share the actuarial liability "given up" by those who either die, terminate, or become disabled.[4]

The actuarial liability at the end of each successive age is determined by the following, which again exhibits the benefit of interest and survivorship:

$$(AL)_x = \frac{[(AL)_{x-1} + (NC)_x](1 + i)}{p_x^{(T)}}. \tag{9.14}$$

Alternatively, the actuarial liability may be calculated by using normal cost values only, rather than successive actuarial liability values:

$$(AL)_x = \sum_{t=0}^{x-y-1} \frac{(NC)_{y+t}(1 + i)^{x-y-t}}{{}_{x-y-t}p_{y+t}^{(T)}}. \tag{9.15}$$

Once the employee retires, however, the retroactive equation must be modified to reflect the depletion of the actuarial liability through the annual payment of B_r. The retrospective valuation of the actuarial

---

[4] The benefit of survivorship, of course, is reduced or even eliminated if non-surviving employees receive some type of a benefit, the precise effect being determined by the benefit amount and the underlying actuarial cost method.

liability in retirement at the end of age x, based on the actuarial liability at the end of age $x - 1$, is given by equation (9.16).

$$(AL)_x = \frac{[(AL)_{x-1} - B_r](1 + i)}{p_x'^{(m)}}. \tag{9.16}$$

Once again we see the presence of the benefit of interest and the benefit of survivorship, but in this case $p_x'^{(m)}$ includes a mortality decrement only.

TABLE 9–4

Normal Cost Accumulated without the Benefit of Interest and Survivorship as a Percentage of the Actuarial Liability

Age	ABCM Normal Cost Accumulated without Benefit of:			^{CA}PBCM Normal Cost Accumulated without Benefit of:		
	Interest	*Survivorship*	*Interest or Survivorship*	*Interest*	*Survivorship*	*Interest or Survivorship*
35 . . .	82.9	74.1	62.5	79.7	68.3	55.5
40 . . .	75.2	74.0	58.0	63.9	58.9	39.9
45 . . .	69.6	73.4	54.1	50.4	51.0	28.5
50 . . .	65.3	72.0	50.6	39.1	43.5	19.8
55 . . .	61.9	69.6	47.1	29.9	36.2	13.4
60 . . .	58.9	75.9	49.3	22.7	34.7	10.3
65 . . .	56.1	73.1	45.3	17.1	30.3	7.2

Table 9–4 has been constructed to illustrate the significance of the benefit of survivorship and the benefit of interest in the determination of an age-30 entrant's actuarial liability at various ages during his active working life. Since the impact of each of these components is importantly a function of the slope of the normal cost values from age y to age r, Table 9.4 includes an analysis of the two most extreme cases in this respect by using the ABCM, which has a steeply increasing normal cost, and the ^{CA}PBCM, which has a level normal cost.

Looking first at the age-65 data of the ABCM, one will observe that the normal cost, accumulated *without* the benefit of interest, is about one-half the true age-65 actuarial liability, while the normal cost accumulated without the benefit of survivorship is about three fourths of the proper value. In this example the benefit of interest has a more significant impact on the actuarial liability of the ABCM than the benefit of survivorship. The third column in Table 9–4 shows the normal cost accumulated without either of these two factors. The accumulated value by age 65 totals 45 percent of the actuarial liability.

The data associated with the ^{CA}PBCM are considerably different from those of the ABCM. For example, the accumulated normal cost, exclusive of the benefit of interest, amounts to less than 20 percent of the age-65 actuarial liability, while the accumulated normal cost without the benefit of survivorship is 30 percent of this value. The normal cost accumulation without either of these factors (that is, a straight summation of the normal cost values) totals a mere 7 percent of the age-65 actuarial liability, as given in the right-most column of Table 9–4.

Two points are worth noting in conjunction with the data in Table 9–4. First, the flatter the normal cost values at each age, the greater are the benefit of interest and survivorship in employment. Secondly, the impact of both factors is greater for younger employees than for older employees.

Chapter 10

Basic Ancillary Benefit Functions

In this chapter we consider the cost of various ancillary benefits, that is, benefits associated with vested termination, disability, and death. The standard vesting provision assumed in this book provides full vesting after ten years of service, the disability provision pays the attained age accrued benefit for life if the employee becomes disabled after 15 years of service and age 40, and the death benefit provides 50 percent of the participant's accrued benefit to a surviving spouse if death occurs after the employee has 20 years of service and is age 55 or older. In this chapter the analysis is confined to the $(PVFB)_x$ function and the so-called term cost of ancillary benefits. The following chapter considers the cost of ancillary benefits under various actuarial cost methods.

TERM COST OF ANCILLARY BENEFITS

The annual term cost associated with various ancillary benefits is the simplest approach of all those that will be discussed in this chapter and the next for dealing with the cost of ancillary benefits. Because of its simplicity, it is frequently used in pension plans in spite of the fact that the plan's retirement benefits may be costed according to a particular actuarial cost method.

In general, the term cost of a particular benefit is the related liability that is *expected* to be created during the year. For example, if the benefit under consideration were simply a lump sum death benefit equal to one times the employee's annual salary at death, then the annual term cost would be equal to the cost of a one-year term insurance policy (exclusive of expenses) with a face value equal to the employee's salary. If the actual death payments deviate from the pension plan's expected payments, an actuarial gain or loss will occur. In terms of funding, this actuarial deviation is generally carried forward each year, rather than used to increase or reduce the next year's contribution, under the theory that the random fluctuations in the "experience account" will wash out over time.

COST OF VESTING

Term Cost

The term cost associated with vesting for an employee age x is given by

$$^v(TC)_x = g^{(v)}_{x+1/2} B_{x+1/2} q^{(w)}_x {}_{r-x-1/2} p'^{(m)}_{x+1/2} v^{r-x} \ddot{a}_r, \qquad (10.1)$$

where

$$g^{(v)}_{x+1/2} = \text{the proportion of the accrued benefit, } B_{x+1/2},$$
$$\text{vested at age } x + \tfrac{1}{2}$$

$$q^{(w)}_x = \text{the probability that an employee age } x \text{ withdraws}$$
$$\text{during that age.}$$

This formulation shows that the term cost of vesting is the *expected* liability associated with the contingency that the employee may terminate vested during age x. An approximation to providing a fractional year's credit is made in equation (10.1) by evaluating the grading function and benefit function at age $x + \tfrac{1}{2}$. The mortality-based survival function is also based on the midpoint of the age interval.

The term cost of vesting is directly related to (1) the accrued benefit, and hence all of the factors making up this benefit, (2) the grading function, and (3) the withdrawal probability, whereas $^v(TC)_x$ is inversely related to the assumed mortality rate and interest rate.

All of the components making up $^v(TC)_x$ are increasing or non-decreasing functions of x, except for the withdrawal probability, which is a decreasing function of x. Thus, the precise attained age pattern of $^v(TC)_x$ is not readily discernible. Clearly, $^v(TC)_x$ is zero up to age z, the first vesting age, and it is zero at and beyond age r', the employee's first early retirement qualification age. If $^v(TC)_x$ does not take on its largest value at age z, then its attained age pattern must be one that increases for a period of time, and then decreases to zero by age r'. On the other hand, it may be that z is the point at which $^v(TC)_x$ is the largest, in which case the function decreases from age z to age r'.

Present Value of Future Vested Benefits

The present value of future vested benefits can be expressed by taking the present value of the employee's future term costs associated with vesting:

$$^v(\text{PVFB})_x = \sum_{k=m}^{r'-1} {}_{k-x}p_x^{(T)} v^{k-x} \, {}^v(\text{TC})_k \tag{10.2a}$$

$$= \left[\sum_{k=m}^{r'-1} g_{k+1/2}^{(v)} B_{k+1/2} \; {}_{k-x}p_x^{(T)} q_k^{(w)} {}_{r-k-1/2}p_{k+1/2}^{\prime(m)} \right] v^{r-x} \ddot{a}_r, \tag{10.2b}$$

where m is the larger of x or z, the latter assumed to be the first vesting age.

The $^v(\text{PVFB})_x$, therefore, is the present value of the current and future expected liability associated with the contingency that the employee may terminate vested from age x (or age z if larger) up to age r'. This function increases in value from age y to age z, a result more easily seen by rewriting (10.2b) in the following manner for $y \leqslant x \leqslant z$:

$$^v(\text{PVFB})_x$$

$$= {}_{z-x}p_x^{(T)} v^{z-x} \left[\sum_{k=z}^{r'-1} g_{k+1/2}^{(v)} B_{k+1/2} \; {}_{k-z}p_z^{(T)} q_k^{(w)} {}_{r-k-1/2}p_{k+1/2}^{\prime(m)} \right] v^{r-z} \ddot{a}_r. \tag{10.3}$$

Since the first two factors in (10.3) are increasing functions of age from y to z, while all terms to the right of these are constant over this age interval, $^v(\text{PVFB})_x$ is clearly an increasing function during this period. As the employee's age exceeds age z (his first vesting age) successive terms in the summation of equation (10.2b) are lost. This suggests that $^v(\text{PVFB})_x$ might be a decreasing function of x after age z, if it were not for the fact that ${}_{k-x}p_x^{(T)}$ and v^{r-x} both continue to increase. Consequently, it is not clear mathematically whether $^v(\text{PVFB})_x$ continues to increase in value for a period beyond age z, or begins to decrease immediately. Its behavior, of course, depends on the precise assumptions underlying the function, and no general pattern necessarily exists. In any event, it is clear that $^v(\text{PVFB})_x$ is zero for $x \geqslant r'$, which means that the function must turn downward at some age between z and r'.

If we consider the sensitivity of $^v(\text{PVFB})_x$ to its underlying parameters, it is directly related to (1) the accrued benefit and (2) the grading function. However, whereas $^v(\text{TC})_x$ was found to be directly related to the withdrawal probability, $^v(\text{PVFB})_x$ may not have this relationship. While it is true that an increase in the withdrawal rates for ages prior to age z reduces the $^v(\text{PVFB})_x$ function, as can be seen from (10.3), an increase in a termination rate at some post vesting age has an opposite effect on the probability of surviving to ages beyond the age at which the increase occurs. To look at an extreme case, assume that $q_z^{(w)}$ is increaded to a value of unity. The $^v(\text{PVFB})_x$ function then becomes equal to

$$^v(\text{PVFB})_x = g_{z+1/2}^{(v)} B_{z+1/2} \; _{z-x}p_x^{(T)} \; _{r-z-1/2}p_{z+1/2}^{\prime(m)} v^{r-z} \ddot{a}_r,$$

and it is not clear whether this is larger or smaller than (10.2b) for a typical set of termination rates. In other words, an increase in the termination rate at, say, age k, reduces the persistency probability, $_{t-x}p_x^{(T)}$, for $t > k$. This, in turn, reduces the *expected* vested termination benefit at age t. Thus, when an increase in post vesting termination rates occurs, the change in $^v(\text{PVFB})_x$ will be positive, zero, or negative according to whether the incremental cost resulting from the increase in the termination rates exceeds, equals, or is exceeded by the reduction in costs resulting from the decreased persistency rates. An increase in the termination rates at older ages in conjunction with a decrease at younger ages will increase the cost of vesting if the probability of surviving to retirement from age z remains unchanged. This effect will be amplified by a greater slope in the benefit function. Finally, as with the $^v(\text{TC})_x$ function, the $^v(\text{PVFB})_x$ function is inversely related to the mortality rates and to the assumed interest rate.

Relative Cost

The relative cost of vesting is measured by the vesting cost ratio, (VCR), which is defined below.

$$(\text{VCR})_x = \frac{^v(\text{PVFB})_x}{^r(\text{PVFB})_x}$$

$$= \frac{\sum_{k=m}^{r'-1} g_{k+1/2}^{(v)} B_{k+1/2} \; _{k-x}p_x^{(T)} q_k^{(w)} \; _{r-k-1/2}p_{k+1/2}^{\prime(m)} v^{r-x} \ddot{a}_r}{B_r \; _{r-x}p_x^{(T)} v^{r-x} \ddot{a}_r}. \qquad (10.4a)$$

This simplifies to

$$(VCR)_x = \sum_{k=m}^{r'-1} g_{k+1/2}^{(v)} \frac{B_{k+1/2}}{B_r} \frac{1}{r-k p_k^{(T)}} q_k^{(w)}{}_{r-k-1/2} p_{k+1/2}^{'(m)}. \quad (10.4b)$$

The $(VCR)_x$ is seen to be independent of mortality rates beyond age r, and independent of both termination rates and mortality rates prior to age z. Moreover, the ratio is independent of the assumed interest rate. Thus, the vesting cost ratio is attained age independent from age y to age z, that is, $(VCR)_x = (VCR)_z$ for $y \leqslant x \leqslant z$. On the other hand, $(VCR)_x$ is a function of (1) the initial vesting age z, (2) the grading function, (3) the accrued benefit, (4) the rates of mortality and termination from age z (or x if larger) to age r, and (5) the first age for which the individual qualifies for early retirement, r'. Finally, it can be seen from (10.4b) that the attained age pattern of the vesting cost ratio is constant from age y to age z and decreases to zero by age r'.

Table 10–1 presents characteristics of the vesting cost functions for an age-30 entrant under the standard assumptions used elsewhere

TABLE 10–1

Measures of the Cost of Vesting

x	$100 \dfrac{{}^{v}(TC)_x}{{}^{v}(TC)_{40}}$	$100 \dfrac{{}^{v}(TC)_x}{S_x}$	$100 \dfrac{{}^{v}(PVFB)_x}{{}^{v}(PVFB)_{40}}$	$100 \dfrac{{}^{v}(PVFB)_x}{{}^{r}(PVFB)_x}$
30. . . .	0.0	0.00	42.0	17.8
31. . . .	0.0	0.00	49.7	17.8
32. . . .	0.0	0.00	57.0	17.8
33. . . .	0.0	0.00	63.7	17.8
34. . . .	0.0	0.00	69.8	17.8
35. . . .	0.0	0.00	75.2	17.8
36. . . .	0.0	0.00	80.2	17.8
37. . . .	0.0	0.00	85.1	17.8
38. . . .	0.0	0.00	90.1	17.8
39. . . .	0.0	0.00	95.0	17.8
40. . . .	100.0	1.01	100.0	17.8
41. . . .	111.4	1.13	100.6	17.0
42. . . .	124.0	1.26	100.5	16.2
43. . . .	137.9	1.40	99.7	15.3
44. . . .	153.4	1.55	98.3	14.4
45. . . .	170.9	1.73	96.1	13.5
46. . . .	190.1	1.93	93.1	12.4
47. . . .	212.3	2.15	89.0	11.4
48. . . .	236.3	2.39	83.9	10.2
49. . . .	263.6	2.67	77.4	9.0
50. . . .	293.5	2.97	69.5	7.7
51. . . .	326.1	3.30	60.0	6.3
52. . . .	361.7	3.66	48.5	4.8
53. . . .	398.3	4.03	34.8	3.3
54. . . .	438.0	4.43	18.8	1.7
55. . . .	0.0	0.00	0.0	0.0

in this book. The first column gives the $^v(TC)_x$ function as a percentage of its value at age 40, the first vesting age for the participant. This function increases continuously from age 40 to age 55, at which point it becomes zero. As noted previously, this function might turn downward at an earlier point, if the benefit function were flatter and/or if the interest assumption were lower. The second column of Table 10–1 shows the term cost of vesting as a percentage of the participant's salary at each age, amounting to 1.01 percent of salary at the first vesting age and increasing to 4.43 percent by age 54. Prior to age 40 and after age 54, however, the term cost of vesting is zero.

Column three of Table 10–1 gives the $^v(PVFB)_x$ function as a percentage of its age-40 value. This function increases steadily from the employee's entry age up to his first vesting age, and then continues to increase slightly for two years before turning downward. This function, like the $^v(TC)_x$ function, attains zero by age 55, since this is the age at which the employees first qualifies for early retirement and termination rates beyond this point are assumed to be zero. Column four of Table 10–1 gives the vesting cost ratio, that is, $^v(PVFB)_x$ as a percentage of $^r(PVFB)_x$. This measure of the cost of vesting is constant at 17.8 percent from the employee's entry age up to his first vesting age, after which the percentage declines to zero by age 55.

COST OF DISABILITY

Term Cost

The term cost of disability for an employee age x is given by

$$^d(TC)_x = g^{(d)}_{x+1/2} B_{x+1/2} q^{(d)}_x {}^d_w p'^{(m)}_{x+1/2} v^{w+1/2} \ddot{a}^d_{x+w+1/2}, \qquad (10.5)$$

where

$g^{(d)}_{x+1/2}$ = the proportion of the accrued benefit, $B_{x+1/2}$, provided as a disability benefit at age $x + \frac{1}{2}$

$q^{(d)}_x$ = the probability that an employee age x becomes disabled during that age

w = the waiting period before disability benefits commence

${}^d_n p'^{(m)}_x$ = the probability that a *disabled* life age x lives n years

$\ddot{a}^d_x$ = a life annuity based on disabled-life mortality.

As was the case for the term cost of vesting, the term cost of disability is the expected liability arising out of the possibility that the employee age x may become disabled during the year. Note that the grading function, $g_x^{(d)}$, which determines the proportion of the attained age benefit accrual payable as a disability benefit, is equal to zero if the employee's attained age is less than the first disability qualification age. The survival probability, $_np_x'^{(m)}$, and annuity function, $\ddot{a}_x^d$, are both based on mortality applicable to disabled lives. Moreover, the disabled-life annuity should also include the possibility that the employee would recover from disability after the waiting period and prior to age r. This contingency can be accounted for by increasing the mortality decrement, since either death or recovery would cause a cessation of benefit payments.

Generally, all of the components of the $^d(\text{TC})_x$ function, except the survival probability and annuity function, are increasing functions of age. Thus, the term cost of disability will increase, remain constant, or decrease with advancing age beyond the first qualification age, depending on whether the decrease in the survival probability and the annuity are less than, equal to, or greater than the combined increase in the remaining components of (10.5).

Present Value of Future Disability Benefits

The present value of future disability benefits, $^d(\text{PVFB})_x$, is found by taking the present value of the employee's future term costs associated with disability:

$$^d(\text{PVFB})_x = \sum_{k=m}^{r-1} {}_{k-x}p_x^{(T)} v^{k-x} \, {}^d(\text{TC})_k \tag{10.6a}$$

$$= \sum_{k=m}^{r-1} g_{k+1/2}^{(d)} B_{k+1/2} \, {}_{k-x}p_x^{(T)} q_k^{(d)} \, {}_w^d p_{k+1/2}'^{(m)} v^{k+1/2+w-x} \ddot{a}_{k+1/2+w}^d, \tag{10.6b}$$

where m is the greater of age x or the first disability qualification age. Unlike the case of the $^v(\text{PVFB})_x$ function with respect to changes in post vesting termination rates where the cost implications were unclear, a change in disability rates beyond the first qualification age will always increase the present value of future benefits. The relationship of $^d(\text{PVFB})_x$ to the other parameters is straightforward.

Relative Cost

The relative cost of disability is the ratio of the present value of future disability benefits to the present value of retirement benefits:

$$(DCR)_x = \frac{{}^d(PVFB)_x}{{}^r(PVFB)_x}$$

$$= \frac{\displaystyle\sum_{k=m}^{r-1} g_{k+1/2}^{(d)} B_{k+1/2} \,_{k-x}p_x^{(T)} q_k^{(d)} \,_w^d p_{k+1/2}^{\prime(m)} v^{k+1/2+w-x} \ddot{a}_{k+w+1/2}^d}{B_r \,_{r-x}p_x^{(T)} v^{r-x} \ddot{a}_r}$$

(10.7a)

$$= \sum_{k=m}^{r-1} g_{k+1/2}^{(d)} \frac{B_{k+1/2}}{B_r}$$

$$\times \frac{1}{\,_{r-k}p_k^{(T)}} q_k^{(d)} \,_w^d p_{k+1/2}^{\prime(m)} (1+i)^{r-k-1/2-w} \frac{\ddot{a}_{k+1/2+w}^d}{\ddot{a}_r}. \quad (10.7b)$$

The $(DCR)_x$ is affected by all of the parameters that affect the ${}^d(PVFB)_x$ and ${}^r(PVFB)_x$ functions except for decrements that occur prior to the first age at which disability benefits become payable.

The cost of disability for the age-30 entrant under standard assumptions is given in Table 10–2, using the same format as was used in Table 10–1. Since the first age for which disability benefits are applicable is age 45, the term cost of disability is zero up to this age and increases rapidly thereafter through age 64, at which point it is 25 times greater than the cost at age 45. Column two shows that the term cost, as a percentage of salary, starts out at 0.37 percent and climbs to 9.28 percent of salary at age 64. The latter cost is more than double the largest term cost associated with vesting, and it also corresponds to the employee's largest attained age salary.

The ${}^d(PVFB)_x$ function as a percentage of ${}^d(PVFB)_{45}$ is given in the third column of Table 10–2. This cost measure increases from age 30 up through age 45, the first disability qualification age, and continues to increase through age 55, after which it declines to zero by age 65. The $(DCR)_x$, that is, the ratio of ${}^d(PVFB)_x$ to ${}^r(PVFB)_x$, shows a cost of disability for the age-30 entrant equal to 14.9 percent up through age 45. Beyond this age, however, the $(DRC)_x$ decreases in spite of the fact that the dollar value of ${}^d(PVFB)_x$ continues to increase for ten years.

TABLE 10–2

Measures of the Cost of Disability

x	$100 \dfrac{{}^d(TC)_x}{{}^d(TC)_{45}}$	$100 \dfrac{{}^d(TC)_x}{s_x}$	$100 \dfrac{{}^d(PVFB)_x}{{}^d(PVFB)_{45}}$	$100 \dfrac{{}^d(PVFB)_x}{{}^r(PVFB)_x}$
30. . . .	0.0	0.00	33.1	14.9
31. . . .	0.0	0.00	39.2	14.9
32. . . .	0.0	0.00	45.0	14.9
33. . . .	0.0	0.00	50.3	14.9
34. . . .	0.0	0.00	55.0	14.9
35. . . .	0.0	0.00	59.3	14.9
36. . . .	0.0	0.00	63.2	14.9
37. . . .	0.0	0.00	67.1	14.9
38. . . .	0.0	0.00	71.0	14.9
39. . . .	0.0	0.00	74.9	14.9
40. . . .	0.0	0.00	78.9	14.9
41. . . .	0.0	0.00	82.9	14.9
42. . . .	0.0	0.00	86.9	14.9
43. . . .	0.0	0.00	91.1	14.9
44. . . .	0.0	0.00	95.5	14.9
45. . . .	100.0	0.37	100.0	14.9
46. . . .	116.9	0.43	103.3	14.7
47. . . .	134.8	0.49	106.5	14.5
48. . . .	159.9	0.59	109.7	14.2
49. . . .	186.4	0.68	112.7	13.9
50. . . .	214.2	0.78	115.7	13.6
51. . . .	243.1	0.89	118.5	13.2
52. . . .	280.4	1.03	121.1	12.8
53. . . .	319.2	1.17	123.5	12.4
54. . . .	359.3	1.32	125.6	11.9
55. . . .	407.5	1.49	127.4	11.4
56. . . .	450.2	1.65	124.2	10.9
57. . . .	510.8	1.87	120.6	10.3
58. . . .	590.0	2.16	116.2	9.7
59. . . .	706.1	2.59	110.9	9.0
60. . . .	878.5	3.22	104.0	8.1
61. . . .	1127.1	4.13	94.6	7.1
62. . . .	1472.2	5.39	81.6	5.9
63. . . .	1934.5	7.09	63.1	4.3
64. . . .	2534.3	9.28	36.9	2.4
65. . . .	0.0	0.00	0.0	0.0

COST OF SURVIVING SPOUSE BENEFIT

Term Cost

Equation (10.8) represents the term cost of a surviving spouse benefit, where the benefit paid is some fraction of the deceased employee's accrued benefit.

$$ {}^s(TC)_x = Mg^{(s)}_{x+1/2}B_{x+1/2}q^{(m)}_x v^{1/2}\ddot{a}^{rm}_{x+u+1/2}, \tag{10.8}$$

where

M = the probability that the participant is married at his death

$g^{(s)}_{x+1/2}$ = the proportion of the accrued benefit, $B_{x+1/2}$, that is provided as a surviving spouse benefit at age $x + \frac{1}{2}$

$q^{(m)}_x$ = the probability that the employee dies during age x

u = the number of years (positive or negative) that, when added to the participant's age, yields an assumed age for the spouse

$\ddot{a}^{rm}_{x+u+1/2}$ = a life annuity based on the spouse's age at the death of the participant, taking into account a remarriage decrement which is denoted by the rm superscript.

The expected liability created by the possibility that the employee age x may die during the year has the same general form as the expected vested liability and the expected disability liability. The grading function, $g^{(s)}_{x+1/2}$, controls the portion of the accrued benefit payable to the surviving spouse once the employee attains the age for which such benefits become payable, while the spouse's annuity represents the cost of providing the benefit for the life of the spouse, or until the spouse remarries. The annuity used in (10.8) assumes the spouse is, on average, age $x + u + \frac{1}{2}$ at the participant's death. The value of u is often assumed to be -3 if the participant is a male and 3 if the participant is a female. Although the exact spouse age could be used, this is generally not done in the interest of of simplicity. The interest function, $v^{1/2}$, and the $\frac{1}{2}$-year increment to the spouse's assumed age on the annuity symbol in (10.8) reflect the fact benefits will begin, on average, halfway through the year. Finally, the coefficient M reflects the probability that the participant is married at the time of his death. In the interest of simplicity, this value is often assumed to be a constant (for example, .80).

The benefit function, grading function, and mortality probability in (10.8) are increasing or non-decreasing functions of x, while the annuity function is basically a decreasing function of x. This may not be the case, however, since the annuity includes remarriage rates, which could cause it to increase over some ages. Thus, the attained age pattern of $^s(TC)_x$ could take on any one of a number of different patterns from the employee's initial qualification age to age r. The sensitivity of $^s(TC)_x$ to changes in its underlying parameters is easily determined.

PRESENT VALUE OF FUTURE SURVIVING SPOUSE BENEFITS

Taking the present value of future term costs associated with the surviving spouse benefit, we have the following expression for the $^s(PVFB)_x$ function:

$$^s(PVFB)_x = M \sum_{k=m}^{r-1} g_{k+1/2}^{(s)} B_{k+1/2\ k-x}p_x^{(T)} q_k^{(m)} v^{k+1/2-x} \ddot{a}_{k+u+1/2}^{rm}. \quad (10.9)$$

where m is the greater of the employee's age x or the age he first qualifies for a surviving spouse benefit. Notice that (10.9) does not take into account the probability that the spouse survives to each potential future age for which the employee might die. Rather, the M coefficient is used to approximate the probability that the participant has a living spouse at all ages from age x to age $r - 1$. It would be possible to define M as the probability of having a spouse at age x only, and to use $_{k+1/2-x}p_{x+u}^{\prime(m)}$ to account for the spouse's probability of living to age $k + u + \frac{1}{2}$, but this procedure creates an unwarranted degree of complexity when this cost is considered in the context of an actuarial cost method, the subject of the following chapter.

Relative Cost

The surviving spouse benefit cost ratio (SCR) for an employee age x is

$$(SCR)_x = \frac{^s(PVFB)_x}{^r(PVFB)_x}$$

$$= \frac{M \sum_{k=m}^{r-1} g_{k+1/2}^{(s)} B_{k+1/2\ k-x}p_x^{(T)} q_k^{(m)} v^{k+1/2-x} \ddot{a}_{k+u+1/2}^{rm}}{B_{r\ r-x}p_x^{(T)} v^{r-x} \ddot{a}_r}, \quad (10.10a)$$

which can be written

$$(SCR)_x = M \sum_{k=m}^{r-1} g_{k+1/2}^{(s)} \frac{B_{k+1/2}}{B_r} \frac{1}{_{r-k}p_k^{(T)}} q_k^{(m)} (1+i)^{r-k-1/2} \frac{\ddot{a}_{k+u+1/2}^{rm}}{\ddot{a}_r}. \quad (10.10b)$$

Although (10.10b) is not a simple function, it is relatively straightforward to reason through the effect of a given parameter change.

Table 10–3 shows the cost of the surviving spouse benefit under the standard assumptions for an age-30 entrant. The standard provision, it will be remembered, is a 50 percent life annuity payable to a surviving spouse, the latter assumed to be three years younger than the male employee. The requirements for the benefit are that the employee attain age 55 with 20 years of service; hence, the employee's first qualification age in the illustration is age 55. Finally, the data in Table 10–3 are based on an 80 percent chance that the employee is married at his death.

TABLE 10–3

Measures of the Cost of Survivorship

x	$100\dfrac{{}^s(TC)_x}{{}^s(TC)_{55}}$	$100\dfrac{{}^s(TC)_x}{S_x}$	$100\dfrac{{}^s(PVFB)_x}{{}^s(PVFB)_{55}}$	$100\dfrac{{}^s(PVFB)_x}{{}^r(PVFB)_x}$
30. . . .	0.0	0.00	19.9	6.7
31. . . .	0.0	0.00	23.5	6.7
32. . . .	0.0	0.00	27.0	6.7
33. . . .	0.0	0.00	30.2	6.7
34. . . .	0.0	0.00	33.0	6.7
35. . . .	0.0	0.00	35.6	6.7
36. . . .	0.0	0.00	37.9	6.7
37. . . .	0.0	0.00	40.3	6.7
38. . . .	0.0	0.00	42.6	6.7
39. . . .	0.0	0.00	45.0	6.7
40. . . .	0.0	0.00	47.3	6.7
41. . . .	0.0	0.00	49.7	6.7
42. . . .	0.0	0.00	52.2	6.7
43. . . .	0.0	0.00	54.7	6.7
44. . . .	0.0	0.00	57.3	6.7
45. . . .	0.0	0.00	60.0	6.7
46. . . .	0.0	0.00	62.9	6.7
47. . . .	0.0	0.00	65.9	6.7
48. . . .	0.0	0.00	69.2	6.7
49. . . .	0.0	0.00	72.6	6.7
50. . . .	0.0	0.00	76.4	6.7
51. . . .	0.0	0.00	80.4	6.7
52. . . .	0.0	0.00	84.7	6.7
53. . . .	0.0	0.00	89.4	6.7
54. . . .	0.0	0.00	94.5	6.7
55. . . .	100.0	1.26	100.0	6.7
56. . . .	112.3	1.41	95.4	6.2
57. . . .	125.3	1.58	90.0	5.7
58. . . .	139.7	1.76	83.8	5.2
59. . . .	156.7	1.97	76.7	4.6
60. . . .	176.2	2.22	68.4	4.0
61. . . .	197.8	2.49	58.6	3.3
62. . . .	220.9	2.78	47.3	2.5
63. . . .	245.9	3.10	34.0	1.7
64. . . .	274.0	3.45	18.4	0.9
65. . . .	0.0	0.00	0.0	0.0

The $^s(TC)_x$ function is seen to increase monotonically, beginning at age 55 and ending at age 64 with a value nearly three times greater than the initial value. As a percentage of salary, the term cost of survivorship starts out at 1.26 percent at age 55 and reaches a value of 3.45 percent at age 64. This cost is the lowest of the three ancillary benefits analyzed in this chapter; but the cost would be double the value shown if the surviving spouse were to receive 100 percent instead of 50 percent of the employee's accrued benefit.

The $^s(PVFB)_x$ function gradually increases from age 30 to a maximum value at age 55 and decreases thereafter to zero by age 64. This is the same general pattern as that associated with the $^v(PVFB)_x$, whereas the $^d(PVFB)_x$ function continued to increase for a while after the first eligibility age for the benefit. The (SCR), that is, the ratio of $^d(PVFB)_x$ to $^r(PVFB)_x$, is constant from age 30 to the participant's first eligibility age, a value equal to 6.7 percent for the data in Table 10–3. The $(SCR)_x$ for ages greater than the first eligibility age decreases to zero by age 65.

EMPLOYEE CONTRIBUTIONS

In previous chapters the assumption was made that, if the plan was contributory, employees were not entitled to a refund of their contributions at death or termination. This is unrealistic, and for most plans contributions accumulated with interest are automatically refunded at death, and refunded upon request at termination. The latter, in most cases, would cause a forfeiture of the employer-related pension benefits prior to ERISA, but now a refund-based forfeiture can occur only if the employee is vested in less than 50 percent of his accrued benefits.

The symbol $(PVFC)_x$ has been defined as the present value of future employee contributions. This value was deducted from the $(PVFB)_x$ function in determining the accrued liability of the various individual-based actuarial cost methods, from the numerator of the aggregate projected benefit cost methods, and from the $(PVFB)_y$ function in determining the normal cost under the projected benefit cost methods. If the plan refunds contributions at death or termination, another quantity representing the present value of future refunds, $(PVFR)_x$, must be added at every point that $(PVFC)_x$ was subtracted. In essence, the $(PVFC)_x$ function is transformed to the present value of future *net* contributions, net of those expected to be refunded, by the addition of the $(PVFR)_x$ function.

The $(\text{PVFR})_x$ function is given by

$$(\text{PVFR})_x = \sum_{k=x}^{r-1} \left[\sum_{t=y}^{k} Cs_t(1 + i')^{k+1/2-t} \right]_{k-x}p_x^{(T)}v^{k+1/2-x}[q_k^{(w)} + q_k^{(m)}],$$

$$(10.11)$$

where C is the employee's contribution rate based on his attained age salary.

The summation inside the first set of brackets represents the accumulated contributions from age y up through age $k + \frac{1}{2}$, accumulated at a rate of interest equal to i'. The outer summation considers, for all ages from x to $r - 1$, the probability of persisting to each of these ages and the chance that withdrawal or death *will cause a refund*.[1] The interest discount factor in equation (10.11) may or may not be evaluated at i, depending on the provisions of the plan.

Although (10.11) represents the general form of the $(\text{PVFR})_x$ function, the details of a particular plan would no doubt require modification to this basic equation.

---

[1] Since the employee's withdrawal or death may generate a deferred vested benefit or survivor's benefit instead of a return of contributions, $q_k^{(w)}$ and $q_k^{(m)}$, when used in equation (10.11), must reflect only the chance that contributions are returned.

Chapter 11

Retirement and Ancillary Benefits under Actuarial Cost Methods

In this chapter we consider the total cost of the plan, inclusive of ancillary benefits, under the various individual actuarial cost methods studied earlier. The aggregate versions of each cost method are not considered, but the principles are the same. The cost under the plan termination cost method is unaffected by the existence of ancillary benefits, since this method focuses only on the benefits applicable at plan termination, that is, the retirement benefits under the plan. As noted in the previous chapter, it is common to use the term cost of ancillary benefits instead of integrating this cost into the total costs of the plan according to one of the conventional actuarial cost methods. This practice, however, is giving way to the use of actuarial cost methods for all benefits of the plan, a trend made possible by the availability of more powerful computers.

ACCRUED BENEFIT COST METHOD

The normal cost under the accrued benefit cost method, consistent with the underlying theory of this approach, is equal to the present value of b_x (the attained age benefit accrual), where the present value is based on the possibility that the employee may either terminate vested and be entitled to a deferred vested benefit, become disabled and receive a disability benefit, die and leave his surviving spouse with a benefit, or retire and receive a retirement benefit. The total normal cost, $^{T}(NC)_x$, for a participant age x is given by

$$
{}^{T}(NC)_x = b_x \left\{ \left[\sum_{k=x}^{r-1} c_{k-x} p_x^{(T)} v^{k-x} (g_{k+1/2}^{(v)} q_k^{(w)}{}_{r-k-1/2} p_{k+1/2}^{\prime(m)} v^{r-k} \ddot{a}_r \right. \right.
$$
$$
+ g_{k+1/2}^{(d)} q_k^{(d)} {}_{w}^{d} p_{k+1/2}^{\prime(m)} v^{1/2+w} \ddot{a}_{k+1/2+w}^{d}
$$
$$
\left. + M g_{k+1/2}^{(s)} q_k^{(m)} v^{1/2} \ddot{a}_{k+u+1/2}^{rm}) \right] + {}_{r-x} p_x^{(T)} v^{r-x} \ddot{a}_r \right\}. \tag{11.1}
$$

The constant c is $\frac{1}{2}$ when k equals x and unity otherwise to reflect the fact that on average, only $\frac{1}{2} b_x$ is accrued if withdrawal, disability, or death occurs during the employee's current age. The actuarial liability associated with the participant is found by substituting B_x for b_x in equation (11.1) and defining the constant, c, equal to unity for all values of k.

Table 11-1 shows the normal cost associated with various ancillary benefits as a percentage of the retirement-related cost under the ABCM for the age-30 entrant. In this table the normal cost associated with each ancillary benefit is denoted by a superscript to the $(NC)_x$ symbol, where v denotes the vested benefit, d the disability benefit, s the surviving spouse benefit, and r the retirement benefit. These various cost components are derived by taking the appropriate portion of equation (11.1). Finally, all of the data in Table 11-1, except the last column and the first row, are equally applicable to the actuarial liability under the ABCM.

The cost of vesting is seen to be slightly greater than the cost of retirement from the employee's entry age to age 40, after which the relative cost scales down to zero by age 55. The cost of disability is equal to 29.2 percent of the cost of retirement from the employee's entry age to age 45, a cost which is considerably less than the cost of vesting over these ages. This cost, however, exists up through age 64 whereas the cost of vesting is zero after age 54. The cost of the surviving spouse benefit is 9.6 percent of the retirement-benefit cost from the employee's entry age to age 55 and reduces to zero by age 65.

Column four of Table 11-1 shows that ancillary benefits increase the retirement-based normal cost under the ABCM by nearly two and one-half times at the younger ages and by a continually smaller amount as the age is increased. However, even by age 50 the total normal cost is 50 percent greater with ancillary benefits included than the cost of retirement benefits only. The last column of Table 11-1 is important in that it gives the total normal cost for the employee as a percentage of this attained age salary. These data show that the

TABLE 11–1

Pension Cost Components as a Percentage of the Retirement Cost Component under the ABCM

x	$100\dfrac{^v(NC)_x}{^r(NC)_x}$	$100\dfrac{^d(NC)_x}{^r(NC)_x}$	$100\dfrac{^s(NC)_x}{^r(NC)_x}$	$100\dfrac{^T(NC)_x}{^r(NC)_x}$	$100\dfrac{^T(NC)_x}{s_x}$
30	102.2	29.2	9.6	241.1	0.4
31	102.2	29.2	9.6	241.1	0.6
32	102.2	29.2	9.6	241.1	0.7
33	102.2	29.2	9.6	241.1	0.8
34	102.2	29.2	9.6	241.1	1.0
35	102.2	29.2	9.6	241.1	1.4
36	102.2	29.2	9.6	241.1	1.7
37	102.2	29.2	9.6	241.1	2.0
38	102.2	29.2	9.6	241.1	2.4
39	102.2	29.2	9.6	241.1	2.9
40	102.2	29.2	9.6	241.1	3.4
41	91.0	29.2	9.6	229.8	3.8
42	80.8	29.2	9.6	219.7	4.3
43	71.6	29.2	9.6	210.4	4.8
44	63.1	29.2	9.6	202.0	5.3
45	55.3	29.2	9.6	194.2	5.9
46	48.1	27.7	9.6	185.4	6.5
47	41.4	26.2	9.6	177.2	7.2
48	35.0	24.8	9.6	169.4	7.9
49	29.1	23.2	9.6	162.0	8.7
50	23.5	21.9	9.6	155.0	9.5
51	18.2	20.5	9.6	148.3	10.4
52	13.3	19.1	9.6	142.0	11.4
53	8.6	17.8	9.6	136.0	12.5
54	4.1	16.5	9.6	130.3	13.7
55	0.0	15.3	9.6	124.9	15.0
56	0.0	14.1	8.6	122.7	16.3
57	0.0	13.0	7.6	120.6	17.6
58	0.0	11.8	6.6	118.4	19.1
59	0.0	10.6	5.6	116.2	20.7
60	0.0	9.3	4.7	114.0	22.4
61	0.0	7.9	3.7	111.6	24.3
62	0.0	6.3	2.8	109.1	26.4
63	0.0	4.5	1.8	106.3	28.7
64	0.0	2.4	0.9	103.3	31.3

All columns, except the last one, are equally applicable to the actuarial liability ratios under the ABCM, except for the values at age 30.

dramatic increase brought about by ancillary benefits occurs at those ages where the total normal cost as a percentage of salary is quite low, while at those ages for which the normal cost is quite high, the added cost of ancillary benefits is relatively modest. Thus, the fact that ancillary benefits increase the normal cost under the ABCM by nearly two and one-half times at the employee's younger ages is somewhat deceptive and should be viewed in terms of the total costs at this age as a percentage of salary.

MODIFIED ACCRUED BENEFIT COST METHOD

It will be remembered that the ^{CA}ABCM allocates a constant benefit accrual to each age, while the ^{CS}ABCM allocates a benefit accrual representing a constant percentage of the participant's attained age salary to each age. The normal cost, in turn, was seen to be equal to the present value of these benefit allocations. If we apply these modifications in connection with ancillary benefits, it is necessary to derive an expression for the appropriate benefit allocation. The derivation of this benefit accrual involves equating the present value of future retirement and ancillary benefits at the employee's entry age to the present value of his future normal costs associated with these benefits, where the normal cost expression includes the benefit accrual in notational form. This equality can then be solved for the correct benefit accrual. This was the same approach used in deriving the benefit allocation associated with the retirement benefit of the plan participant. It is important to note, however, that the present value of *all* benefits, both ancillary and retirement-related, must be used in the equation of value in order to develop an appropriate benefit accrual function. If we let

$$^{T}(\text{PVFB})_x = {}^{v}(\text{PVFB})_x + {}^{d}(\text{PVFB})_x + {}^{s}(\text{PVFB})_c + {}^{r}(\text{PVFB})_x \quad (11.2)$$

and $^{T}(\text{NC})_t$ represent the total normal cost when all benefits are included, then the equation of value becomes

$$^{T}(\text{PVFB})_y = \sum_{x=y}^{r-1} {}_{x-y}p_y^{(T)}v^{x-y}\,{}^{T}(\text{NC})^x. \quad (11.3)$$

Note that under the ^{CA}ABCM the value of $^{T}(\text{NC})_x$ is found by substituting $^{CA}b_x$ into (11.1) for b_x, and under the ^{CS}ABCM the normal cost is found by substituting $^{CS}b_x$ for b_x. Substituting the value of $^{T}(\text{NC})_x$ from (11.1) with b_x replaced by $^{CA}b_x$ into (11.3) and then solving for $^{CA}b_x$, we have

$$^{CA}b_x = \frac{{}^{T}(\text{PVFB})_y}{\sum\limits_{x=y}^{r-1} {}_{x-y}p_y^{(T)}v^{x-y}\left[\sum\limits_{k=x}^{r-1} c_{k-x}p_x^{(T)}v^{k-x}(g_{k+1/2}^{(v)}q_k^{(w)}{}_{r-k-1/2}p_{k+1/2}^{\prime(m)}v^{r-k}\ddot{a}_r \right.}$$
$$+ g_{k+1/2}^{(d)}q_k^{(d)}\,{}_{w}^{d}p_{k+1/2}^{\prime(m)}v^{1/2+w}\ddot{a}_{k+1/2+w}^{d}$$
$$\left. + Mg_{k+1/2}^{(s)}q_k^{(m)}v^{1/2}\ddot{a}_{k+u+1/2}^{rm}) + {}_{r-x}p_x^{(T)}v^{r-x}\ddot{a}_r\right]. \quad (11.4a)$$

The first two components to the right of first summation sign in (11.4a) combine with other terms to leave the denominator independent of the x index. Reversing the order of summation we have the following expression for $^{CA}b_x$:

$$^{CA}b_x = \frac{^T(\text{PVFB})_y}{\begin{array}{l} \sum_{k=y}^{r-1} (k + \tfrac{1}{2} - y)_{k-y}p_y^{(T)}v^{k-y}(g_{k+1/2}^{(v)}q_k^{(w)}{}_{r-k-1/2}p_{k+1/2}^{\prime(m)}v^{r-k}\ddot{a}_r \\ + g_{k+1/2}^{(d)}q_k^{(d)}{}_w^d p_{k+1/2}^{\prime(m)}v^{1/2+w}\ddot{a}_{k+1/2+w}^d \\ + Mg_{k+1/2}^{(s)}q_k^{(m)}v^{1/2}\ddot{a}_{k+u+1/2}^{rm}) + (r - y)_{r-y}p_y^{(T)}v^{r-y}\ddot{a}_r. \end{array}}$$ (11.4b)

This value of $^{CA}b_x$, once determined, would be substituted into equation (11.1) to derive the total normal cost for the participant age x. The value of $^{CS}b_x$ would be equal to Ks_x, where K is found by substituting $S_{x+1/2}$ for $(k + \tfrac{1}{2} - y)$ and S_r for $(r - y)$ in the denominator of (11.4b). The actuarial liability under each version of the modified accrued benefit cost method would be found by the conventional prospective valuation approach, that is, $^T(\text{PVFB})_x$ less the present value of future normal costs.

An alternative approach to the modified accrued benefit cost methods when ancillary benefits are included is to define a separate benefit accrual for each type of benefit. These benefit accruals, using the ^{CA}ABCM as the example, would be as follows:

$$^{CA}b_x^v = \frac{^v(\text{PVFB})_y}{\sum_{k=y}^{r-1} (k + \tfrac{1}{2} - y)_{k-y}p_y^{(T)}g_{k+1/2}^{(v)}q_k^{(w)}{}_{r-k-1/2}p_{k+1/2}^{\prime(m)}v^{r-y}\ddot{a}_r}$$ (11.5a)

$$^{CA}b_x^d = \frac{^d(\text{PVFB})_y}{\sum_{k=y}^{r-1} (k + \tfrac{1}{2} - y)_{k-y}p_y^{(T)}g_{k+1/2}^{(d)}q_k^{(d)}{}_w^d p_{k+1/2}^{\prime(m)}v^{k+1/2+w-y}\ddot{a}_{k+1/2+w}^d}$$

  (11.5b)

$$^{CA}b_x^s = \frac{^s(\text{PVFB})_y}{M\sum_{k=y}^{r-1} (k + \tfrac{1}{2} - y)_{k-y}p_y^{(T)}g_{k+1/2}^{(s)}q_k^{(m)}v^{k+1/2-y}\ddot{a}_{k+u+1/2}^{rm}}$$ (11.5c)

$$^{CA}b_x^r = \frac{^r(\text{PVFB})_y}{(r - y)_{r-y}p_y^{(T)}v^{r-y}\ddot{a}_r} = \frac{B_r}{r - y}.$$ (11.5d)

The various values of K for the ^{CS}ABCM would be determined by substituting $S_{k+1/2}$ for $(k + \tfrac{1}{2} - y)$ and S_r for $(r - y)$ in the above equations. The normal cost under this approach would be found by taking the present value, at age x, of the benefit accruals defined above. For example, the cost of vesting under the ^{CA}ABCM would be

$$^{v}(NC)_x = \ ^{CA}b_x^v \sum_{k=x}^{r-1} c_{k-x}p_x^{(T)}g_{k+1/2}^{(v)}q_k^{(w)}{}_{r-k-1/2}p_{k+1/2}^{\prime(m)}v^{r-x}\ddot{a}_r. \qquad (11.6)$$

This alternative to the modified accrued benefit cost method maintains consistency with the underlying theory of the modification with

TABLE 11–2

Total Normal Cost as a Percentage of Retirement Cost and as a Percentage of Salary under Accrued Benefit Cost Methods

	ABCM		^{CS}ABCM		^{CA}ABCM	
x	$100\ \dfrac{^T(NC)_x}{^r(NC)_r}$	$100\ \dfrac{^T(NC)_x}{S_x}$	$100\ \dfrac{^T(NC)_x}{^r(NC)_x}$	$100\ \dfrac{^T(NC)_x}{S_x}$	$100\ \dfrac{^T(NC)_x}{^r(NC)_x}$	$100\ \dfrac{^T(NC)_x}{S_x}$
30 . . . 241.1	0.4	227.4	0.9	187.8	3.0
31 . . . 241.1	0.6	227.4	1.1	187.8	3.5
32 . . . 241.1	0.7	227.4	1.4	187.8	4.1
33 . . . 241.1	0.8	227.4	1.7	187.8	4.5
34 . . . 241.1	1.0	227.4	2.0	187.8	5.0
35 . . . 241.1	1.4	227.4	2.3	187.8	5.4
36 . . . 241.1	1.7	227.4	2.7	187.8	5.7
37 . . . 241.1	2.0	227.4	3.0	187.8	6.1
38 . . . 241.1	2.4	227.4	3.5	187.8	6.4
39 . . . 241.1	2.9	227.4	4.0	187.8	6.8
40 . . . 241.1	3.4	227.4	4.5	187.8	7.1
41 . . . 229.8	3.8	216.7	4.8	179.0	7.1
42 . . . 219.7	4.3	207.2	5.2	171.1	7.2
43 . . . 210.4	4.8	198.5	5.6	163.9	7.2
44 . . . 202.0	5.3	190.5	6.1	157.4	7.2
45 . . . 194.2	5.9	183.1	6.5	151.3	7.3
46 . . . 185.4	6.5	174.9	7.0	144.5	7.3
47 . . . 177.2	7.2	167.1	7.5	138.0	7.3
48 . . . 169.4	7.9	159.8	8.1	132.0	7.3
49 . . . 162.0	8.7	152.8	8.6	126.2	7.4
50 . . . 155.0	9.5	146.2	9.3	120.8	7.4
51 . . . 148.3	10.4	139.9	10.0	115.6	7.5
52 . . . 142.0	11.4	133.9	10.7	110.6	7.5
53 . . . 136.0	12.5	128.3	11.5	105.9	7.6
54 . . . 130.3	13.7	122.9	12.4	101.5	7.7
55 . . . 124.9	15.0	117.8	13.3	97.3	7.8
56 . . . 122.7	16.3	115.8	14.2	95.6	7.9
57 . . . 120.6	17.6	113.7	15.1	93.9	7.9
58 . . . 118.4	19.1	111.7	16.2	92.2	8.0
59 . . . 116.2	20.7	109.6	17.3	90.6	8.1
60 . . . 114.0	22.4	107.5	18.5	88.8	8.2
61 . . . 111.6	24.3	105.3	19.8	87.0	8.3
62 . . . 109.1	26.4	102.9	21.3	85.0	8.5
63 . . . 106.3	28.7	100.3	23.0	82.8	8.7
64 . . . 103.3	31.3	97.4	24.8	80.5	8.9

Columns 1, 3, and 5 are applicable also to $100^T(AL)_x \div {}^r(AL)_x$ under each cost method, except for the values at age 30.

respect to each type of benefit (that is, the allocation of a constant benefit accrual, either as a constant dollar amount or as a constant percent of salary), but the total benefit allocated for the participant will no longer follow these patterns. For this reason, the approach given by equation (11.4b) will be used throughout the remaining portion of this text.

Table 11–2 shows, for all three versions of the accrued benefit cost method, a comparison of total costs as a percentage of each method's retirement-benefit cost and as a percentage of attained age salary. These data are based on an age-30 entrant under standard assumptions. The first two columns of Table 11–2 are identical to the last two columns of Table 11–1, both being applicable to the ABCM. The third and fourth column show that the cost effect of ancillary benefits on the ^{CS}ABCM is quite similar to the impact on the ABCM, although the percentage increase in the retirement-benefit costs is smaller at each attained age than the percentage increase associated with the ABCM.

The last two columns of Table 11–2 indicate that the ^{CS}ABCM is increased by the introduction of ancillary benefits to a considerably smaller extent than the impact on either the ABCM or the ^{CA}ABCM. Moreover, at ages beyond age 54, the "cost" effect of ancillary benefits is negative. This phenomenon is due to allocating a constant benefit accrual to each age in spite of the fact that the cost functions underlying the ancillary benefits do not increase monotonically up to retirement. Note that the introduction of ancillary benefits under each version of the accrued benefit cost methods causes the total cost as a percentage of salary to increase less steeply with attained age than the increase associated with retirement benefits only.

PROJECTED BENEFIT COST METHOD

The normal cost associated with ancillary benefits under either version of the projected benefit cost method is determined by dividing the age-y present value of future ancillary benefits by the appropriate employment-based life annuity. Thus, for the ^{CA}PBCM, we have the following normal cost associated with the ancillary benefits and retirement benefits:

$$^{T}(NC)_x = \frac{^{T}(PVFB)_y}{\ddot{a}^{T}_{y:\overline{r-y}|}}, \tag{11.7a}$$

and the actuarial liability is found by

$$^{CA}(AL)_x = {}^T(PVFB)_x - {}^T(NC)_x \ddot{a}^T_{x:\overline{r-x}|} \tag{11.7b}$$

The value of K to be used in determining the attained age normal cost under the ^{CS}PBCM is found by substituting $s_y {}^s\ddot{a}^T_{y:\overline{r-y}|}$ for $\ddot{a}^T_{y:\overline{r-y}|}$ in (11.7a) and the last term in equation (11.7b) would be $Ks_x {}^s\ddot{a}^T_{x:\overline{r-x}|}$.

The above shows that, regardless of the benefit being costed or funded under the projected benefit cost method, the denominator used in determining the normal cost is the same. Thus, unlike the modified accrued benefit cost methods where the benefit accruals are defined in terms of all of the plan's benefits, the projected benefit cost method can be applied to each benefit separately in determining its respective normal cost and actuarial liability.

If one were to look at the actuarial liability of each plan benefit separately, he would find some interesting results. For example, consider the actuarial liability associated with vesting under the ^{CA}PBCM:

$$^v(AL)_x = {}^v(PVFB)_x - \frac{{}^v(PVFB)_y}{\ddot{a}^T_{y:\overline{r-y}|}} \ddot{a}^T_{x:\overline{r-x}|}. \tag{11.8}$$

We know that the first term, $^v(PVFB)_x$, is zero at and beyond age r', yet the second term in equation (11.4) is positive up through age $r - 1$. Consequently, the actuarial liability associated with vesting is *negative* from at least r' to r, and it will generally turn negative prior to r'. Since the ^{CS}PBCM normal cost is a function of attained age salary, and since salary increases with age, the negative actuarial liability under this version will be *greater* than the negative actuarial liability under the ^{CA}PBCM given in (11.8).

It might be somewhat surprising to observe a plan's total actuarial liability being reduced when vesting is introduced, but this can occur for a plan consisting of a large number of older employees for whom the vesting-related actuarial liability is negative. Some would argue that this is an inappropriate way to fund the cost of vesting, and for these persons the term cost of vesting might be more appropriate. Another approach is to use the conventional accrued benefit cost method in connection with the ancillary benefits of a plan, while maintaining the projected benefit cost method for the retirement benefit sector. In any event, it is perfectly consistent and logical for the actuarial liability associated with a particular ancillary benefit to be negative over some ages if the $(PVFB)_x$ function is not monotonically increasing (as is the case for $^v(PVFB)_x$) while the normal cost function is either flat or monotonically increasing, as it is under the two versions of the projected benefit cost method.

Table 11–3 shows the impact of introducing ancillary benefits on the normal cost and actuarial liability under the ^{CS}PBCM and the ^{CA}PBCM for an age-30 entrant under standard assumptions. It can be seen that the percentage increase in the normal cost of the two methods is 39.4 percent, a value applicable to all attained ages. This is a smaller value at the younger ages and a larger value at the older

TABLE 11–3

Total Normal Cost and Actuarial Liability Percentages under Various Projected Benefit Cost Methods

x	$^{CS}PBCM$ $100\dfrac{^T(NC)_x}{^r(NC)_x}$	$100\dfrac{^T(NC)_x}{s_x}$	$100\dfrac{^T(AL)_x}{^r(AL)_x}$	$^{CA}PBCM$ $100\dfrac{^T(NC)_x}{^r(NC)_x}$	$100\dfrac{^T(NC)_x}{s_x}$	$100\dfrac{^T(AL)_x}{^r(AL)_x}$
30	139.4	6.1	0.0	139.4	12.1	0.0
31	139.4	6.1	139.4	139.4	11.1	139.4
32	139.4	6.1	139.4	139.4	10.2	139.4
33	139.4	6.1	139.4	139.4	9.4	139.4
34	139.4	6.1	139.4	139.4	8.7	139.4
35	139.4	6.1	139.4	139.4	8.0	139.4
36	139.4	6.1	139.4	139.4	7.4	139.4
37	139.4	6.1	139.4	139.4	6.9	139.4
38	139.4	6.1	139.4	139.4	6.4	139.4
39	139.4	6.1	139.4	139.4	5.9	139.4
40	139.4	6.1	139.4	139.4	5.5	139.4
41	139.4	6.1	137.9	139.4	5.1	138.4
42	139.4	6.1	136.6	139.4	4.7	137.4
43	139.4	6.1	135.3	139.4	4.4	136.4
44	139.4	6.1	134.0	139.4	4.1	135.4
45	139.4	6.1	132.7	139.4	3.8	134.4
46	139.4	6.1	131.2	139.4	3.6	133.0
47	139.4	6.1	129.6	139.4	3.3	131.6
48	139.4	6.1	127.9	139.4	3.1	130.2
49	139.4	6.1	126.2	139.4	2.9	128.6
50	139.4	6.1	124.4	139.4	2.8	127.0
51	139.4	6.1	122.6	139.4	2.6	125.2
52	139.4	6.1	120.7	139.4	2.4	123.4
53	139.4	6.1	118.8	139.4	2.3	121.4
54	139.4	6.1	116.7	139.4	2.1	119.4
55	139.4	6.1	114.7	139.4	2.0	117.3
56	139.4	6.1	114.0	139.4	1.9	116.4
57	139.4	6.1	113.2	139.4	1.8	115.4
58	139.4	6.1	112.4	139.4	1.7	114.3
59	139.4	6.1	111.4	139.4	1.6	113.1
60	139.4	6.1	110.3	139.4	1.5	111.7
61	139.4	6.1	108.9	139.4	1.4	110.1
62	139.4	6.1	107.3	139.4	1.4	108.2
63	139.4	6.1	105.3	139.4	1.3	105.9
64	139.4	6.1	102.9	139.4	1.2	103.2
65	0.0	0.0	100.0	0.0	0.0	100.0

ages than the impact under the various accrued benefit cost methods. The second and fifth columns give the total normal cost under each method as a percentage of attained age salary. As before, the ^{CS}PBCM normal cost is a constant percentage of salary, while the ^{CA}PBCM is a decreasing percentage of salary, but the decrease in the latter is amplified by the introduction of ancillary benefits.

The third and sixth columns of Table 11–3 show the increase in the actuarial liability, a value identical to the increase in the normal cost up to age 40. Beyond age 40, the incremental impact of ancillary benefits scales down towards zero by age 65. This decreasing pattern is nearly identical for the ^{CS}PBCM and the ^{CA}PBCM actuarial liability.

Chapter 12

Basic Early Retirement Cost Functions

In this chapter the cost of early retirement is examined in relation to the $(PVFB)_x$ function for a given employee. The following chapter considers the cost of early retirement under various actuarial cost methods. First, however, the concept of actuarially equivalent early retirement benefits is analyzed.

ACTUARIALLY EQUIVALENT EARLY RETIREMENT

It is not uncommon to find plans providing employees who elect to retire early with a so-called actuarially equivalent early retirement benefit. It is of interest at this point to derive an expression for a retirement grading function, $*g_x^{(r)}$, which when multiplied by a participant's attained age accrued benefit, B_x, produces the actuarially equivalent benefit.[1]

Mathematics

The principle underlying the concept of an actuarially equivalent early retirement benefit is one which seeks to provide the participant with a reduced benefit such that the present value of this benefit, if payable at the early retirement age, is equal to the present value of the *unreduced* benefit payable at the normal retirement age. This relationship for early retirement at age k is given by

$$*g_k^{(r)}B_k\ddot{a}_k = B_k \,_{r-k}p_k^{\prime(m)}v^{r-k}\ddot{a}_r, \tag{12.1}$$

---

[1] The asterisk on the grading function is used to denote the special case when its value is equal to the *actuarially equivalent* grading function.

146

where $*g_k^{(r)}$ denotes the actuarially equivalent grading function and the survival probability from age k to r considers the mortality decrement only. The left side of (12.1) is the present value at age k of the early retirement benefit payable immediately, while the right side represents the present value (at age k) of the participant's attained age accrued benefit payable at age r. An expression for the actuarially equivalent grading function is obtained by solving (12.1) for $*g_k^{(r)}$:

$$*g_k^{(r)} = \frac{_{r-k}p_k^{\prime(m)}v^{r-k}\ddot{a}_r}{\ddot{a}_k} = \frac{_{r-k|}\ddot{a}_k}{\ddot{a}_k}. \qquad (12.2)^2$$

The actuarially equivalent grading function, consisting of the ratio of the present value of an $(r - k)$-year deferred life annuity issued at age k to the present value of a non-deferred life annuity issued at age k, is clearly less than unity for all $k < r$. The impact of a change in the rate of interest or mortality on the actuarial equivalent grading function can be reasoned through by rewriting (12.2) in the following form:

$$*g_k^{(r)} = \frac{_{r-k}p_k^{\prime(m)}v^{r-k}\ddot{a}_r}{\ddot{a}_{k:\overline{r-k}|} + _{r-k}p_k^{\prime(m)}v^{r-k}\ddot{a}_r}. \qquad (12.3)$$

Although both the numerator and denominator in (12.3) are affected by changes in the interest rate and mortality rate, the denominator is *less* sensitive to these parameters than the numerator because of the temporary annuity factor, $\ddot{a}_{k:\overline{r-k}|}$. Thus, the actuarial equivalent grading function is inversely related to the interest and the mortality assumptions, implying that the actuarially equivalent benefits for an early retired employee will be *smaller* if either a higher rate of interest or mortality is assumed.

Mathematically, male lives can be interpreted as *impaired* female lives since males have a higher mortality rate at every age. Thus, it follows that the actuarial equivalent benefit associated with male employees will be smaller than the corresponding benefit for female employees at the same attained age.

Table 12–1 gives the value of $*g_k^{(r)}$ for $50 \leqslant k \leqslant 65$ and the results of a sensitivity study of equation (12.2) for various interest rates and mortality rates. Interestingly, the actuarially equivalent grading function under the standard assumptions (7 percent interest and GAM-71

---

[2] The general symbol, $_{n|}\ddot{a}_x$, denotes the present value of an n-year deferred annuity with payments beginning at age $x + n$. Unless otherwise indicated, the deferral period assumes an interest and mortality discount only.

TABLE 12–1

Attained Age and Sensitivity Analysis of the Actuarially Equivalent Grading Function

Age	$*g_k^{(r)}$ (based on standard assumptions)	Actuarial Equivalent Grading Function under Alternative Assumptions as a Percentage of the Grading Function under Standard Assumptions			
		$i = 0.05$	$i = 0.09$	$0.5q_x'^{(m)}$	$1.5q_x'^{(m)}$
65.	1.000	100.00	100.00	100.00	100.00
64.	0.893	101.50	98.48	101.79	98.46
63.	0.800	103.03	96.99	103.49	97.06
62.	0.719	104.57	95.52	105.10	95.77
61.	0.647	106.15	94.07	106.62	94.60
60.	0.584	107.74	92.63	108.05	93.52
59.	0.529	109.36	91.22	109.41	92.52
58.	0.479	111.01	89.82	110.70	91.61
57.	0.435	112.69	88.44	111.92	90.76
56.	0.396	114.40	87.08	113.07	89.98
55.	0.361	116.13	85.73	114.16	89.25
54.	0.329	117.90	84.40	115.19	88.58
53.	0.301	119.70	83.09	116.16	87.95
52.	0.276	121.53	81.79	117.09	87.37
51.	0.253	123.40	80.51	117.96	86.83
50.	0.232	125.30	79.24	118.78	86.32

mortality assumptions) decreases by nearly 10 percent for each successively younger early retirement age. In other words, the grading function is approximately equal to $.9^{k-r}$ for $r - 15 \leqslant k \leqslant r$. An employee retiring early at age 61 would receive about two-thirds of his attained age accrued benefit, while an employee retiring at age 55 would receive about one-third of his accrued benefit.

The data in Table 12–1 show that rather wide variations in the interest rate and mortality rate assumptions have only a modest impact on the early retirement actuarial reduction factor for ages down to 60. Below this age however, the value of $*g_k^{(r)}$ becomes more sensitive to changes in these assumptions. Based on the data in Table 12–1, a 25 percent deviation in the interest rate has about the same effect on $*g_k^{(r)}$ as a 50 percent deviation in the mortality rates.

If a plan provides full accrued benefit at early retirement instead of actuarially reduced benefits, the added cost is represented by the reciprocal of $*g_k^{(r)}$. Table 12–2 gives $*g_k^{(r)}$ and its reciprocal for $30 < k \leqslant 65$. Based on these data, early retirement at age 58 on a full accrued benefit basis is twice as costly as early retirement at age 58 on an actuarially reduced benefit basis. At age 54 the cost is three times as great and at age 51 it is four times as great. Early retirement at age 40 with full benefit accruals is seen to be ten times more costly

TABLE 12–2

**Actuarially Equivalent Early Retirement Grading Function
(based on normal retirement at age 65)**

k	$*g_k^{(r)}$	$\dfrac{1}{*g_k^{(r)}}$	k	$*g_k^{(r)}$	$\dfrac{1}{*g_k^{(r)}}$
65. . . .	1.000	1.000	47. . . .	0.180	5.553
64. . . .	0.893	1.119	46. . . .	0.166	6.027
63. . . .	0.800	1.250	45. . . .	0.153	6.536
62. . . .	0.719	1.391	44. . . .	0.141	7.082
61. . . .	0.647	1.545	43. . . .	0.130	7.668
60. . . .	0.584	1.711	42. . . .	0.121	8.296
59. . . .	0.529	1.892	41. . . .	0.111	8.969
58. . . .	0.479	2.087	40. . . .	0.103	9.690
57. . . .	0.435	2.297	39. . . .	0.096	10.463
56. . . .	0.396	2.525	38. . . .	0.089	11.292
55. . . .	0.361	2.771	37. . . .	0.082	12.179
54. . . .	0.329	3.036	36. . . .	0.076	13.130
53. . . .	0.301	3.322	35. . . .	0.071	14.148
52. . . .	0.276	3.629	34. . . .	0.066	15.239
51. . . .	0.253	3.960	33. . . .	0.061	16.407
50. . . .	0.232	4.316	32. . . .	0.057	17.658
49. . . .	0.213	4.699	31. . . .	0.053	18.998
48. . . .	0.196	5.111			

than retirement with actuarially reduced benefits, and the cost continues to grow as the retirement age is lowered.

EARLY RETIREMENT COST FUNCTION

Mathematics

The present value of future retirement benefits associated with a plan participant currently age x who is eligible to retire at any age from r' to r is given by

$$
\begin{pmatrix} (\text{PVFB})_x \\ \text{with early} \\ \text{retirement} \\ \text{permitted} \end{pmatrix} = \sum_{k=m}^{r} \begin{Bmatrix} \text{Average} \\ \text{accrued} \\ \text{benefit} \\ \text{during} \\ \text{age } k \end{Bmatrix} \begin{Bmatrix} \text{Probability} \\ \text{of surviving} \\ \text{in active} \\ \text{service to} \\ \text{integral} \\ \text{age } k \end{Bmatrix} \begin{Bmatrix} \text{Probability} \\ \text{of leaving the} \\ \text{active group} \\ \text{due to the} \\ \text{retirement} \\ \text{decrement} \\ \text{any time} \\ \text{during} \\ \text{one-year} \\ \text{period} \\ \text{at age } k \end{Bmatrix} \begin{Bmatrix} \text{Interest} \\ \text{discount} \\ \text{from age} \\ x \text{ to age} \\ k + \frac{1}{2} \end{Bmatrix} \begin{Bmatrix} \text{Average} \\ \text{present} \\ \text{value of} \\ \text{straight} \\ \text{life} \\ \text{annuity} \\ \text{during} \\ \text{age } k \end{Bmatrix}
$$

$$
{}^{r'}(\text{PVFB})_x = \sum_{k=m}^{r} g_{k+1/2}^{(r)} B_{k+1/2\ k-} \, {}^{r}_x p_x^{(T)} q_k^{(r)} v^{k+1/2-x} \ddot{a}_{k+1/2}, \tag{12.4}
$$

where

r' = the first age for which the employee qualifies for early retirement

r = the first age for which all employees will have retired

m = the greater of r' or x

$g^{(r)}_{k+1/2}$ = the proportion of the participant's accrued benefit, $B_{k+1/2}$, payable if retirement occurs during age k

$_n p^{(T)}_x$ = the probability of surviving in employment n years, where retirement decrements are assumed as well as mortality, withdrawal, and disability decrements

$q^{(r)}_k$ = probability of retiring during age k

$$\doteq q'^{(r)}_k \left[1 - \tfrac{1}{2} q'^{(m)}_k \right] \left[1 - \tfrac{1}{2} q'^{(w)}_k \right] \left[1 - \tfrac{1}{2} q'^{(d)}_k \right]$$

$$\doteq q'^{(r)}_k {}_{1/2} p'^{(m)}_k {}_{1/2} p'^{(w)}_k {}_{1/2} p'^{(d)}_k .$$

The r' superscript to the $(\text{PVFB})_x$ function is used to signify that costs are determined according to multiple retirement ages, whereas the r superscript will denote this function based on a single retirement age, usually the normal retirement age but not restricted to this age. It is important to note that for $k = r$, the $\tfrac{1}{2}$ is dropped from $k + \tfrac{1}{2}$ in equation (12.4) and other equations presented in this chapter and the next. This is consistent with the assumption that retirement occurs at the *beginning* of the plan's normal retirement age.

The grading function in (12.4), $g^{(r)}_{k+1/2}$, gives the average portion of the participant's attained age accrued benefit available to him if he should retire during age k. If full benefits are payable at early retirement, this function takes on the value of unity for all ages and could be eliminated from (12.4). More likely, however, the participant at early retirement will be entitled to something less than his attained age accrued benefit, and in some cases, his benefit will be actuarially reduced. In any event, the grading function is designed to account for whatever reduction (or increase) that takes place in the employee's accrued benefit at each possible early retirement age.

$^{r'}(\text{PVFB})_x$ is a constant percentage of $^r(\text{PVFB})_x$ over the ages $y \leqslant x \leqslant r'$, the attained age pattern of the latter function having been studied in Chapter 5. The early retirement-based function approaches $^r(\text{PVFB})_x$ from above or below from age r' to r, depending on the value of the grading function. If $g^{(r)}_x$ is equal to unity for all early retirement ages, $^r(\text{PVFB})_x$ will be approached from above over this period. We will show subsequently that if $g^{(r)}_x$ is equal to an actuarial reduction

TABLE 12–3

$^r(PVFB)_x$ Calculation under a Uniform Early Retirement Assumption

k	$g^{(r)}_{k+1/2}$	$\dfrac{100}{s_{30}}B_{k+1/2}$	$_{k-30}p^{(T)}_{30}$	$q^{(r)}_k$	$v^{k+1/2-30}$	$\ddot{a}_{k+1/2}$	Product
55. . . .	1.000	197.227	0.180	0.090	0.178	11.182	6.399
56. . . .	1.000	217.863	0.162	0.099	0.166	10.993	6.403
57. . . .	1.000	240.078	0.143	0.110	0.156	10.797	6.377
58. . . .	1.000	263.950	0.125	0.124	0.145	10.593	6.321
59. . . .	1.000	289.552	0.108	0.141	0.136	10.383	6.233
60. . . .	1.000	316.959	0.091	0.165	0.127	10.167	6.111
61. . . .	1.000	346.245	0.074	0.197	0.119	9.946	5.953
62. . . .	1.000	377.482	0.057	0.246	0.111	9.719	5.754
63. . . .	1.000	410.740	0.042	0.327	0.104	9.487	5.514
64. . . .	1.000	446.088	0.027	0.489	0.097	9.251	5.229
65. . . .	1.000	464.292	0.013	1.000	0.094	9.130	5.072

$$\frac{100}{s_{30}}{}^r(PVFB)_{30} = 65.366$$

For $k = 65$, the $\frac{1}{2}$ is dropped from $k + \frac{1}{2}$.

in the employee's accrued benefit, $^r(PVFB)_x$ will be approached from below as x approaches r.

Table 12–3 provides a step-by-step calculation of the $^r(PVFB)_{30}$ function for an age 30-entrant under the standard assumptions used throughout this book, with the exception that the retirement rates, $q'^{(r)}_k$, are designed to result in a uniform distribution of retirements at each age from 55 through 65. Note that Table 12–3 shows the retirement probabilities, $q^{(r)}_k$, instead of the retirement rates.[3] The grading function for this illustration is assumed to be unity, implying that early retirement takes place on a full accrued benefit basis. Finally, the benefit function and the $^r(PVFB)_{30}$ are both expressed as a percentage of the participant's age-30 salary.

The benefit function and the retirement probabilities are sharply increasing functions of attained age, while the survival probability, the interest function, and the annuity function decrease with age. The product of these factors is seen to be a gradually decreasing function of attained age. The sum of the seventh column gives the value of $^r(PVFB)_{30}$, which is equal to 65 percent of the participant's salary at age 30. This value, by way of comparison, is 17 percent greater than the value derived under the assumption of an age-65 retirement.

---

[3] The average retirement age, given that one will retire instead of decrementing from other causes, under the uniform retirement distribution assumption from age 55 through age 65 is 60.2. This value reflects an assumption that retirement will occur at mid-age for all ages except age 65, for which the beginning-of-age assumption is made, and it reflects the effects of other decrements (death and disability) that do not allow an employee age 55 or less to be exposed to retirement equally at all ages, in spite of the uniform retirement distribution assumption.

Actuarially Equivalent Benefits

The $^{r'}(\text{PVFB})_x$ function evaluated under the assumption of actuarially equivalent early retirement benefit is denoted by $^{*r'}(\text{PVFB})_x$ and found by substituting $^*g^{(r)}_{k+1/2}$ from equation (12.2) into (12.4) for $g^{(r)}_{k+1/2}$:

$$^{*r'}(\text{PVFB})_x = \sum_{k=m}^{r} \left[\frac{r-k-1/2 p'^{(m)}_{k+1/2} v^{r-k-1/2} \ddot{a}_r}{\ddot{a}_{k+1/2}} \right]$$
$$\times \ B_{k+1/2} \ {}_{k-x}p^{(T)}_x q^{(r)}_k v^{k+1/2-x} \ddot{a}_{k+1/2}. \tag{12.5}$$

Now, if we write the survival probability in terms of survival rates,

$$_{k-x}p^{(T)}_x = {}_{k-x}p'^{(m)}_x {}_{k-x}p'^{(w)}_x {}_{k-x}p'^{(d)}_x {}_{k-x}p'^{(r)}_x, \tag{12.6a}$$

and the retirement probability in terms of rates,

$$q^{(r)}_k = q'^{(r)}_k [1 - \tfrac{1}{2} q'^{(m)}_k][1 - \tfrac{1}{2} q'^{(w)}_k][1 - \tfrac{1}{2} q'^{(d)}_k] \tag{12.6b}$$
$$= q'^{(r)}_k {}_{1/2}p'^{(m)}_k {}_{1/2}p'^{(w)}_k {}_{1/2}p'^{(d)}_k, \tag{12.6c}$$

equation (12.5) may be simplified to

$$^{*r'}(\text{PVFB})_x = \left[\sum_{k=m}^{r} B_{k+1/2} \ {}_{k+1/2-x}p'^{(d)}_x {}_{k-x}p'^{(r)}_x q'^{(r)}_k \right]$$
$$\times \ {}_{r-x}p'^{(m)}_x {}_{r-x}p'^{(w)}_x v^{r-x} \ddot{a}_r. \tag{12.7a}$$

Note that the withdrawal survival probability, which would normally be retained in the summation as $_{k+1/2-x}p'^{(w)}_x$, can be extracted and written as $_{r-x}p'^{(w)}_x$ since there are no termination rates assumed beyond the participant's first early retirement qualification age, r'.

An intuitively appealing approximation to the $^{*r'}(\text{PVFB})_x$ function evaluated at an actuarially equivalent grading function is found by assuming no disability rates beyond r', that is, assuming that the disability survival probability is constant from r' to r. This assumption allows one to extract $_{k+1/2-x}p'^{(d)}_x$ from the summation in (12.7a) as follows:

$$^{*r'}(\text{PVFB})_x \doteq \left[\sum_{k=m}^{r} B_{k+1/2} \ {}_{k-x}p'^{(r)}_x q'^{(r)}_k \right] {}_{r-x}p^{(T)}_x v^{r-x} \ddot{a}_r. \tag{12.7b}$$

Note the use of $_{r-x}p^{(T)}_x$ for $_{r-x}p'^{(m)}_x {}_{r-x}p'^{(w)}_x {}_{r-x}p'^{(d)}_x$ in (12.7b). The quantity in brackets represents the *expected* early retirement benefit. If we let $E(B)$ denote the expected retirement benefit, that is,

$$E(B) = \sum_{k=m}^{r} B_{k+1/2} \ {}_{k-x}p'^{(r)}_x q'^{(r)}_k, \tag{12.8}$$

TABLE 12–4

$*^{r'}$(PVFB)$_x$ **Calculation under a Uniform Early Retirement Assumption**

k	$*g^{(r)}_{k+1/2}$	$\dfrac{100}{s_{30}} B_{k+1/2}$	$_{k-30}p^{(T)}_{30}$	$q^{(r)}_k$	$v^{k+1/2-30}$	$\ddot{a}_{k+1/2}$	Product
55. . . .	0.378	197.227	0.180	0.090	0.178	11.182	2.419
56. . . .	0.415	217.863	0.162	0.099	0.166	10.993	2.658
57. . . .	0.457	240.078	0.143	0.110	0.156	10.797	2.912
58. . . .	0.503	263.950	0.125	0.124	0.145	10.593	3.181
59. . . .	0.556	289.552	0.108	0.141	0.136	10.383	3.464
60. . . .	0.615	316.959	0.091	0.165	0.127	10.167	3.758
61. . . .	0.682	346.245	0.074	0.197	0.119	9.946	4.060
62. . . .	0.758	377.482	0.057	0.246	0.111	9.719	4.364
63. . . .	0.845	410.740	0.042	0.327	0.104	9.487	4.661
64. . . .	0.945	446.088	0.027	0.489	0.097	9.251	4.941
65. . . .	1.000	464.292	0.013	1.000	0.094	9.130	5.072

$$\frac{100}{s_{30}} *^{r'}(\text{PVFB})_{30} = \overline{41.491}$$

For $k = 65$, the $\tfrac{1}{2}$ is dropped from $k + \tfrac{1}{2}$.

an approximation for the actuarially equivalent early retirement function is

$$*^{r'}(\text{PVFB})_x \doteq E(B)_{r-x}p^{(T)}_x v^{r-x}\ddot{a}_r = \frac{E(B)}{B_r} {}^{r'}(\text{PVFB})_x. \qquad (12.9)$$

Equation (12.9) shows that, if early retirement is permitted on an actuarially equivalent basis, the $^{r'}$(PVFB)$_x$ function evaluated at $E(B)$ instead of B_r provides an approximation to $*^{r'}$(PVFB)$_x$. The approximation underestimates the true value of $*^{r'}$(PVFB)$_x$, but the error would be relatively small for the typical case.[4]

The ratio $E(B) \div B_r$ is less than unity, implying that the retirement-related liability under a plan which assumes actuarially equivalent early retirement is *less* than the liability associated with the plan if only normal retirement is permitted. This ratio for a new entrant at age 30 based on the benefit function shown in Table 12–3 is 0.699. In general, the reduction in the PVFB liability associated with providing actuarially equivalent early retirement benefits is dependent upon the incidence of early retirement, the level of disability rates from r' to r, and the slope of the benefit function.

Table 12–4 provides a step-by-step calculation of the $*^{r'}$(PVFB)$_x$ similar to the data previously presented in Table 12–3 except that

---

[4] The error associated with (12.9) for the age-30 entrant based on the standard assumptions used in this book is about 6 percent at ages below 55 and smaller at the older ages, assuming the uniform retirement distribution from age 55 through age 65.

$*g_{k+1/2}^{(r)}$ is used instead of unity. Since the actuarially equivalent grading function is a steeply increasing function of age, the product of the various factors shown in Table 12–4 is also an increasing function of age, as compared to the product of these factors in Table 12–3 which yielded a decreasing function. The $*r'(\text{PVFB})_{30}$ function expressed as a percentage of s_{30} for the age-30 entrant is 41 percent. This is in contrast to 65 percent for the $r'(\text{PVFB})_{30}$ calculated in Table 12–3.

Relative Cost of Early Retirement

The relative cost of early retirement is first considered under the assumption of a single early retirement age and then under the more general assumption of multiple early retirement ages. In both cases, the cost of early retirement is expressed as a ratio of the cost of normal retirement.

Single Early Retirement Age. The early retirement cost ratio at attained age x for early retirement at age k, $_k(\text{ERCR})_x$, has as its numerator the present value associated with retirement at the beginning of age k, and as its denominator the present value associated with retirement at the beginning of age r, that is, the $r'(\text{PVFB})_x$ function:

$$_k(\text{ERCR})_x = \frac{g_k^{(r)} B_k \, _{k-x}p_x^{(T)} v^{r-x} \ddot{a}_k}{B_r \, _{r-x}p_x^{(T)} v^{r-x} \ddot{a}_r}. \tag{12.10a}$$

Note that there are no retirement decrements assumed in either of the survival probabilities, since it is assumed in this section that retirement occurs with certainty at one of the two ages k or r. Equation (12.10a) reduces to

$$_k(\text{ERCR})_x = g_k^{(r)} \frac{B_k}{B_r} \frac{1}{_{r-k}p_k^{(T)} v^{r-k}} \frac{\ddot{a}_k}{\ddot{a}_r}. \tag{12.10b}$$

An examination of (12.10b) indicates that the cost of early retirement at age k relative to the cost at age r is reduced by the benefit ratio $(B_k \div B_r)$ and increased by the reciprocal of the survival probability $(_{r-k}p_k^{(T)})$, by the recriprocal of the interest factor (v^{r-k}), and by the annuity ratio $(\ddot{a}_k \div \ddot{a}_r)$. The early retirement grading function could conceivably have an increasing, decreasing, or neutral effect on the cost of early retirement, depending on the design of the plan. The most likely value for this function among pension plans, however, would be unity or less, and hence it would have either a neutral or reducing impact. Even if the grading function were equal to unity, it is not clear which variables will dominate the $_k(ERCR)_x$, that is, the benefit ratio which tends to lower its value for successively younger early retirement ages or the other three factors that tend to increase its value.

Table 12–5 illustrates the $_k(ERCR)_x$ for $30 \leqslant k \leqslant 65$ and $r = 65$ for an age-30 entrant under the standard assumptions used in previous chapters, and assuming that the early retirement grading function is equal to unity. The first five columns of this table show the components

TABLE 12–5

Ratio of $(PVFB)_x$ for Retirement at Age k to $(PVFB)_x$ for Retirement at Age r ($r = 65$, $x = 30$)

k	$g_k^{(r)}$	$\dfrac{B_k}{B_r}$	$\dfrac{1}{r-kp_k^{(T)}}$	$\dfrac{1}{v^{r-k}}$	$\dfrac{\ddot{a}_k}{\ddot{a}_r}$	$_k(ERCR)_x$
65. . . . 1		1.000	1.000	1.000	1.000	1.000
64. . . . 1		0.922	1.048	1.070	1.026	1.060
63. . . . 1		0.848	1.089	1.145	1.052	1.112
62. . . . 1		0.778	1.125	1.225	1.077	1.155
61. . . . 1		0.713	1.155	1.311	1.102	1.190
60. . . . 1		0.652	1.182	1.403	1.125	1.217
59. . . . 1		0.595	1.206	1.501	1.149	1.238
58. . . . 1		0.542	1.228	1.606	1.172	1.252
57. . . . 1		0.492	1.248	1.718	1.193	1.260
56. . . . 1		0.446	1.266	1.838	1.215	1.262
55. . . . 1		0.403	1.284	1.967	1.235	1.258
54. . . . 1		0.364	1.347	2.105	1.255	1.294
53. . . . 1		0.327	1.414	2.252	1.274	1.327
52. . . . 1		0.293	1.484	2.410	1.292	1.355
51. . . . 1		0.262	1.556	2.579	1.310	1.379
50. . . . 1		0.234	1.631	2.759	1.327	1.396
49. . . . 1		0.208	1.710	2.952	1.344	1.409
48. . . . 1		0.184	1.792	3.159	1.361	1.414
47. . . . 1		0.162	1.879	3.380	1.376	1.414
46. . . . 1		0.142	1.969	3.617	1.392	1.406
45. . . . 1		0.124	2.066	3.870	1.406	1.392
44. . . . 1		0.108	2.168	4.141	1.420	1.371
43. . . . 1		0.093	2.278	4.430	1.434	1.343
42. . . . 1		0.080	2.397	4.741	1.447	1.308
41. . . . 1		0.068	2.527	5.072	1.459	1.265
40. . . . 1		0.057	2.670	5.427	1.471	1.214
39. . . . 1		0.047	2.829	5.807	1.482	1.156
38. . . . 1		0.039	3.008	6.214	1.493	1.089
37. . . . 1		0.032	3.211	6.649	1.503	1.012
36. . . . 1		0.025	3.443	7.114	1.513	0.924
35. . . . 1		0.019	3.711	7.612	1.522	0.824
34. . . . 1		0.015	4.046	8.145	1.530	0.741
33. . . . 1		0.011	4.485	8.715	1.538	0.634
32. . . . 1		0.007	5.080	9.325	1.546	0.494
31. . . . 1		0.003	5.912	9.978	1.553	0.296
30. . . . 1		0.000	7.116	10.677	1.560	0.000

of equation (12.10b), while the sixth column gives the $_k(\text{ERCR})_x$ itself, equal to the product of the first five columns. The results show that the cost of early retirement below age 65 on a full benefit basis is greater for each successively younger retirement age down to age 48, at which point the cost is 41 percent greater than it is at age 65. For retirement at younger ages, the reduction in the benefit accruals due to a shorter service period and a smaller salary average becomes more significant than the continued increase in the other three variables, causing the relative cost of early retirement to become lower. For example, the cost of an employee (age 37 or less) retiring at age 37 with a benefit of B_{37} payable immediately for life has approximately the same cost as the cost associated with him working to age 65 and receiving a benefit of B_{65} for life at that point. The component factors given in Table 12–5 provide a complete explanation of the increasing and then decreasing pattern of the relative cost of early retirement associated with successively younger retirement ages.

If we substitute the actuarial equivalent early retirement grading function into (12.10b) we get

$$_k^*(\text{ERCR})_x = \frac{B_k \; _{r-k}p_k'^{(m)}}{B_r \; _{r-k}p_k'^{(T)}}. \tag{12.11a}$$

If the withdrawal decrement is zero after age k, $_{r-k}p_k'^{(T)}$ is equal to $_{r-k}p_k'^{(m)} \, _{r-k}p_k'^{(d)}$ and the early retirement cost ratio may be written as

$$_k^*(\text{ERCR})_x = \frac{B_k}{B_r} \frac{1}{_{r-k}p_k'^{(d)}}. \tag{12.11b}[5]$$

The third column of Table 12–5 gives the benefit ratio in (12.11b), which would represent a good approximation to $_k^*(\text{ERCR})_x$ in those cases where disability rates are low or nonexistent. Using these data, the cost associated with retirement at age 60 is two thirds of the cost of retirement at age 65, and the cost at age 55 is 40 percent of the age-65 retirement cost. If the slope of the benefit function were less, for example, as under a career average benefit formula or if the slope of the salary function were less, the cost saving due to actuarially

---

[5] It may not be appropriate to assume $q_k'^{(w)} = 0$ for all k under investigation. For example, if one is comparing the cost of early retirement for a plan that currently does not permit early retirement, then there would logically be withdrawal rates from age k to r. In this case equation (12.11a) would be the appropriate equation to use. In addition, the cost of vesting could be included in the analysis. On the other hand, if one is comparing the cost at each possible early retirement age for a plan that currently allows early retirement at the various ages under investigation, then the withdrawal rates would be zero and equation (12.11b) could be used.

equivalent early retirement would be less than that illustrated by column one of Table 12–5.

Multiple Early Retirement Ages. Although it is important to analyze the relative cost of retiring early at a specific age, a more general measure of the relative cost of early retirement is found by considering all possible retirement ages and the related possibilities of retiring at each age. Thus we have the early retirement cost ratio based on multiple retirement ages defined as follows:

$$(\text{ERCR})_x = \frac{\sum\limits_{k=m}^{r} g_{k+1/2}^{(r)} B_{k+1/2} \, _{k-x}p_x^{(T)} q_k^{(r)} v^{k+1/2-x} \ddot{a}_{k+1/2}}{B_r \, _{r-x}p_x^{(T)} v^{r-x} \ddot{a}_r}, \tag{12.12a}$$

where $(\text{ERCR})_x$ assumes multiple early retirement ages, whereas $_k(\text{ERCR})_x$ was used for the case of early retirement at age k only. If the retirement decrements are extracted from $_{k-x}p_x^{(T)}$ in the numerator of (12.12a) and written explicitly as $_{k-x}p_x'^{(r)} \, _{k-x}p_x^{(T)}$, and if $q_k^{(r)}$ is written as $q_k'^{(r)} \, _{1/2}p_k^{(T)}$, equation (12.12a) may be approximated by

$$(\text{ERCR})_x \doteq \sum_{k=m}^{r} g_{k+1/2}^{(r)} \frac{B_{k+1/2}}{B_r} \, _{k-x}p_x'^{(r)} q_k'^{(r)} \frac{\ddot{a}_{k+1/2}}{_{r-k-1/2}p_{k+1/2}^{(T)} v^{r-k-1/2}\ddot{a}_r} \tag{12.12b}$$

$$\doteq \sum_{k=m}^{r} \, _{k-x}p_x'^{(r)} q_k'^{(r)} \, _{k+1/2}(\text{ERCR})_x. \tag{12.12c}$$

In this form, the cost of early retirement is approximately equal to the weighted average of equation (12.10b), that is, the cost of early retirement for each specific early retirement age, where the weights are equal to the conditional probability that retirement occurs at age k given that retirement will occur between r' and r.

An estimate of the value of $(\text{ERCR})_{30}$ can be made by taking a weighted average of the last column in Table 12–5, where the weights reflect the probability of retiring at each age. It turns out that the value of $(\text{ERCR})_{30}$ under a uniform retirement distribution assumption from age 55 to age 65 for an age-30 entrant under standard assumptions, and assuming $g_k^{(r)}$ is equal to unity, is equal to 1.17.

If the plan provides actuarially reduced early retirement benefits, (12.12b) becomes

$$*(\text{ERCR})_x = \sum_{k=m}^{r} \frac{B_{k+1/2}}{B_r} \, _{k-x}p_x'^{(r)} q_k'^{(r)} \frac{1}{_{r-k-1/2}p_{k+1/2}^{(d)}} \doteq \frac{E(B)}{B_r}. \tag{12.13}$$

Thus, the ratio of the employee's expected early retirement benefit to his normal retirement benefit gives an approximation to the relative cost of actuarially reduced early retirement. This relative cost measure is likely to be considerably less than one. In fact, its value for an age-30 entrant under standard assumptions, and assuming a uniform distribution of retirements from age 55 to age 65, is 0.74.

Chapter 13

Early Retirement under Actuarial Cost Methods

The purpose of this chapter is to analyze the cost of early retirement under various actuarial cost methods. The analysis begins with the accrued benefit cost method and proceeds to the projected benefit cost method. Although the aggregate cost methods are not considered explicitly, the previously discussed analogies of weighting the numerator and denominators of the individual cost methods to obtain the results under the aggregate methods hold. The plan termination cost method is unaffected by an early retirement provision since costs and liabilities are based on deferred pensions beginning at the plan's normal retirement age.

ACCRUED BENEFIT COST METHOD

The normal cost and actuarial liability under the conventional accrued benefit cost method when early retirement is permitted are given by equations (13.1) and (13.2):

$$^{r'}(\text{NC})_x = b_x \sum_{k=m}^{r} cg^{(r)}_{k+1/2} \; {}_{k-x}p^{(T)}_x q^{(r)}_k v^{k+1/2-x} \ddot{a}_{k+1/2} \qquad (13.1)$$

$$^{r'}(\text{AL})_x = B_x \sum_{k=m}^{r} g^{(r)}_{k+1/2} \; {}_{k-x}p^{(T)}_x q^{(r)}_k v^{k+1/2-x} \ddot{a}_{k+1/2}. \qquad (13.2)$$

The constant c in (13.1) is $\frac{1}{2}$ if k has as its first value x and unity for other values of k. The value of $\frac{1}{2}$ accounts for a fractional year of credit if retirement occurs at age x. As in previous chapters, the ABCM actuarial liability is a $B_x \div b_x$ multiple of its normal cost for $x < r'$, and nearly equal to this multiple for $x \geqslant r'$.

The normal cost under each modification of the accrued benefit cost method requires the calculation of $^{CA}b_x$ and $^{CS}b_x$ under the assumptions of early retirement. These values, once determined, are substituted into (13.1) to obtain the normal cost. It will be remembered that the ^{CA}ABCM allocates a constant amount of B_r to each attained age, while the ^{CS}ABCM allocates B_r according to a constant percentage of salary. In order to derive the appropriate attained age benefit allocation under these methods in the context of early retirement, it is necessary to equate the participant's entry age $^{r'}(\text{PVFB})_y$ function to the present value of future normal costs. Thus, for the ^{CA}ABCM, we have

$$^{r'}(\text{PVFB})_y$$

$$= \sum_{x=y}^{r} \left[c \cdot {}^{CA}b_x \sum_{k=m}^{r} g_{k+1/2}^{(r)} \, {}_{k-x}p_x^{(T)} q_k^{(r)} v^{k+1/2-x} \ddot{a}_{k+1/2} \right] {}_{x-y}p_y^{(T)} v^{x-y}.$$

$$(13.3a)$$

Again, the constant c is $\frac{1}{2}$ when k equals x and unity otherwise to reflect the fact that on average, only $\frac{1}{2}{}^{CA}b_x$ is accrued in the year of retirement. The survival probabilities and the interest factors can be combined into two symbols based on a $(k - y)$-year age span. Since $g_{k+1/2}^{(r)}$ is zero for $k < r'$, the second summation can begin at age x rather than m (where m is the greater of r' or x):

$$^{r'}(\text{PVFB})_y = \sum_{x=y}^{r} c \cdot {}^{CA}b_x \sum_{k=x}^{r} g_{k+1/2}^{(r)} \, {}_{k-y}p_y^{(T)} q_k^{(r)} v^{k+1/2-y} \ddot{a}_{k+1/2}. \quad (13.3b)$$

An equivalent expression to (13.3b) can be formed by reversing the order of summation and noting that the sum from y to k of $c^{CA}b_x$ is equal to $^{CA}b_x(k + \frac{1}{2} - y)$:

$$^{r'}(\text{PVFB})_y = \sum_{k=y}^{r} {}^{CA}b_x(k + \tfrac{1}{2} - y)g_{k+1/2}^{(r)} \, {}_{k-y}p_y^{(T)} q_k^{(r)} v^{k+1/2-x} \ddot{a}_{k+1/2}.$$

$$(13.3c)$$

Finally, solving for $^{CA}b_x$ we have an expression for the appropriate benefit allocation under the ^{CA}ABCM when early retirement is assumed:

$$^{CA}b_x = \frac{^{r'}(\text{PVFB})_y}{\displaystyle\sum_{k=y}^{r} (k + \tfrac{1}{2} - y)g_{k+1/2}^{(r)} \, {}_{k-y}p_y^{(T)} q_k^{(r)} v^{k+1/2-y} \ddot{a}_{k+1/2}}. \quad (13.4a)$$

Equation (13.4a) shows that the attained age benefit allocated under the ^{CA}ABCM is equal to the present value of future benefits at age y

divided by the "present value" of future years of service, where both present values assume multiple retirement ages. If there were just one retirement age, say age r, and if retirement were assumed to occur at the beginning of this age, equation (13.4a) reduces to $B_r \div (r - y)$. This relationship, it will be remembered, was the definition of $^{CA}b_x$ under the single retirement age assumption.

The corresponding percentage, $100K$, which would be used to find the attained age benefit allocation under the ^{CS}ABCM, is given by

$$K = \frac{^{r'}(\text{PVFB})_y}{\sum\limits_{k=y}^{r} S_{k+1/2} g_{k+1/2}^{(r)} {}_{k-y} p_y^{(T)} q_k^{(r)} v^{k+1/2-y} \ddot{a}_{k+1/2}}. \qquad (13.4b)$$

The attained age benefit accrual, $^{CS}b_x$, which is used to determine the normal cost, is found by multiplying the above value of K by the participant's attained age salary, that is, $^{CS}b_x = K s_x$.

Here again we see that the value of K is equal to the present value of future benefits at age y divided by the present value of future salary, both assuming early retirement decrement. If there were just one retirement age, say at age r, and if retirement were assumed to occur at the beginning of this age, equation (13.4b) reduces to $B_r \div S_r$. This definition of K was derived earlier for the ^{CS}ABCM under the assumption of a single retirement age.

The actuarial liability under the modified accrued benefit cost methods cannot be found by taking the present value of all benefit allocations to date, as is the case under these methods when early retirement is not assumed and as is the case under the ABCM with or without the early retirement assumption. This is illustrated by deriving the actuarial liability under the ^{CA}ABCM using the standard prospective valuation procedure, that is, by subtracting the present value of future normal costs from the present value of future benefits:

$$^{r'}(\text{AL})_x = {}^{r'}(\text{PVFB})_x - \sum\limits_{t=x}^{r} {}^{r'}(\text{NC})_t \, {}_{t-x}p_x^{(T)} v^{t-x}. \qquad (13.5a)$$

Substituting the expression for the normal cost under the ^{CA}ABCM into (13.5a), we have

$$^{r'}(\text{AL})_x = {}^{r'}(\text{PVFB})_x$$
$$- \sum\limits_{t=x}^{r} \left[c^{CA}b_t \sum\limits_{k=m}^{r} g_{k+1/2}^{(r)} {}_{k-t}p_t^{(T)} q_k^{(r)} v^{k+1/2-t} \ddot{a}_{k+1/2} \right] {}_{t-x}p_x^{(T)} v^{t-x},$$
$$(13.5b)$$

where m is the greater of r' or t. The right side of this equation can be changed in precisely the same way equations (13.3a) through (13.3c) were changed to yield the following:

$$^{r'}(AL)_x = {}^{r'}(PVFB)_x$$

$$- \sum_{k=m}^{r} {}^{CA}b_x(k + \tfrac{1}{2} - x)g^{(r)}_{k+1/2}\,{}_{k-x}p^{(T)}_x q^{(r)}_k v^{k+1/2-x}\ddot{a}_{k+1/2}.$$

$$(13.5c)$$

Finally, combining the two terms on the right side of (13.5c), we have

$$^{r'}(AL)_x$$

$$= \sum_{k=m}^{r} \left[B_{k+1/2} - {}^{CA}b_x(k + \tfrac{1}{2} - x) \right] g^{(r)}_{k+1/2}\,{}_{k-x}p^{(T)}_x q^{(r)}_k v^{k+1/2-x}\ddot{a}_{k+1/2}$$

$$(13.5d)$$

Thus the actuarial liability at age x is equal to the present value of the bracketed term in (13.5d), where this term represents the projected benefit at each potential retirement age k, less the benefit allocations which will be made from age x to age k. Since the benefits accrued to date, amounting to ${}^{CA}b_x(x - y)$, are not necessarily equal to the bracketed term in (13.5d), the actuarial liability cannot be determined by taking the present value of the accrued benefits under the modified accrued benefit cost methods.

It can be shown that the attained age actuarial liability under the ^{CS}ABCM is equal to equation (13.5d) with $K(S_{k+1/2} - S_x)$ substituted for ${}^{CA}b_x(k + \tfrac{1}{2} - x)$.

PROJECTED BENEFIT COST METHOD

The normal cost under the ^{CA}PBCM in the context of multiple retirement ages is equal to the ratio

$$^{r'}(NC)_x = \frac{{}^{r'}(PVFB)_y}{{}^{r'}\ddot{a}^T_{y:\overline{r-y|}}},$$

$$(13.6)$$

where ${}^{r'}\ddot{a}^T_{y:\overline{r-y|}}$ denotes the present value of a temporary employment based annuity including early retirement decrements from age r' to r. The corresponding equation for the normal cost under the ^{CS}PBCM is given by

$$^{r'}(NC)_x = \frac{{}^{r'}(PVFB)_y}{s_y \cdot {}^{r's}\ddot{a}^T_{y:\overline{r-y|}}}\, s_x,$$

$$(13.7)$$

where the r' superscript to the temporary annuity symbol again denotes the assumption of early retirement decrements.

The actuarial liability under the ^{CA}PBCM, evaluated prospectively, may be expressed as

$$^{r'}(AL)_x = {}^{r'}(PVFB)_x - \frac{^{r'}(PVFB)_y}{^{r'}\ddot{a}^T_{y:\overline{r-y}|}}\, {}^{r'}\ddot{a}^T_{x:\overline{r-x}|}, \tag{13.8}$$

while that of the ^{CS}PBCM is denoted by replacing the annuities in (13.8) with salary-based annuities multiplied by the appropriate salary function.

It can be shown that for $x \leqslant r'$, the actuarial liability under the projected benefit cost method can be expressed as a portion of the $^{r'}(PVFB)_x$ function. In the case of the ^{CA}PBCM, the expression analogous to (7.4d) becomes

$$^{r'}(AL)_x = \frac{^{r'}\ddot{a}^T_{y:\overline{x-y}|}}{^{r'}\ddot{a}^T_{y:\overline{r-y}|}}\, {}^{r'}(PVFB)_x \qquad (x \leqslant r'), \tag{13.9}$$

while for the ^{CS}PBCM, the coefficient of $^{r'}(PVFB)_x$ is equal to the corresponding salary-based temporary annuity ratio.

The attained age normal cost and actuarial liability function under the early retirement assumption follow the corresponding attained age function based on *normal* retirement in a predictable manner. Like the relation of $^{r'}(PVFB)_x$ to $^{r}(PVFB)_x$ discussed in the previous chapter, the normal cost and actuarial liability under the PBCM form a constant percentage of their corresponding normal retirement-based function up to age r'. At ages r' and over, each function approaches its normal retirement-based counterpart (unless already equal to it). The approach may be from above or below, depending on the value of the early retirement benefit grading function.

ACTUARIALLY EQUIVALENT BENEFITS

In the previous chapter we found that the present value of future benefits is lower under actuarially equivalent early retirement than it is for normal retirement. In this section, the effect of introducing actuarially equivalent early retirement benefits under each cost method is examined.

Accrued Benefit Cost Method

The effect of actuarially equivalent benefits under the conventional accrued benefit cost method can be observed by substituting $^*g^{(r)}_{k+1/2}$

from (12.2) for $g_{k+1/2}^{(r)}$ in equation (13.1), writing the survival probabilities in their single decrement form, and combining terms:

$$*^{r'}(\mathrm{NC})_x = b_x \left[\sum_{k=m}^{r} c_{k+1/2-x} p_x'^{(d)}{}_{k-x} p_x'^{(r)} q_k'^{(r)} \right]_{r-x} p_x'^{(m)}{}_{r-x} p_x'^{(w)} v^{r-x} \ddot{a}_r.$$

$$(13.10)^{1}$$

If the disability survival probability from r' to r is reasonably constant (that is, low or nonexistent disability rates), it too can be extracted from the summation sign without introducing a serious error. The remaining terms in the bracket sum to unity if $x < r'$. Thus, an approximation to (13.10) for $x < r'$, is simply the ABCM evaluated at normal retirement. The same procedure can be used to show that the actuarial liability under actuarially equivalent early retirement is also approximated by the normal retirement actuarial liability.

The above results, unlike the results obtained for the $^{r'}(\mathrm{PVFB})_x$, show that the normal cost and actuarial liability are practically unaffected for a plan allowing early retirement to take place on an actuarially equivalent basis as opposed to a plan not permitting early retirement.

Actuarially equivalent early retirement under each of the modified accrued benefit cost methods affects both the attained age benefit accruals, $^{CA}b_x$ and $^{CS}b_x$, and also the present value of these accruals. Once the benefit accruals are obtained by introducing the actuarial equivalent grading function into equations (13.4a) and (13.4b), the normal cost values can be approximated by substituting these accruals into the regular normal retirement present value function.

Equation (13.4a), evaluated at an actuarially equivalent early retirement grading function, reduces to the following approximation by extracting the disability survival probability from the summation as before:

$$^{CA}b_x \doteqdot \frac{E(B)}{E(Y)}. \tag{13.11}$$

where

$$E(Y) = \sum_{k=m}^{r} (k + \tfrac{1}{2} - y)_{k-y} p_y'^{(r)} q_k'^{(r)}. \tag{13.12}$$

In other words, $E(Y)$ is equal to the expected years of service based on multiple early retirement ages. The approximations in the numerator and denominator of (13.11) are both related to the disability

---

[1] See equations (12.5), (12.6), and (12.7) for a guide to the development of this equation.

survival probability and would tend to cancel out, making the approximation in (13.11) quite good. Thus, an approximation to normal cost and actuarial liability under the ^{CA}ABCM can be found by substituting $E(B) \div E(Y)$ into the normal cost equation based on retirement at age r. Moreover, if $E(B) \div E(Y)$ were approximately equal to $B_r \div (r - y)$, the ^{CA}ABCM based on normal retirement would provide an approximation to the normal cost and actuarial liability under early retirement on an actuarially equivalent basis.

The $^{CS}b_x$ under the ^{CS}ABCM when actuarially equivalent early retirement is considered can be found by substituting (12.2) into (13.4b) to obtain the correct value of K to be multiplied times the attained age salary. An approximation to K, however, is the ratio of $E(B)$ to $E(S)$, where

$$E(S) = \sum_{k=m}^{r} S_{k+1/2} \, _{k-y}p'^{(r)}_y q'^{(r)}_k. \tag{13.13}$$

Thus, $E(S)$ is equal to the expected total salary paid to the participant based on multiple early retirement ages. Once again, if $E(B) \div E(S)$ were approximately equal to $B_r \div S_r$, the ^{CS}ABCM evaluated at normal retirement would represent an approximation to the cost under actuarially equivalent early retirement.

The actuarial liability under the ^{CA}ABCM when actuarially equivalent benefits are provided may be written in the following manner:

$$*^{r'}(\text{AL})_x = \left\{ \sum_{k=m}^{r} [B_{k+1/2} - {}^{CA}b_x \cdot (k + \tfrac{1}{2} - x)]_{k+1/2-x}p'^{(d)}_x \, _{k-x}p'^{(r)}_x q'^{(r)}_k \right\}$$
$$\times \, _{k-x}p'^{(m)}_x \, _{k-x}p'^{(w)}_x v^{r-x} \ddot{a}_r. \tag{13.14}$$

Equation (13.14) shows that the actuarial liability is equal to the present value of the participant's expected early retirement benefit less the expected benefits yet to be allocated for the age-x participant. It can be shown that, for $x \leq r'$, the above may be approximated by

$$*^{r'}(\text{AL})_x \doteqdot (x - y)^{CA}b_x \, _{r-x}p^{(T)}_x v^{r-x} \ddot{a}_r, \tag{13.15}$$

where the approximation involves assuming the disability survival probability is constant from r' to r. Equation (13.15) shows that, for $x \leq r'$, the actuarial liability, assuming actuarial equivalent early retirement benefits, can be found by taking the present value of benefit accruals allocated to date. This relationship does not hold beyond age r', however.

The actuarial liability under the ^{CS}ABCM is equal to (13.14) with $^{CA}b_x(k + \frac{1}{2} - x)$ replaced by $K(S_{k+1/2} - S_x)$. Similarly, this liability for $x \leqslant r'$ may be written by replacing $(x - y)^{CA}b_x$ by KS_x in (13.15).

Projected Benefit Cost Method

An equation for the normal cost under the ^{CA}PBCM for actuarially equivalent early retirement can be found by substituting the actuarial equivalent grading function into the numerator of equation (13.6). The following represents an approximation to the normal cost value by assuming the disability survival probability is constant from r' to r:

$$^{*r'}(NC)_x \doteqdot \frac{E(B)_{r-y}p_y^{(T)}v^{r-y}\ddot{a}_r}{^{r'}\ddot{a}^T_{y:\overline{r-y}|}}. \tag{13.16}$$

In words, (13.16) equals the expected early retirement benefit evaluated at normal retirement age, divided by an $r - y$ year employment based life annuity, where the latter includes the retirement decrements from r' to r. The decrease in $E(B)$ relative to B_r is generally greater than the decrease in the employment based life annuity under early retirement relative to its value when only retirement at age r is considered. Thus, it can be concluded that actuarially reduced early retirement under the ^{CA}PBCM generally produces a *lower* cost than the cost for retirement at normal retirement only.

This same conclusion holds for the ^{CS}PBCM, and the equation corresponding to (13.16) is

$$^{*r'}(NC)_x \doteqdot \frac{E(B)_{r-y}p_y^{(T)}v^{r-y}\ddot{a}_r}{S_y\,^{r's}\ddot{a}^T_{y:\overline{r-y}|}} S_x. \tag{13.17}$$

The actuarial liability associated with actuarially equivalent early retirement benefits is given by (13.18a), which can be expressed more compactly for $x \leqslant r'$ by (13.18b). In both cases the disability survival probability is assumed to be constant from r' to r.

$$^{*r'}(AL)_x = E(B)_{r-x}p_x^{(T)}v^{r-x}\ddot{a}_r - \frac{E(B)_{r-y}p_y^{(T)}v^{r-y}\ddot{a}_r}{^{r'}\ddot{a}^T_{y:\overline{r-y}|}}\,^{r'}\ddot{a}^T_{x:\overline{r-x}|} \tag{13.18a}$$

$$^{*r'}(AL)_x = E(B)_{r-x}p_x^{(T)}v^{r-x}\ddot{a}_r \frac{^{r'}\ddot{a}^T_{y:\overline{x-y}|}}{^{r'}\ddot{a}^T_{y:\overline{r-y}|}} \qquad (x \leqslant r'). \tag{13.18b}$$

The corresponding actuarial liability equations for the ^{CS}PBCM can be obtained by substituting the salary-based temporary annuities for the temporary annuities in (13.18a) and (13.18b). The annuities in

(13.18a) must be multiplied by the appropriate salary function, s_x in the numerator and s_y in the denominator, whereas the salary functions cancel out in (13.18b), since s_y is required for both the numerator and the denominator.

It turns out that, like the normal cost of the projected benefit cost method under actuarially equivalent early retirement benefits, the actuarial liability given by the above equations is *less* than the corresponding liability based on normal retirement.

RELATIVE COST OF EARLY RETIREMENT

The relative cost of early retirement under the various actuarial cost methods is first analyzed in terms of one early retirement age and then the more general assumption of multiple early retirement ages is considered.

Single Early Retirement Age

The normal cost or actuarial liability associated with retirement at age k expressed as a ratio of the normal cost or actuarial liability associated with retirement at age r ($k \leqslant r$) yields the following early retirement cost ratios:

$$_k(\text{ERCR})_x = g_k^{(r)} \frac{B_k}{B_r} \frac{1}{_{r-k}p_k^{(T)}} \frac{1}{v^{r-k}} \frac{\ddot{a}_k}{\ddot{a}_r} C_k, \qquad (13.19)$$

where

$$C_k = \frac{B_r}{B_k} \qquad \text{for the conventional ABCM normal cost and actuarial liability}$$

$$= \frac{S_r}{S_k} \qquad \text{for the } {}^{\text{CS}}\text{ABCM normal cost and actuarial liability}$$

$$= \frac{r-y}{k-y} \qquad \text{for the } {}^{\text{CA}}\text{ABCM normal cost and actuarial liability}$$

$$= \frac{{}^s\ddot{a}_{y:\overline{r-y}|}^T}{{}^s\ddot{a}_{y:\overline{k-y}|}^T} \qquad \text{for the } {}^{\text{CS}}\text{PBCM normal cost and actuarial liability}$$

$$= \frac{\ddot{a}_{y:\overline{r-y}|}^T}{\ddot{a}_{y:\overline{k-y}|}^T} \qquad \text{for the } {}^{\text{CA}}\text{PBCM normal cost and actuarial liability}$$

$$= 1 \qquad \text{for the } (\text{PVFB})_x \text{ function.}$$

In other words, equation (13.19) is the $_k(\mathrm{ERCR})_x$ for the $(\mathrm{PVFB})_x$, and the $_k(\mathrm{ERCR})_x$ for each of the actuarial cost methods is found by multiplying this value by some coefficient C_k. All of the definitions of C_k exceed unity, implying that the relative cost of early retirement under each of the actuarial cost methods is *greater* than the relative cost of early retirement under the $(\mathrm{PVFB})_x$ function.

Table 13–1 gives the $_k(\mathrm{ERCR})_x$ based on equation (13.19) for each of the actuarial cost methods under the standard assumptions and

TABLE 13–1

$_k(\mathrm{ERCR})_x$ **Assuming Full Benefit Accruals under Various Actuarial Cost Methods (age-30 entrant, $g'_k = 1$)**

			Cost Measure			
k	$ABCM$	$^{CS}ABCM$	$^{CA}ABCM$	$^{CS}PBCM$	$^{CA}PBCM$	$PVFB$
65. . . .	1.000	1.000	1.000	1.000	1.000	1.000
64. . . .	1.151	1.135	1.092	1.073	1.063	1.060
63. . . .	1.312	1.276	1.179	1.139	1.117	1.112
62. . . .	1.484	1.422	1.263	1.198	1.164	1.155
61. . . .	1.668	1.575	1.343	1.251	1.203	1.190
60. . . .	1.866	1.734	1.420	1.299	1.235	1.217
59. . . .	2.080	1.900	1.494	1.341	1.260	1.238
58. . . .	2.310	2.074	1.565	1.378	1.280	1.252
57. . . .	2.559	2.256	1.633	1.410	1.294	1.260
56. . . .	2.828	2.446	1.698	1.437	1.302	1.262
55. . . .	3.118	2.646	1.761	1.459	1.305	1.258
54. . . .	3.558	2.958	1.888	1.531	1.351	1.294
53. . . .	4.056	3.302	2.019	1.602	1.395	1.327
52. . . .	4.620	3.680	2.156	1.674	1.435	1.355
51. . . .	5.256	4.093	2.298	1.745	1.473	1.379
50. . . .	5.975	4.545	2.444	1.815	1.507	1.396
49. . . .	6.787	5.038	2.595	1.883	1.537	1.409
48. . . .	7.703	5.577	2.750	1.950	1.563	1.414
47. . . .	8.739	6.165	2.911	2.015	1.585	1.414
46. . . .	9.910	6.806	3.076	2.079	1.603	1.406
45. . . .	11.240	7.508	3.249	2.141	1.617	1.392
44. . . .	12.751	8.277	3.428	2.201	1.627	1.371
43. . . .	14.473	9.121	3.616	2.260	1.634	1.343
42. . . .	16.443	10.051	3.814	2.318	1.637	1.308
41. . . .	18.706	11.079	4.024	2.375	1.637	1.265
40. . . .	21.321	12.223	4.250	2.431	1.634	1.214
39. . . .	24.358	13.503	4.495	2.488	1.629	1.156
38. . . .	27.909	14.946	4.763	2.545	1.622	1.089
37. . . .	32.091	16.583	5.059	2.602	1.612	1.012
36. . . .	37.052	18.455	5.392	2.660	1.600	0.924
35. . . .	42.985	20.615	5.768	2.716	1.585	0.824
34. . . .	50.422	24.182	6.480	2.895	1.637	0.741
33. . . .	60.116	28.832	7.402	3.113	1.703	0.634
32. . . .	73.221	35.116	8.639	3.388	1.790	0.494
31. . . .	91.606	43.934	10.358	3.745	1.906	0.296

assuming $g_k^{(r)} = 1$ for the age-30 entrant. The last column of this table is the $_k(ERCR)_x$ of the $(PVFB)_x$ function given earlier in Table 12–5. The data in Table 13–1 show that the relative cost of early retirement, based on full accrued benefits, is significantly higher under the accrued benefit actuarial cost methods than it is under the projected benefit actuarial cost methods. Moreover, the CS versions of these two basic types of actuarial cost methods produce higher relative costs than the CA versions.

The cost of early retirement at age k on an actuarially reduced benefit basis, relative to the cost of normal retirement, is found by substituting the definition of $*g_k^{(r)}$ from equation (12.2) into (13.19):

$$*_k(ERCR)_x = \frac{B_k \;_{r-k}p_k'^{(m)}}{B_r \;_{r-k}p_k^{(T)}} C_k, \tag{13.20}$$

where C_k is defined by (13.19).

The benefit ratio in (13.20) is less than unity, while the survival probability ratio exceeds unity. Nevertheless, the product of these two ratios generally will be less than unity, implying that the $*_k(ERCR)_x$ for the $(PVFB)_x$ will be less costly than normal retirement. This conclusion was reached in the previous chapter. Since the value of C_k associated with each individual actuarial cost method is greater than unity, it is not mathematically clear whether the $*_k(ERCR)_x$ will be less than, equal to, or greater than unity for the various actuarial cost methods.

Table 13–2 gives the $*_k(ERCR)_x$ based on equation (13.20) for an age-30 entrant under standard assumptions. The $*_k(ERCR)_x$ for the two projected benefit cost methods is similar to that of the $(PVFB)_x$ function, all of which are considerably less than unity and decrease as the age is lowered. The ABCM, at the other extreme, exceeds unity and represents an increasing function of age. The two versions of the ABCM fall in between the conventional ABCM and the projected benefit cost methods, and both have attained age patterns that are not monotonic. In general, the cost impact under actuarial equivalent early retirement for the ABCM and the ^{CS}ABCM is relatively minor, while a fairly significant cost saving is associated with the projected benefit cost methods and to a lesser extent with the ^{CA}ABCM.

Although the analysis up to this point has been in terms of the cost of early retirement at age k relative to the cost at age r, it is often of interest to calculate the cost of early retirement at age k on a full benefit basis relative to the cost on an actuarially equivalent basis. This cost measure, as noted in the previous chapter, is equal to the

TABLE 13–2

$\overset{*}{k}$(ERCR)$_x$ Assuming Actuarially Reduced Benefit Accruals under Various Actuarial Cost Methods (age-30 entrant)

			Cost Measure			
k	ABCM	^{CS}ABCM	^{CA}ABCM	^{CS}PBCM	^{CA}PBCM	PVFB
65. . . .	1.000	1.000	1.000	1.000	1.000	1.000
64. . . .	1.028	1.014	0.975	0.958	0.949	0.947
63. . . .	1.050	1.021	0.944	0.911	0.894	0.890
62. . . .	1.067	1.022	0.908	0.861	0.837	0.830
61. . . .	1.080	1.019	0.870	0.810	0.779	0.770
60. . . .	1.091	1.013	0.830	0.759	0.722	0.711
59. . . .	1.100	1.004	0.790	0.709	0.666	0.654
58. . . .	1.107	0.994	0.750	0.660	0.613	0.600
57. . . .	1.114	0.982	0.711	0.614	0.563	0.548
56. . . .	1.120	0.969	0.673	0.569	0.516	0.500
55. . . .	1.125	0.955	0.636	0.526	0.471	0.454
54. . . .	1.172	0.974	0.622	0.504	0.445	0.426
53. . . .	1.221	0.994	0.608	0.482	0.420	0.400
52. . . .	1.273	1.014	0.594	0.461	0.396	0.373
51. . . .	1.327	1.033	0.580	0.441	0.372	0.348
50. . . .	1.384	1.053	0.566	0.420	0.349	0.324
49. . . .	1.444	1.072	0.552	0.401	0.327	0.300
48. . . .	1.507	1.091	0.538	0.382	0.306	0.277
47. . . .	1.574	1.110	0.524	0.363	0.285	0.255
46. . . .	1.644	1.129	0.510	0.345	0.266	0.233
45. . . .	1.720	1.149	0.497	0.328	0.247	0.213
44. . . .	1.800	1.169	0.484	0.311	0.230	0.194
43. . . .	1.888	1.190	0.472	0.295	0.213	0.175
42. . . .	1.982	1.212	0.460	0.279	0.197	0.158
41. . . .	2.086	1.235	0.449	0.265	0.183	0.141
40. . . .	2.200	1.261	0.439	0.251	0.169	0.125
39. . . .	2.328	1.291	0.430	0.238	0.156	0.110
38. . . .	2.472	1.324	0.422	0.225	0.144	0.096
37. . . .	2.635	1.362	0.415	0.214	0.132	0.083
36. . . .	2.822	1.406	0.411	0.203	0.122	0.070
35. . . .	3.038	1.457	0.408	0.192	0.112	0.058
34. . . .	3.309	1.587	0.425	0.190	0.107	0.049
33. . . .	3.664	1.757	0.451	0.190	0.104	0.039
32. . . .	4.146	1.989	0.489	0.192	0.101	0.028
31. . . .	4.822	2.312	0.545	0.197	0.100	0.016

reciprocal of $^*g_k^{(r)}$ and is valid for all actuarial cost methods. Table 12–2 shows this relative cost measure for the standard assumptions used in this book.

Multiple Early Retirement Ages

The early retirement cost ratio for the (PVFB)$_x$ function under multiple early retirement ages was found to be equal to the expected value of $_k(ERCR)_x$, where the expectation was based on this function evaluated at the midpoint of the age intervals (except at age r) and weighted by the retirement factors: $_{k-x}p_x'^{(r)}q_k'^{(r)}$. For $x \leqslant r'$, the $(ERCR)_x$ of the normal cost and actuarial liability of the various actuarial cost methods can likewise be found by taking this same weighted average of (13.19). This approach works also for the actuarial liability of the various accrued benefit cost methods at age r' and over, and except for a minor approximation, for the normal cost of three methods at age r' and over. The approximation associated with the normal cost is that of assuming the coefficient, c, in the early retirement equation is unity for all ages instead of being equal to $\frac{1}{2}$ when the summation index is equal to x for $x \geqslant r'$. Finally, a weighted average of (13.19) represents an approximation to the true value of $(ERCR)_x$ for the actuarial liability of the two projected benefit cost methods at and beyond age r', but again the error is not significant. Note that the value of C_k in (13.19) for the ABCM, ^{CS}ABCM, and ^{CA}ABCM would also be evaluated at $k + \frac{1}{2}$. The annuity ratios associated with the ^{CS}PBCM and the ^{CA}PBCM would be evaluated at integral k, but they would be based on the survival probability that reflects early retirement decrements.

Table 13–3 shows the values of $(ERCR)_{30}$ and $*(ERCR)_{30}$ for various actuarial cost methods and the $(PVFB)_x$ function under the assumption of a uniform retirement distribution from age 55 to age 65 for the age-30 entrant under standard assumptions. The $(ERCR)_{30}$, that is, the relative cost of early retirement when full attained age benefit accruals are provided, is largest for the conventional ABCM and smallest for the $(PVFB)_{30}$ function. Early retirement on this basis for the ABCM is 84 percent more costly than retirement at age 65, while for the ^{CA}PBCM the cost increase is 19 percent.

TABLE 13–3

Measures of the Cost of Early Retirement under a Uniform Early Retirement Distribution

Cost Measure	$(ERCR)_{30}$	$*(ERCR)_{30}$
ABCM. . . .	1.844	1.074
^{CS}ABCM. . . .	1.761	1.041
^{CA}ABCM. . . .	1.410	0.867
^{CS}PBCM. . . .	1.237	0.785
^{CA}PBCM. . . .	1.186	0.753
PVFB	1.171	0.744

The $*(ERCR)_{30}$, that is, the relative cost of early retirement when actuarially reduced benefits are provided, follows the same cost pattern as the $(ERCR)_{30}$. However, in this case, there is a 7 percent increase in costs under the ABCM and a 25 percent cost saving under the ^{CA}PBCM. One implication of these results is that a somewhat smaller reduction in benefits could be provided than a full actuarial reduction under several actuarial cost methods without increasing costs more than the cost of age-65 retirement.

Chapter 14

Effect of Plan Design on Pension Costs

This chapter is devoted to analyzing the effect of plan design on pension costs, using a hypothetical plan population. The plan population assumed is the one existing in the 25th year of simulation for the population given in Chapter 4 (see Table 4–7). The analysis is segregated according to benefit category—that is, retirement, vested, disability, and surviving spouse benefits—and the effects of various benefit formulas and eligibility requirements within each category are studied. The numerical results are based on active employees only, since it would have required far too extensive a simulation to create populations of nonactive employees whose benefits would correspond to the various plan designs analyzed in this chapter. Consequently, the results in some cases may not hold for the plan actuarial liability when the liability of nonactives is included. Finally, it should be noted at this point that the sensitivity analysis in each area is conducted according to the $(PVFB)_x$ function, and the normal cost and actuarial liability under the ABCM and ^{CS}PBCM. The results under these two actuarial cost methods, however, are presented only when they deviate substantially from the results under the $(PVFB)_x$ function.

RETIREMENT BENEFITS

Career and Final Average Benefit Formulas

The precise manner in which the benefit formula of a pension plan is tied to the participant's salary will have an important effect on plan costs. A final five-year average benefit formula, it will be remembered, is used as the standard assumption, and salaries are projected by approximately 7 percent per year to reflect merit, productivity, and inflation. Table 14–1 has been constructed to illustrate the effect of averaging more or fewer years of salary in the benefit formula, and to test the related importance of the salary projection factors. Since the results were found to be nearly identical among the various cost measures, only the data associated with the present value of future benefits is given in Table 14–1.

TABLE 14–1

Effect of the Benefit Formula on Pension Costs

	Percentage Increase in $\sum(PVFB)_x$	
Years of Final Average Salary Used in Benefit Formula	*Interest = 7% Salary Scale ≐ 7% (standard assumptions)*	*Interest = 4% Salary Scale ≐ 4%*
1 year	111.0	105.1
5 years	100.0	100.0
10 years	87.8	93.5
15 years	77.3	87.2
20 years	68.8	81.5
Career average	52.3	68.4

Column one of Table 14–1 shows that a career average plan is only half as costly as a final five-year average plan. If the formula uses the final year's salary, rather than a five-year average, costs are about 10 percent greater, while a ten-year average would reduce costs by about 10 percent. Interestingly, another five years added into the benefit formula, making a total of 15 years, continues to reduce costs by nearly 10 percent. Thus, costs under a final five-year average benefit formula are reduced by about 10 percent for each five years added to the averaging period.

Column two of Table 14–1 shows the results of assuming both a 4 percent rate of interest, instead of the standard 7 percent, and a salary projection that is approximately equal to 4 percent, instead of the standard assumption, which is approximately equal to 7 percent. In effect, 3 percentage points of inflation are subtracted out of both assumptions. It can be seen that the resulting flatter salary scale lessens the sensitivity of costs to the number of years used in the benefit formula. The career average plan under these assumptions is two-thirds as expensive as the final five-year average plan and the benefit formula generalization given above must be modified to state that costs are affected by 5 to 6 percent instead of 10 percent for each five years added to, or subtracted from, the final five-year average formula.

The effect of excluding the liability of nonactive plan participants is minor for the data presented in this section, because of the direct relationship between the level of plan benefits and the corresponding plan liability, and because the benefit levels of nonactives under each variation in the benefit formula would follow the change in projected benefits of actives. While it is true that the cost differential between a career average and final five-year average benefit formula is substantial, and that variations in the salary projection (or experience) are likewise important, the cost difference between a final five and a final ten-year average formula—amounting to 5 or 10 percent—is relatively modest.

The costs given in Table 14–1 represent long-run differences. The cost of shifting from a less expensive benefit formula to a more expensive benefit formula would also depend on whether or not the change applies retroactively to past service and, in the likely event that it *is* retroactive, the supplemental cost related to the supplemental liability created by the plan amendment must also be considered. The transitional cost of benefit formula changes is studied in Chapter 17.

Early Retirement Benefits

The benefits provided at early retirement, like the basic benefit formula itself, can have a significant effect on plan costs. The trend in recent years is not to reduce early retirement accrued benefits according to a full actuarial reduction, and, in many cases, no reduction whatsoever is made—at least down to certain ages. The cost effect of providing nonreduced early retirement benefits relative to actuarially reduced benefits is shown in Table 14–2. The data depict the relative cost of early retirement, as measured by the plan $(PVFB)_x$ function, under the assumption that all employees retire at age r' (or their attained age if greater), for r' equal to successively younger ages from age 65 down to age 55.

The increase in cost of providing nonreduced early retirement benefits, as Table 14–2 demonstrates, is roughly 10 percent for each year by which retirement precedes age 65, a rule that holds down through age 55. Thus, it would cost 50 percent more to give full benefits, instead of actuarially reduced benefits, if all employees were to retire at age 60; while the cost would be doubled if all employees were to retire at age 55 with full benefits instead of actuarially reduced benefits. Where multiple retirement ages are present, the fact that $\sum(PVFB)_x$ is nearly linear from age 55 to 65 allows one to approximate accurately the added cost to the plan of providing nonreduced benefits in place of actuarially reduced benefits by using the average retirement age. For example, if a plan had an average early retirement age of 63, it would cost 20 percent more to provide full accrued benefits as opposed to actuarially reduced benefits.

TABLE 14–2

Effect of Nonreduced Early Retirement Benefits

Assumed Retirement Age (r')	Cost of Nonreduced Early Retirement as Percentage of Cost for Actuarially Reduced Benefits
65	100.0
64	109.2
63	119.0
62	129.3
61	140.1
60	151.1
59	162.1
58	173.1
57	184.0
56	194.4
55	204.4

The cost impact of nonreduced early retirement benefits is somewhat higher below age 60 for the ^{cs}PBCM normal cost (at age 55 equal to 221.3 percent as opposed to 204.4), but not for the actuarial liability. For the ABCM, on the other hand, the impact on both its normal cost and actuarial liability is somewhat less than the impact on the $\sum(PVFB)_x$ function at all ages (at age 55 equal to 190.5 percent and 185.5 percent, respectively). As was the case for Table 14–1, Table 14–2 illustrates the long-run costs of providing nonreduced early retirement benefits, and there would be an additional cost created by shifting from actuarially reduced to nonreduced benefits. The data in Table 14–2 must not be interpreted as showing the cost of nonreduced early retirement at age r' relative to the cost of age-65 retirement; rather, the data show the cost of *nonreduced* early retirement at age r' relative to the cost of *actuarially* reduced retirement at age r'. The cost of *early* retirement relative to the cost of *normal* retirement, on both an actuarially reduced and a nonreduced benefit basis, is given in the next chapter.

Cost-of-Living Provision

Some plans, mostly or perhaps exclusively in the public sector, allow the benefits of retired employees to increase automatically, usually according to a rate which is tied to a national inflation index, rather than simply to increase retirement benefits *ad hoc*. The purpose of this section is to investigate the cost consequences of an automatic benefit escalator under various rates of inflation in relationship to the cost of assuming a fixed benefit in retirement (the standard assumption used up to this point).

The cost impact on the $\sum(PVFB)_x$ function (which is affected to about the same degree as the cost measures under the $^{CS}PBCM$ and the ABCM) is given in Table 14-3 for rates of inflation up to 6 percent. These data clearly show that retirement costs are quite sensitive to cost-of-living escalators—a 3 percent inflation assumption increasing costs by about 20 percent and a 6 percent assumption increasing costs over 40 percent.

TABLE 14-3

Effect of Cost-of-Living Escalators

Inflation Rate	Cost of $\sum(PVFB)_x$ with C-O-L Provision as a Percentage of the Cost under the Standard Assumptions
0	100.0
1	105.4
2	111.5
3	118.2
4	125.9
5	134.5
6	144.2

Since *ad hoc* benefit improvements are more the rule than the exception, these results suggest that plan costs determined under a constant retirement benefit assumption may significantly understate best-estimate costs even if a cost-of-living clause is not part of the plan. Since, in all likelihood, benefit improvements will be made, it might be argued that the continuation-of-plan liability should reflect the cost of this contingency.

VESTED BENEFITS

ERISA Vesting Standards

It was pointed out in Chapter 1 that there are three alternative vesting standards under ERISA: full vesting after ten years (the standard assumption used in this book), graded vesting from the fifth to the fifteenth year, and the rule-of-45. The cost of each provision, expressed as a percentage of the cost of retirement, is given in Table 14–4.

TABLE 14–4

Vesting Cost under ERISA as a Percentage of Retirement Cost

	ERISA Vesting Provisions		
Cost Measure	*Full after Ten Years*	*Graded from 5th to 15th Years*	*Rule-of-45*
$\sum(\text{PVFB})_x$.	11.3	11.3	11.4
^{CS}PBCM			
NC	17.5	19.9	19.3
AL.	7.4	6.4	6.9
ABCM			
NC	18.9	20.8	20.4
AL.	13.9	14.3	14.3

As Table 14–4 shows, the vesting cost percentages differ significantly among the various cost measures used, but the difference in the cost of vesting among the three ERISA standards is trivial. It appears that the 15-year graded provision is slightly more costly than the full-after-ten-years provision, but these results are more likely due to the underlying actuarial assumptions than to the provisions themselves. These data suggest that the choice of an ERISA vesting standard can be made on criteria other than cost, such as administrative simplicity, employee understanding, and so forth.

It may be of interest to note that the full-after-ten-years provision vests 40 percent of all active employees in the hypothetical plan population, the 15-year-graded provision vests 61 percent of all active employees in at least some portions of their attained age accrued benefits, and the rule-of-45 vests 55 percent on this same basis.

As for the specific vesting cost percentages, the $(\text{PVFB})_x$ function shows an 11 percent value. The ^{CS}PBCM generates a normal cost percentage nearly double that of the $\sum(\text{PVFB})_x$ function, while its actuarial liability percentage is nearly one-half the $\sum(\text{PVFB})_x$ percentage. Although not obvious, it turns out that the normal cost vesting percentage (17 to 20 percent) is the value both the $\sum(\text{PVFB})_x$ and $^{\text{CS}}\text{PBCM}_x$ actuarial liability will eventually attain over time, provided the liability of vested terminated employees is included in the cost measure. In other words, if the plan had a full complement of vested terminated employees from the earliest vesting age to the end of the assumed human life span, and a full set of retired employees, the $\sum(\text{PVFB})_x$ function and the $^{\text{CS}}\text{PBCM}$ actuarial liability would both develop vesting cost percentages approximately equal to those of the $^{\text{CS}}\text{PBCM}$ normal cost. If the benefits of vested terminated employees are not increased for inflation, which is the typical procedure, the $^{\text{CS}}\text{PBCM}$ normal cost vesting percentages may never be reached, and this would certainly be the case if the benefits of retired employees were increased for inflation while those of vested terminated employee were not.

The vesting cost percentages for the ABCM normal cost tend to be close in value to those of the $^{\text{CS}}\text{PBCM}$ normal cost, but the latter are heavily dependent on the entry ages of employees, while the vesting cost percentages of the ABCM normal cost depend more strongly upon the employee's attained age and service. For example, if all employees were age r' or older, the vesting cost percentage for the ABCM normal cost would be zero. In general, it is difficult to predict the vesting cost percentage under the ABCM, and its relationship to that of the $^{\text{CS}}\text{PBCM}$ in Table 14–4 is not one that would hold for all plan populations. The same is true for the ABCM actuarial liability which is seen to average about 14 percent.

The vesting cost percentage *for a given individual* is identical for both the normal cost and actuarial liability under the ABCM, yet Table 14–4 seems to contradict this finding. The reason is that the vesting cost percentages given in Table 14–4 are based on the aggregate of active employees, and the averaging process causes a smaller actuarial liability percentage than the corresponding normal cost percentage. This is attributable to the differential rates of change in the age specific normal cost and actuarial liability associated with retirement and vested benefits.

Because of the similarity in costs among the three alternative vesting standards, the analysis of vesting in the following section, and in the next chapter, deals with the full-vesting-after-ten-years provision only. It should be noted that just as the liability-based vesting cost percentages are deceptively low without a full complement of vested terminated employees included, the normal cost vesting percentages also may be misleading in that they do not show the transitional cost of changing from no vesting to one of the ERISA standards. This transitional cost is examined in Chapter 17.

Effect of Vesting Provision

The purpose of this section is to analyze the sensitivity of the vesting cost percentage to changes in the years-of-service requirement for full vesting. Although ERISA requires non-graded vesting to occur after ten years of service, it is nevertheless interesting to consider more restrictive, as well as more liberal provisions that are set out in Table 14–5.

TABLE 14–5

Effect of Eligibility Requirements for Vesting (vesting cost as a percentage of retirement cost)

Cost Measure	*Years of Service Required for Full Vesting*				
	20	*15*	*10*	*5*	*0*
$\sum(PVFB)_x$	5.7	9.1	11.3	12.3	12.6
CSPBCM					
NC	6.3	12.1	17.5	21.9	25.6
AL	4.9	6.9	7.4	6.8	5.3
ABCM					
NC	7.3	13.6	18.9	22.9	26.1
AL	6.4	10.9	13.9	15.6	16.1

The 20-year service requirement generates a vesting cost percentage of one-half the ten-year service requirement, but the $\sum(PVFB)_x$ function is rather insensitive to vesting more rapidly than ten years. Although approximately 60 percent of the active employees in the underlying plan population have less than ten years of service, their impact on the vesting-related $\sum(PVFB)_x$ (the numerator of the vesting cost percentage) is minimal for more rapid vesting because they tend to be young employees for whom the interest discount is strongest, and their accrued benefits are relatively small because of their short service and low salaries.

The normal cost of the CSPBCM is seen to be somewhat sensitive to the vesting requirement, increasing from a vesting cost percentage of 17 percent for ten-year vesting to 22 percent for five-year vesting and 26 percent for immediate vesting. It may seem inconsistent that the ^{CS}PBCM actuarial liability vesting cost percentage actually decreases in value as the vesting provision is liberalized beyond the ten-year service requirement, but the reasoning is as follows. The actuarial liability is determined by subtracting the present value of future normal costs from the present value of future benefits. The data in Table 14–5 indicate that the vesting related $\sum(\text{PVFB})_x$ is hardly affected by vesting more liberal than ten years, yet the vesting related normal cost of the ^{CS}PBCM is increased substantially, which implies a commensurate increase in the present value of *future* normal costs. Thus, in this case the vesting-related actuarial liability is lowered by more liberal vesting since $\sum(\text{PVFB})_x$ remains nearly constant while $\sum^{v}(\text{PVFNC})_x$ increases. As a matter of fact, for overmature populations, it is possible that $^{v}(\text{PVFNC})_x$ could exceed $\sum^{v}(\text{PVFB})_x$, causing the vesting cost percentage associated with the ^{CS}PBCM actuarial liability to be negative.

The normal cost of the ABCM is seen to follow that of the ^{CS}PBCM, while its actuarial liability follows the pattern set by the $\sum(\text{PVFB})_x$ function. The vesting related actuarial liability under this method, unlike that of the ^{CS}PBCM, can never be negative. In the most extreme case, when all employees are over age r', the vesting cost percentage would be zero for both the normal cost and the actuarial liability of this method. On the other hand, the percentage would take on its largest value if all employees were at their initial vesting age, but, unless this were a single age, the normal cost and actuarial liability percentages would vary due to the averaging process inherent in an aggregate ratio.

DISABILITY BENEFITS

The disability provision used as the standard assumption in this treatise requires 15 years of service and the attainment of age 40 for payment of the accrued pension upon disability. Nearly 25 percent of all active employees in the standard population meet the age and service requirements to be eligible for disability benefits. The cost of disability, expressed as a percentage of the basic retirement benefit cost, is 11 to 12 percent, depending on the cost measure used. This cost tends to be somewhat greater when measured in terms of a normal cost rather than the $\sum(\text{PVFB})_x$ function or an actuarial liability.

Table 14–6 shows the sensitivity of the disability cost percentage to various age and service eligibility requirements. The data are given for the normal cost and actuarial liability of the ^{CS}PBCM only, since the disability cost percentage of the ABCM normal cost is nearly identical to that of the ^{CS}PBCM, as are their respective actuarial liability percentages and the $\sum(\text{PVFB})_x$ liability percentage.

TABLE 14–6

Effect of Eligibility Requirements for Disability Benefits

Eligibility Requirement		Disability Cost as a Percentage of Retirement Cost under $^{CS}PBCM$	
Age	Service (years)	Normal Cost	Actuarial Liability
60	25.	5.6	6.4
55	20.	8.8	9.1
40	15*.	12.3	11.1
None	15.	12.3	11.2
40	None.	14.7	11.4
None	None.	15.1	11.4

* Standard provision.

The age 40 and 15 years service provision is nearly as expensive as having no eligibility requirements whatsoever. Moreover, eliminating the age requirement while retaining the 15 year service requirement has no noticeable effect on the cost of disability. Finally, as was the case for the cost of vesting, the disability cost percentages associated with the actuarial liability will tend toward those of the normal cost over time.

SURVIVING SPOUSE BENEFIT

The standard assumption for the surviving spouse benefit is an eligibility requirement of age 55 and 20 years of service, and a benefit equal to 50 percent of the decedent's accrued benefits. It is further assumed that 80 percent of the employees who die have a surviving spouse, the spouse is three years younger than the employee, and the survivor is subject to a clause that terminates the annuity upon remarriage. The cost under these assumptions, generated by less than 10 percent of all active employees who qualify, amounts to about 5 percent of the retirement cost of the pension plan. Since costs are directly proportional to the amount of the surviving spouse benefit, the cost would be 10 percent if full attained age accrued benefits were to be provided. Moreover, costs increase in direct proportion to the assumed marriage percentage. Thus, if full benefit accruals were given, and if virtually all employees had a surviving spouse, costs would amount to about 12 percent of the plan's retirement cost.

Table 14–7 shows the effect of various age and service requirements for the surviving spouse benefit on the related cost, expressed as a percentage of the retirement costs under the ^{CS}PBCM. The age 55 and 20-year provision is about half as expensive as immediate qualification. As was the case for the disability benefit, the service requirement is seen to be the dominant restriction, there being no noticeable difference between the straight 15-year service requirement and an age 40 and 15-year requirement. Finally, the actuarial liability is affected somewhat less than the impact on the normal cost of the ^{CS}PBCM, and the same percentages hold for the normal cost and actuarial liability of the ABCM.

TABLE 14–7

Effect of Eligibility Requirements for Surviving Spouse Benefits

Eligibility Requirements		Cost of Surviving Spouse Benefit as a Percent of the Cost of Retirement under $^{CS}PBCM$	
Age	Service (years)	Normal Cost	Actuarial Liability
60	25	2.8	3.1
55	20*	5.0	5.1
40	15	7.6	6.6
None	15	7.6	6.6
40	None	9.3	6.7
None	None	9.6	6.7

* Standard provision.

SUMMARY OF PENSION COST COMPONENTS

The cost of the various benefits provided under the so-called standard pension plan is summarized in Table 14–8. The first section shows the component cost as a percentage of the basic retirement cost, which corresponds to the way each ancillary benefit was dealt with in this chapter. The second portion of the table shows the percentage of the total pension cost made up by the various benefit components.

An obvious, but nevertheless important, fact revealed by Table 14–8 is that retirement benefits account for 75 to 80 percent of total

TABLE 14–8

Pension Cost Components

Cost Measure	Component Cost as a Percentage of Retirement Cost				Component Cost as a Percentage of Total Cost			
	Retirement Benefits	Vested Benefits	Disability Benefits	Surviving Spouse Benefits	Retirement Benefits	Vested Benefits	Disability Benefits	Surviving Spouse Benefits
$\sum(\text{PVFB})_x$ . .	100	11.3	11.9	5.3	77.9	8.8	9.3	4.1
^{cs}PBCM								
NC.	100	17.5	12.3	5.0	74.2	13.0	9.1	3.7
AL	100	7.4	11.1	5.1	80.9	6.0	9.0	4.1
ABCM								
NC.	100	18.9	12.9	5.5	72.8	13.8	9.4	4.0
AL	100	13.9	12.5	5.7	75.7	10.5	9.5	4.3

plan costs for the assumed benefit structure. The percentage would
be somewhat higher if fewer or less generous ancillary benefits were
provided, and vice versa. The underlying actuarial assumptions also
play an important part in the value of retirement benefits relative to
ancillary benefits. It would be a rare case, however, if the cost of
retirement benefits fell outside a 65 to 90 percent cost interval, and
a 70 to 85 percent interval no doubt would include the vast majority
of plans. This perspective on the relative magnitude of retirement and
ancillary benefit costs will be helpful in the following chapter, where
the effects of varying the actuarial assumptions on the various cost
components given in Table 14–8 are considered.

Chapter 15

Effect of Actuarial Assumptions on Pension Costs

The purpose of this chapter is to investigate the sensitivity of pension costs to changes in the underlying assumptions of a hypothetical pension plan in order to gain a perspective on the relative importance of the various actuarial assumptions. The cost results obtained using different actuarial assumptions can be viewed as the costs of two plans with different experience, or the long-run cost differences of the same plan in the event that its experience should change. The cost implications of using actuarial assumptions that do not conform to the future experience of the plan are analyzed in Chapter 17.

The numerical results discussed in this chapter are based on active employees only, as was the case in the preceding chapter, for the $\sum(PVFB)_x$ function. In those cases where the results of the normal cost and actuarial liability under the $^{CS}PBCM$ and ABCM differ from the results of the $\sum(PVFB)_x$ function, a comment to this effect is given and/or the results under these cost methods are shown.

MORTALITY RATES

The impact of mortality on the $\sum(PVFB)_x$ of the plan is shown in Table 15–1, where the mortality rate multiple indicates the change made to the standard assumption. For example, a multiple of 0.5 indicates that the age-specific rates are reduced to one half the standard rates (except for the rate at the assumed end of the life span, which retains a value of unity), while a multiple of 1.5 indicates a

50 percent increase in the age-specific rates (unless a value greater than unity results, in which case unity is used). The first column of Table 15–1 shows the cost effect if the rates applicable to ages below age 65 are changed, the second column shows the effect if the rate for ages 65 and over are changed, while the third column reflects the effect if the change occurs at all ages.

TABLE 15–1

Effect of Mortality

Mortality Rate Multiple	Pension Costs as a Percentage of the Cost under Standard Assumptions for the $\sum(PVFB)_x$ Function		
	Ages Less than 65 Only	Ages 65 and over Only	All Ages
0.50	105.6	116.1	123.0
0.75	102.8	107.0	110.0
1.00	100.0	100.0	100.0
1.25	97.3	94.4	91.9
1.50	98.4	89.7	85.2

A significant change in mortality for ages below age 65 has only a modest impact. For example, a 50 percent change in either direction affects costs by about 5 percent. Although not shown in Table 15–1, eliminating the mortality assumption for ages less than age 65 increases costs by only 11 percent. The effect of changes in the mortality rates at ages over age 65 is more significant, as one would expect. However, a 25 percent deviation in mortality at these ages affects costs less than 10 percent. It is interesting that a 50 percent decrease in retirement mortality increases the age-65 life expectancy by nearly 40 percent, whereas pension costs are increased by only about 16 percent. Similarly, a 50 percent increase in retirement mortality decreases the age-65 life expectancy by 20 percent, but decreases costs by only 10 percent.

Table 15–2 shows a complete breakdown of total costs into their benefit-related components, and the resulting impact of changing the mortality schedule over all ages. The cost of vesting is slightly more sensitive to changes in the mortality assumption than the cost of retirement. Since the rate of mortality among disabled lives was not altered in the experiment, the cost of disability is shown to be quite insensitive to the change in mortality for active employees. The cost of surviving spouse benefits, as expected, is affected significantly, and in the opposite direction from the effect on the other benefit costs. Note that the effect on the cost of surviving spouse benefit is almost equal to the change in the mortality assumption. The counterbalancing influence of the surviving spouse benefit is, however, relatively minor in terms of influencing total costs, as the last column of data in Table 15–2 clearly indicates.

TABLE 15–2

Effect of Mortality on Component Costs

Mortality Rate Multiple	Penion Cost Components as a Percentage of the Cost under Standard Assumptions for the $\sum(PVFB)_x$ Function				
	Retirement Benefits	Vested Benefits	Disability Benefits	Surviving Spouse Benefits	Total Cost
0.50	128.1	130.2	105.1	52.5	123.0
0.75	112.3	113.2	102.5	76.9	110.0
1.00	100.0	100.0	100.0	100.0	100.0
1.25	90.0	89.2	97.6	122.0	91.9
1.50	81.6	80.2	95.2	142.8	85.2

As pointed out in Chapter 2, female mortality is lower than male mortality at the same attained age. It is assumed, by virtue of using the GAM–71 male mortality rates, that the model population consists of all male members. The effect of female members is analyzed by replacing the all-made mortality assumption with an all-female assumption. This change increases total costs by about 20 percent, and the impact on component benefit costs is nearly identical to the 50 percent reduction in mortality as shown in Table 15–2. The cost effects of having only a proportion of females in the plan could be approximated by multiplying the proportion of females times the percentage increase in costs associated with a 50 percent mortality reduction as given in Table 15–2.

In summary, the mortality assumption and the implied mortality experience of the plan can potentially have a significant impact on costs. But probable variations in this factor, for example, a 25 percent deviation across all ages, have a relatively minor impact on costs in comparison to the impact of similar deviations in assumptions yet to be studied. The costs given in this section are based solely on the present value of future benefits for active employees, but the results were found to be nearly identical for the normal cost and actuarial liability of the [CS]PBCM and ABCM.

WITHDRAWAL RATES

The withdrawal rates of active employees are not only greater in value than mortality rates, but are also subject to considerably more variation, both among plans and for a given plan over time. Although a 50 percent deviation in the mortality assumption among a large group of plan members is unlikely, barring a catastrophe, this is not the case for termation rates of active employees. Moreover, a change in the withdrawal rates affects the various cost measures differently, requiring more data to be presented in this section. The analysis begins by considering uniform percentage changes in withdrawal rates over all ages and then considers the effect of changes in only pre-vesting or post-vesting termination rates.

Uniform Termination Rate Changes

Table 15–3 shows the cost results of various termination rate multiples, including a multiple of zero, which eliminates the assumption altogether. The $\sum(PVFB)_x$ function is increased by 84 percent when the withdrawal assumption is eliminated—a significant impact indeed. Note also that a 50 percent deviation in this parameter has a non-symmetrical effect on the $\sum(PVFB)_x$, that is, costs are increased by 28 percent and reduced by 16 percent, respectively, as the withdrawal rates are reduced by 50 percent and then increased by 50 percent.

The normal cost of the ^{CS}PBCM is somewhat more sensitive to changes in the rates of employee termination than the $\sum(PVFB)_x$ function. The effect of equal percentage changes in this assumption

TABLE 15–3

Effect of Termination Rates

Termination Rate Multiple	$\sum(PVFB)_x$	Pension Costs as a Percentage of the Cost under Standard Assumption			
		$^{CS}(PBCM)$		$ABCM$	
		NC	AL	NC	AL
0.0	184.0	163.7	96.0	107.6	103.1
0.50	128.2	132.0	99.0	103.2	101.4
0.75	111.9	115.7	99.8	101.5	100.7
1.00	100.0	100.0	100.0	100.0	100.0
1.25	90.9	85.5	99.5	98.7	99.4
1.50	83.8	72.7	98.5	97.5	98.9

produces a nearly symmetrical cost impact, a 25 percent deviation affecting costs by 15 percent and a 50 percent deviation affecting costs by 30 percent.

The withdrawal assumption has only a minor impact on the ^{CS}PBCM actuarial liability and on both cost measures under the ABCM. The impact on the ^{CS}PBCM actuarial liability is minimal because the present value of future normal costs increases by about the same amount as the increase in the present value of future benefits. As for the ABCM, it turns out that the vast majority of the normal cost and actuarial liability of the plan is in respect to participants who are beyond the ages for which withdrawal rates play a significant role.

Additional data are provided on changes in the rates of termination under the ^{CS}PBCM normal cost in Table 15–4. This single cost measure is given since, in theory, the long-run impact on the $\sum(\text{PVFB})_x$ and ^{CS}PBCM actuarial liability would be about the same. As would be expected, the relative cost of vested benefits increases with higher rates of termination, while the relative cost of retirement, disability, and surviving spouse benefits decrease. The relative cost of vested benefits increases or decreases by about 3 percentage points for each change in the termination rate assumption.

TABLE 15–4

Effect of Termination Rates on Component Costs

	Pension Cost Components as a Percentage of Total Costs under the ^{CS}PBCM Normal Cost				
Termination Rate Multiple	Retirement Benefits	Vested Benefits	Disability Benefits	Surviving Spouse Benefits	Total Costs
0.50	79.3	6.4	10.1	4.2	100.0
0.75	76.7	9.7	9.6	4.0	100.0
1.00	74.2	13.0	9.7	3.7	100.0
1.25	71.8	16.1	8.6	3.5	100.0
1.50	69.7	19.0	8.1	3.2	100.0

In conclusion, it is clear that the withdrawal assumption has a significant impact on the $\sum(\text{PVFB})_x$ function and the ^{CS}PBCM normal cost, but is has practically no effect on the ^{CS}PSCM actuarial liability or either of the two cost measures under the ABCM. Since it is possible that mandatory vesting standards may have different effects on employees depending on their vesting statuses, the following sections consider segmented changes in the termination rates of active employees.

Segmented Termination Rate Changes

It is possible that employees who are not yet vested could experience higher rates of termination than the rates assumed in the standard termination rate schedule, or they could experience lower rates based on the premise that nonvested employees will tend to remain in service until they become vested. The cost impact of changes in termination rates at nonvested ages is given in Table 15–5 under the ^{CS}PBCM normal cost, since this cost represents the *long-run* effect on the $\sum(PVFB)_x$ function and the ^{CS}PBCM actuarial liability.

TABLE 15–5

Effect of Pre-Vesting Termination Rates on Component Costs

Pre-Vesting Termination Rate Multiple	Pension Cost Components as a Percentage of the Cost under Standard Assumptions for the ^{CS}PBCM Normal Cost				
	Retirement Benefits	*Vested Benefits*	*Disability Benefits*	*Surviving Spouse Benefits*	*Total Costs*
0.50	113.8	117.0	115.7	115.9	114.5
0.75	107.1	108.9	108.2	108.3	107.5
1.00	100.0	100.0	100.0	100.0	100.0
1.25	92.5	90.6	91.3	91.2	92.1
1.50	84.7	81.1	82.4	82.1	84.0

The percentage impact on each cost component, as well as the impact on total costs, is given for 25 and 50 percent deviations in pre-vesting termination rates. Vested benefit costs are slightly more sensitive to such changes than retirement benefit costs, but because of magnitude of the latter, the impact on total costs follows that of the retirement benefit component. Comparing the impact of changes in pre-vesting termination rates to the impact of changes in termination rates at all ages, as previously shown in the second column of Table 15–3, one can see that pre-vesting rates influence costs by about half as much as changes at all ages.

The effect of changes in post-vesting termination rates, leaving the pre-vesting rates unaltered, is shown in Table 15–6 for the ^{CS}PBCM normal cost. The vested benefit cost is affected in precisely the opposite direction, and to a greater extent, than the retirement, disability and surviving spouse benefit costs; yet total costs still follow the pattern set by the retirement benefit cost. Thus we see that if the introduction of vesting, for example, brought a significant increase in termination rates among vested employees, total cost would go down in spite of the fact that vesting costs would increase. The parenthetical percentages given in the vested benefit cost column of Table 15–6 show the percentage of total costs accounted for by the vesting cost component. This percentage ranges from a low of 6.3 percent to a high of 19.8 percent.

TABLE 15–6

Effect of Post-Vesting Termination Rates on Component Costs

| Post-Vesting Termination Rate Multiple | Pension Cost Component as a Percentage of the Cost under Standard Assumptions for the $^{CS}PBCM$ Normal Cost | | | | |
	Retirement Benefits	Vested Benefits	Disability Benefits	Surviving Spouse Benefits	Total Cost
0.50	124.8	56.7 (6.3)	127.5	130.7	116.4
0.75	111.8	79.9 (9.6)	113.0	114.5	107.9
1.00	100.0	100.0 (13.0)	100.0	100.0	100.0
1.25	89.5	117.2 (16.4)	88.3	87.2	92.9
1.50	80.2	131.8 (19.8)	78.0	76.0	86.6

Tables 15–5 and 15–6 clearly show that total plan costs are importantly a function of the retirement benefit costs. In fact, one can nearly always predict the effect on total pension costs of a given parameter change by reasoning through the effect on the retirement benefit cost component. An important application of this principle is the effect of termination rate changes on total costs, especially for changes among vested employees.

DISABILITY RATES

It will be remembered that the cost of disability for the standard assumptions amounted to 11 or 12 percent, depending on the cost measure used. In this section the cost impact of various changes in the underlying rates of disability is explored.

Table 15–7 sets forth the basic data, where the disability rate multiple begins at zero and increases to a value of two. Since the cost impact of such changes was found to be roughly equal across all cost measures, only the results under the $\sum(\text{PVFB})_x$ function are given. The percentage change in the cost of disability is approximately equal

TABLE 15–7

Effect of Disability Rates

	Pension Cost Components as a Percentage of the Cost under Standard Assumptions for the $\sum(PVFB)_x$ Function				
Disability Rate Multiple	Retirement Benefits	Vested Benefits	Disability Benefits	Surviving Spouse Benefits	Total Costs
0.0	113.8	101.9	0.0 (0.0)	107.5	102.0
0.50	106.7	101.0	51.6 (4.7)	103.6	101.0
1.00	100.0	100.0	100.0 (9.3)	100.0	100.0
1.50	93.9	99.1	145.5 (13.6)	96.5	99.1
2.00	87.8	98.1	188.1 (17.8)	93.1	98.2

to the percentage change in disability rates. The other component benefit costs, while affected only modestly for such large deviations in the disability assumptions, are impacted in the opposite direction from that of the disability cost. Consequently, consistent with the principle set out in the previous section, total costs are inversely related to changes in the disability parameter, following the pattern set by the retirement benefit costs.

Total costs are practically insensitive to significant changes in disability rates. This occurs because of the offsetting effect such changes have on the various component costs. Nevertheless, the cost of the disability benefit, as disability rates are increased, makes up an ever larger proportion of total costs, as the parenthetical percentages in Table 15–7 point out.

RETIREMENT RATES

The cost implication of providing non-reduced early retirement benefits instead of actuarially reduced benefits was analyzed in the previous chapter. The purpose of this section is to compare the cost of early retirement to the cost of normal retirement, both on a non-reduced and an actuarially reduced basis.

The cost of providing actuarially reduced early retirement benefits under the assumption that all employees retire at specified retirement ages (or their attained age if greater) is given in Table 15–8 for each cost measure. The $\sum(PVFB)_x$ function and the costs under the ^{CS}PBCM are reduced significantly as the retirement age is lowered, while the costs of the ABCM are affected only slightly. For example,

TABLE 15–8

Effect of Early Retirement with Actuarially Reduced Benefits, as a Percentage of the Cost of Normal Retirement

| | | Cost of Early Retirement with Actuarially Reduced Benefits, as a Percentage of the Cost of Normal Retirement | | | |
| | | $^{CS}PBCM$ | | $ABCM$ | |
Retirement Age	$\sum(PVFB)_x$	NC	AL	NC	AL
65.	100.0	100.0	100.0	100.0	100.0
63.	87.0	90.5	89.1	100.0	99.6
61.	75.3	81.6	79.4	99.5	98.8
59.	65.6	73.7	71.5	99.1	98.1
57.	57.7	67.3	65.1	98.9	97.6
55.	51.3	62.0	60.0	98.6	97.2

total costs are reduced by 10 percent under the $^{CS}PBCM$ if retirements occur at age 63, and by 20 percent if retirement occurs at age 61. These results conflict with the conventional wisdom on the cost of actuarially equivalent early retirement which states that plan costs are unaffected. Although this is the case under the ABCM, costs under the $\sum(PVFB)_x$ function and the $^{CS}PBCM$ deviate substantially from this rule.

Table 15–9 shows the results of early retirement when full attained age (nonreduced) accrued benefits are provided. The result is just the reverse of that observed in connection with actuarially reduced benefits, that is, the $\sum(PVFB)_x$ function is affected only minimally, the $^{CS}PBCM$ costs are increased by about 7 percent for each two-year drop in the retirement age, and the ABCM costs are increased by

TABLE 15–9

Effect of Early Retirement without a Benefit Reduction

| | | Cost of Early Retirement with Nonreduced Retirement Benefits, as a Percentage of the Cost of Normal Retirement | | | |
| | | $^{CS}PBCM$ | | $ABCM$ | |
Retirement Age	$\sum(PVFB)_x$	NC	AL	NC	AL
65.	100.0	100.0	100.0	100.0	100.0
63.	103.5	107.4	106.4	117.0	116.8
61.	105.5	114.9	111.4	134.5	133.5
59.	106.4	122.0	115.3	152.4	149.9
57.	106.2	129.7	118.1	170.6	165.7
55.	104.8	137.2	119.5	187.9	180.3

about 15 percent for each two-year decline. Thus, non-actuarially reduced early retirement is quite costly under the ABCM, but the cost increase under the ^{CS}PBCM is only half as great. Moreover, the cost, as measured independently of a given actuarial cost method, (that is, by the $\sum(PVFB)_x$ function) is almost insensitive to the early retirement age if full benefits are provided. Different results may be obtained for a career average or flat unit benefit formula.

The results given in Tables 15–8 and 15–9 are not inconsistent with the early retirement cost data presented in the previous chapter. At that point it was shown that the cost of providing nonreduced benefits in place of actuarially reduced benefits was 10 percent times the number of years retirement takes place below age 65. Early retirement at age 55 under this rule, for example, would be 100 percent more expensive if nonreduced benefits were provided instead of actuarially reduced benefits. This rule can be tested using the data given in this section by dividing the percentage cost found in Table 15–9 by its counterpart in Table 15–8.

In summary, early retirement on an actuarially reduced basis has a neutral effect on costs under the ABCM, and a decreasing impact on the other cost measures (see Table 15–8). If full benefits are provided, early retirement is quite expensive under the ABCM, moderately expensive under the ^{CS}PBCM, and only trivially expensive as measured by the $\sum(PVFB)_x$ function (see Table 15–9). Finally, for a given early retirement age, the cost of providing full benefits upon early retirement as compared to providing actuarially reduced benefits is quite expensive, amounting to 10 percent for each age below age 65 (see Table 14–2).

SALARY RATES

Pension costs are directly proportional to the level of benefits provided under the plan. Consequently, for plans with a salary-based benefit formula, the assumed rate of growth in salaries has an important bearing on costs. The underlying theory on future salary increases, as set out in a Chapter 2, is that merit, productivity and inflation represent the components of increase. The standard merit scale, although conforming to a concave function, has about a 2 percent compounding effect for an age-30 entrant, the productivity factor is assumed to be 1 percent, and the inflation factor 4 percent. The first two components, merit and productivity, are relatively stable as compared to the inflation component. The purpose of this section is to analyze the impact of introducing each salary increase component into the salary assumption, and to study the effects of varying rates of inflation on pension costs.

The sensitivity of total costs to changes in the salary assumption is given in Table 15–10, where all costs are expressed as a percentage of the costs under the standard assumptions. Each cost measure will be discussed separately because of the heterogeneity of results.

TABLE 15–10

Effect of Salary Rate

Salary Assumption	$\sum(PVFB)_x$	Pension Costs as a Percentage of the Cost under Standard Assumptions			
		$^{CS}PBCM$		$ABCM$	
		NC	AL	NC	AL
Flat salary	55.1	35.7	68.7	55.9	119.7
Merit only (approximate 2%). . . .	57.2	46.0	72.8	66.4	115.3
Merit plus productivity of 1% . . .	63.0	53.7	77.4	74.0	111.9
Merit plus productivity plus inflation of:					
2%.	78.1	73.3	87.9	87.8	105.7
4%.	100.0	100.0	100.0	100.0	100.0
6%.	132.4	135.3	113.5	110.8	94.8
8%.	181.5	180.2	127.7	120.5	90.0

The $\sum(PVFB)_x$ function is reduced to almost one half of its value if no salary increases are assumed whatsoever. The introduction of the merit scale increases costs by only 2 percentage points, and the productivity component by another 6 percentage points. Thus, prior to the introduction of the inflation assumption, costs are two thirds of the level under standard assumptions. Variations in the inflation factor about the 4 percent level are seen to be quite significant. A 2 percent decrease in the rate of inflation reduces the cost by 20 percent, while a 2 percent increase in the rate increases costs by over 30 percent.

The impact of the salary scale in the $^{CS}PBCM$ normal cost is somewhat greater than the impact on the $\sum(PVFB)_x$ function, but the corresponding effect on its actuarial liability is less pronounced. For example, a 2 percent decrease in the inflation assumption reduces the $^{CS}PBCM$ normal cost by 25 percent, while a 2 percent increase in the inflation assumption increases costs by 35 percent. The actuarial liability, however, is altered by only about 12 percent. This occurs because the $(PVFB)_x$ component of the actuarial liability equation is less responsive to the salary scale change than is the present value of future normal costs; hence, the actuarial liability is also less responsive.

The effect of the salary assumption on the ABCM is unique indeed. The normal cost impact is less than that of the ^{cs}PBCM normal cost, a 2 percent deviation in the inflation parameter affecting costs by 10 to 15 percent. The impact of the salary scale on the actuarial liability, however, is precisely the opposite of its impact on the other cost measures, that is, a lower salary scale increases the actuarial liability and vice versa. The reason for this is that a change in the salary scale affects each participant's assumed accrued benefits under the ABCM. In particular, the flatter the salary scale the *larger* are the assumed salaries of plan participants for prior years, which in turn increases the assumed accrued benefits. In other words, for a given set of current salaries, the flatter the salary scale the larger will be the actuarial liability under the ABCM. As Table 15–10 amply illustrates, the ABCM actuarial liability is relatively insensitive to significant changes in the inflation assumption.

In theory, at least, it is inappropriate to alter the inflation component in the salary scale without a commensurate change in the assumed investment return. Although the effect of simultaneous changes in these two assumptions is studied at a later point, the data presented in Table 15–10 are nevertheless valuable in showing the overall sensitivity of costs to the inflation component. Moreover, the data show the expected increase in costs of raising the salary assumption from a rate of 3 or 4 percent to a more realistic level. The conservative value for this assumption, of course, is a rate of increase *higher* than one actually expects to experience, an assumption rarely found in practice.

INTEREST RATES

The interest rate assumption, like the salary rate assumption, has associated with it an underlying theory that was discussed at an earlier point. This theory states that this assumption consists also of three components: one to account for the risk-free rate of return, one to account for the risk inherent in the portfolio of assets held, and one to account for inflation. These components, it will be remembered, are 2 percent, 1 percent and 4 percent respectively, for the standard assumptions.

Table 15–11 gives the results of introducing the various interest rate components and varying the inflation rate around the 4 percent standard assumption. A brief inspection of this table shows that costs are more sensitive to the interest rate assumption than they are to any parameter thus far studied. For example, eliminating the interest assumption entirely causes costs to increase by 300 to 700 percent, depending on the cost measure.

TABLE 15–11

Effect of Interest Rate

| | | Pension Costs as a Percentage of the Cost under Standard Assumptions | | | |
| | | $^{CS}PBCM$ | | $ABCM$ | |
Interest Assumption	$\sum(PVFB)_x$	*NC*	*AL*	*NC*	*AL*
Zero rate.	755.1	634.8	322.0	454.5	390.3
Risk-free rate of 2%	387.5	374.3	322.0	454.5	390.3
Risk-free plus risk premium of 1%	285.5	286.9	229.8	217.0	201.3
Risk-free rate plus risk premium, plus inflation of:					
2%	163.5	168.8	138.6	143.5	138.7
4%	100.0	100.0	100.0	100.0	100.0
6%	64.9	60.1	73.3	72.8	74.9
8%	44.3	36.9	54.7	55.1	57.9

A more meaningful analysis is the impact of a change in the inflation assumption. The $^{CS}PBCM$ normal cost is the most sensitive of the various cost measures to such changes. A zero rate of inflation (or a 3 percent rate of interest) has the effect of increasing the $^{CS}PBCM$ normal cost nearly three fold, while an 8 percent inflation rate (or an 11 percent interest rate) reduces costs to one third of the cost under the standard assumption. The impact on the $(PVFB)_x$ function is nearly the same as that on the $^{CS}PBCM$ normal cost, while the costs under the ABCM and the $^{CS}PBCM$ actuarial liability are less sensitive to changes in the interest rate. Nevertheless, for these latter cost measures, a zero inflation rate doubles costs while an 8 percent rate reduces them by 40 percent from the level under the 4 percent standard inflation rate assumption.

Although not shown in Table 15–11, it turns out that each of the component benefit costs making up total costs is affected to the same extent as total costs, except for the vested benefit cost component. The costs of the latter benefit were found to be noticeably more sensitive to changes in the interest rate for each of the various cost measures. Thus, contrary to the vesting cost percentage of an individual plan participant as given in equation (10.4b), which was found to be independent of the interest rate assumption, the vesting cost percentage of the entire plan is somewhat sensitive, and is inversely related to the interest assumption.

The rule-of-thumb that pension costs are altered by 6 to 7 percent for each one fourth of a percentage change in the interest rate is well known and used often in connection with pension plans. If we take the midpoint of this range, or 6.5 percent, the rule tells us that a 1 percent increase in the interest rate assumption will reduce costs by 22 percent $[100 \cdot (1 - 1.065^{-4})]$, while a 1 percent reduction in the interest rate will increase costs by 29 percent $[100 \cdot (1.065^4 - 1)]$. The results of a 2 percent change in the interest rate are $(1.065)^{-8} = 0.60$ and $(1.065)^8 = 1.65$, respectively, and the results of a 4 percent deviation are $(1.065)^{-16} = 0.37$ and $(1.065)^{16} = 2.74$. Both the $\sum(\text{PVFB})_x$ function and the ^{CS}PBCM normal cost conform to this rule remarkably well, but the ^{CS}PBCM actuarial liability and the costs under the ABCM appear to follow a 4 percent rule rather than the 6 to 7 percent rule.

The inflation component of the interest rate assumption was altered in this section without a simultaneous change in the inflation component of the salary scale. While the results are both interesting and important, it is believed that the sensitivity of pension costs to the inflation parameter as analyzed in the next section, is somewhat more meaningful and valuable.

INFLATION RATES

The effects of changing the assumed rate of inflation, a component of both the salary rate and interest rate assumptions, is analyzed in this section. Conventional wisdom suggests that equal changes in the interest rate and salary rate (in this case being brought about by a change in the inflation component of each) will tend to wash out, since these two assumptions have counterbalancing effects on pension costs. Upon some reflection, it is clear that this cannot be the case, since the salary scale operates only up to the participant's age 65, while the interest discount factor extends to the end of the assumed life span.[1] Thus, a change in the inflation component of the interest

---

[1] This would not be true if the plan has a cost-of-living clause, in which case it might be argued that the salary factor also extends beyond the retirement age.

assumption will have a *greater* impact on pension costs than its counterpart in the salary assumption.

The results of assuming an inflation component of zero up through 8 percent are given in Table 15–12 for the $\sum(PVFB)_x$ function only, since nearly identical percentages were found for the other cost measures, except for the ABCM actuarial liability which turned out to be somewhat more sensitive. Pension costs, as expected, are inversely related to changes in the inflation rate. In other words, the higher the rate of inflation the lower will be the dollar cost of the plan *for the current year*. Although the *dollar* cost of a plan experiencing high inflation will eventually be greater at some future point in time than if lower inflation were to be experienced, the cost as a *percentage of salary* will be less the higher the rate of inflation.

TABLE 15–12

Effect of Inflation Rate

Inflation Component	Interest Rate and (approximate) Salary Rate	$\sum(PVFB)_x$ Cost as a Percentage of the Cost under Standard Assumptions
0	3	156.9
2	5	123.4
4	7	100.0
6	9	83.0
8	11	70.3

Theoretically, if a sponsoring firm's earnings were to be perfectly insulated from the effects of inflation, then greater rates of inflation might be viewed as a cost reducing factor in a relative sense. The more typical case, however, is where inflation injures the earning potential of the firm and the corresponding increase in pension dollar costs simply adds to other problems created by inflation. The effects of inflation are even more serious if the inflation component in the salary assumption is allowed to take effect at ages beyond 65. The cost associated with cost-of-living escalators, it will be remembered, was analyzed in the previous chapter. Nevertheless, it is important to point out here that, if the inflation component used in the salary scale were to extend to retirement ages through a cost-of-living escalator, then both the current dollar cost and the future cost as a percent of salary would be insensitive to the rate of inflation assumed in the salary and interest rate parameter.

Chapter 16

Pension Cost Forecasts

GENERAL CONCEPT

The annual actuarial valuation of a pension plan involves the determination of its liabilities and costs for the current year only. A pension cost forecast, on the other hand, involves estimating the liabilities and costs of the pension system both for the current year and for several years into the future, the number of future years being determined according to the purpose of the forecast. One aspect of a pension cost forecast is the projection of the underlying pension plan population, which involves assumptions as to the number of active employees who will die, terminate, become disabled, and retire in each future year, the corresponding number of new employees who will be hired into the population, and the number of nonactive employees who will die during each year. In addition, the salaries of active employees must be projected to reflect increases due to merit, productivity, and inflation, while the assets of the plan are projected to reflect future employer (and possibly employee) contributions, benefit payment, and investment yields. In essence, a pension cost forecast involves a series of annual actuarial valuations, where each valuation is performed on successive years' projections of the current plan population.

Purpose of Forecasts

An annual actuarial valuation has as two of its main objectives the determination of the plan's current funding status and the contributions to be made to the plan. A pension cost forecast also has these objectives, but in addition seeks to determine the funding status and the cost of the plan over some future planning horizon rather than for the current year only. Pension cost forecasts are particularly useful in assessing the long-run financial implications of plan changes. Generally, when a provision of the plan is changed, a supplemental liability is created. For example, shifting from a career average to a final average benefit formula, unless the change does not apply retroactively, creates a supplemental liability and, in turn, a supplemental cost for at least 10 years and possibly as long as 30 years under ERISA. In any event, a static sensitivity analysis, like those provided in the previous two chapters, gives only a point-in-time "snapshot" of the actual cost impact of the change. If the supplemental cost were to be included in the sensitivity analysis, the resulting cost impact would exceed the long-run cost impact on the plan if the supplemental cost is excluded. While calculating the supplemental cost separately for the current year allows one to view both the short-run and long-run cost, the pattern of costs in the intermediate years would be unclear, especially if one were interested in the cost as a percentage of expected salaries in future years.

Similarly, if one or more of the more significant actuarial assumptions were to be changed, or if consideration were being given to the use of another actuarial cost method, a pension cost forecast would provide the future financial consequences of such changes, in terms of both the associated cash flow and the funding status of the plan.

Another broad purpose of pension cost forecasts is to monitor the financial effects of experience deviations from the actuarial assumptions used for the plan. For example, a low salary scale may be assumed in combination with a low interest rate on the theory that investment gains will make up for the "losses" due to higher-than-assumed salary increases. This assumption and other so-called "combination best-estimate" assumptions may be tested by a pension cost forecast, as can the effects of a zero or negative population growth rate. Of particular interest for some pension systems is the future cash flow as the underlying population becomes progressively overmature and/or the implications of the plan's cash flow on investment policy.

Actuarial Assumptions

It is important to make a distinction between valuation assumptions and projection assumptions. Valuation assumptions are those used in the year-to-year actuarial valuations which are conducted on the projected pension plan populations. They are needed to derive the annual contributions to the plan and to calculate the year-to-year liabilities of the projected plan populations. A liability measure based on valuation assumptions, however, may not be the most appropriate one to use in determining the funding status of the plan unless the valuation assumptions are best estimates.

Projection assumptions are those which are used to project the population forward year-by-year during the projection period, that is, they predict the actual experience of the population in future years. It is of utmost importance to the validity of the pension forecast that experience assumptions represent individual, not combination, best estimates. Otherwise, an error associated with the underlying population and salary structure introduces an error into the cash flow of the plan, both in terms of contributions paid in and benefits paid out. This error introduces still another error in the asset position of the plan, an error that is cumulative in nature.

The simplest type of pension forecast is one having identical projection assumptions and valuation assumptions, but this commonality is seldom appropriate. If, in fact, the two types of assumptions are identical, there will be no projected actuarial gains or losses during the projection period. If projection assumptions deviate from valuation assumptions, which is the more typical case, then gains or losses will occur. The financial consequences of these actuarial deviations are factored into the financial forecast of the plan in precisely the same way that such gains or losses are handled in the actual operation of the plan year by year.

The projection assumptions associated with a given pension cost forecast can either be deterministic or stochastic in nature. Deterministic assumptions imply a predetermined set of decrement rates, salary rates, and investment rates for each year of the projection period to which the population is exposed. The experience rates need not be the same year after year, but they are nevertheless predetermined. For example, the yield on assets, which is one of the most important projection assumptions, might be set at 9 percent for the current year, 8 percent for the following year, and so forth to the end of the projection period. Another example of a changing, but nevertheless deterministic projection assumption, is a gradual increase in the number of early retirements taking place over time. As noted previously, the projection assumptions need not be the same as the valuation assumptions. For instance, the valuation assumptions of a plan may assume that all retirements occur at age 63, whereas the early retirements that actually take place during the course of the projections might occur at all possible early retirement ages.

Stochastic projection assumptions, on the other hand, imply a predetermined set of distribution parameters—again not necessarily constant over time—from which random variates representing experience rates are developed. As an example, the rate of return on investments in year t of the projection might be a random variate from a normal distribution with a mean value of 9 percent and a standard deviation of 12 percent. A given forecast may have a mixture of deterministic and stochastic projection assumptions, the most common stochastic assumptions being salary and investment rates. A deterministic forecast produces the future financial status of the plan in expected value form, while a stochastic forecast produces a distribution of the plan's future financial status. Finally, it should be clear that a deterministic forecast involves only one population projection, whereas a stochastic forecast requires multiple projections, the number of which must be sufficient to produce a satisfactory distribution of results from which confidence intervals and probabilistic statements can be derived.

FINANCIAL FORECASTS UNDER VARIOUS ACTUARIAL COST METHODS

The deterministic financial forecast procedure provides an excellent tool for analyzing pension costs under various actuarial cost methods over time. The purpose of this section is to show the results of using different actuarial cost methods in connection with the 50-year simulated plan population as set forth in Chapter 4. In the interest of simplicity, the experience assumptions and the valuation assumptions are identical throughout the 50-year financial forecast period. A total of nine actuarial cost methods are analyzed:[1]

CDCM = Current Disbursement Cost Method.

TBCM = Terminal (Benefit) Cost Method.

ABCM = Accrued Benefit Cost Method.

^{CS}ABCM = Modified Accrued Benefit Cost Method, with the projected benefit allocated as a constant percentage of salary.

---

[1] CDCM, which refers to the current disbursement cost method, reflects the pay-as-you-go costs of the plan. TBCM, which denotes the terminal (benefit) cost method, has a normal cost equal to the lump sum cost of an employee's pension benefit at this date of leaving employment and an actuarial liability equal to the liability of all non-active employees.

^{CA}ABCM = Modified Accrued Benefit Cost Method, with the projected benefit allocated as a constant dollar amount.

^{CS}PBCM = Projected Benefit Cost Method, with costs equal to a constant percentage of salary.

^{CA}PBCM = Projected Benefit Cost Method, with costs equal to a constant dollar amount.

^{CS}APBCM = Aggregate Projected Benefit Cost Method, with costs equal to a constant percentage of salary.

^{CA}APBCM = Aggregate Projected Benefit Cost Method, with costs equal to a constant dollar amount.

Unless otherwise stated, the above noted cost methods represent the "with supplemental" liability versions, and the two aggregate cost methods assume that the actuarial liability under each method's individual counterpart is frozen at the outset of the financial forecast. The projection assumes that the pension plan is first adopted at the beginning of the forecast, with retroactive service credit being given to all active employees, and there are no non-active members in the initial population. Table 4–7 in Chapter 4 provides various statistics on the population used in the experiment.

Normal Cost Comparisons

A comparison of the normal costs under each actuarial cost method is given in Table 16–1. The data are expressed as a percentage of the projected salary in each future year, and the contributions to the pension plan would equal these percentages if there were no supplemental costs, a subject taken up in the following section.

Since pension costs in this chapter and the next are given as a percentage of salary, it is important to remember that the benefit formula provides a benefit equal to 1.5 percent of final average salary per year of service. The cost results, of course, are directly proportional to the 1.5 percent, allowing one to use simple proportions to find the cost of the plan as a percentage of salary under a benefit formula using a larger or smaller percentage than 1.5 percent.

An interesting and intuitively appealing uniformity exists among the data in Table 16–1. The cost methods that are the least expensive at the outset are the most expensive near the end of the forecast period, and vice versa. The ^{CS}APBCM, as expected, develops a cost which is

TABLE 16–1

Normal Cost as a Percentage of Salary under Various Actuarial Cost Methods

Year	CDCM	TBCM	ABCM	$^{CS}ABCM$	$^{CA}ABCM$	$^{CS}PBCM$	$^{CS}APBCM$	$^{CA}PBCM$	$^{CA}APBCM$
0.	0.0	1.1	2.7	3.3	4.9	5.8	5.7	7.2	6.8
1.	0.1	1.1	2.8	3.3	5.0	5.8	5.7	7.1	6.8
2.	0.1	1.2	2.9	3.4	5.0	5.8	5.7	7.1	6.8
3.	0.2	1.3	3.0	3.5	5.1	5.8	5.7	7.0	6.8
4.	0.3	1.4	3.1	3.6	5.1	5.8	5.7	6.9	6.8
5.	0.4	1.5	3.2	3.7	5.2	5.8	5.7	6.8	6.7
6.	0.4	1.6	3.3	3.8	5.2	5.8	5.7	6.8	6.7
7.	0.5	1.7	3.4	3.9	5.3	5.8	5.7	6.7	6.6
8.	0.6	1.8	3.6	4.0	5.3	5.8	5.7	6.6	6.5
9.	0.7	1.9	3.7	4.1	5.4	5.8	5.7	6.5	6.5
10.	0.8	2.1	3.8	4.2	5.4	5.8	5.7	6.5	6.4
11.	0.9	2.3	4.0	4.3	5.5	5.8	5.7	6.4	6.3
12.	1.0	2.4	4.1	4.4	5.5	5.8	5.7	6.3	6.3
13.	1.1	2.6	4.2	4.6	5.6	5.8	5.7	6.2	6.2
14.	1.2	2.8	4.4	4.7	5.6	5.8	5.7	6.2	6.1
15.	1.3	3.0	4.5	4.8	5.6	5.8	5.7	6.1	6.1
16.	1.5	3.2	4.6	4.9	5.7	5.8	5.7	6.0	6.0
17.	1.6	3.4	4.8	5.0	5.7	5.8	5.7	6.0	5.9
18.	1.8	3.6	4.9	5.1	5.7	5.8	5.7	5.9	5.9
19.	1.9	3.7	5.1	5.3	5.8	5.8	5.7	5.8	5.8
20.	2.1	4.0	5.2	5.4	5.8	5.8	5.7	5.8	5.7
21.	2.3	4.2	5.3	5.5	5.8	5.8	5.7	5.7	5.7
22.	2.5	4.4	5.5	5.6	5.9	5.8	5.7	5.6	5.6
23.	2.7	4.6	5.6	5.7	5.9	5.8	5.7	5.6	5.6
24.	3.0	4.9	5.8	5.8	5.9	5.8	5.7	5.5	5.5
25.	3.2	5.1	5.9	5.9	5.9	5.8	5.7	5.5	5.5
26.	3.5	5.3	6.0	6.0	6.0	5.8	5.7	5.4	5.4
27.	3.7	5.6	6.2	6.1	6.0	5.8	5.7	5.4	5.4
28.	4.0	5.8	6.3	6.2	6.0	5.8	5.7	5.3	5.3
29.	4.3	6.1	6.4	6.4	6.0	5.7	5.7	5.3	5.2
30.	4.6	6.4	6.6	6.5	6.1	5.7	5.7	5.2	5.2
31.	4.9	6.6	6.7	6.6	6.1	5.7	5.7	5.2	5.1
32.	5.3	6.9	6.9	6.7	6.1	5.7	5.7	5.1	5.1
33.	5.6	7.2	7.0	6.8	6.1	5.7	5.7	5.1	5.0
34.	6.0	7.4	7.1	6.9	6.1	5.7	5.7	5.0	5.0
35.	6.4	7.8	7.3	7.0	6.2	5.7	5.7	5.0	4.9
36.	6.8	8.1	7.4	7.1	6.2	5.7	5.7	4.9	4.9
37.	7.2	8.3	7.5	7.2	6.2	5.7	5.7	4.8	4.8
38.	7.7	8.6	7.7	7.3	6.2	5.7	5.7	4.8	4.8
39.	8.2	9.0	7.8	7.5	6.3	5.7	5.7	4.7	4.7
40.	8.7	9.3	8.0	7.6	6.3	5.7	5.7	4.7	4.6
41.	9.2	9.6	8.2	7.7	6.3	5.7	5.7	4.6	4.6
42.	9.8	10.0	8.3	7.9	6.4	5.7	5.7	4.5	4.5
43.	10.4	10.3	8.5	8.0	6.4	5.7	5.7	4.5	4.4
44.	11.0	10.7	8.7	8.2	6.5	5.7	5.7	4.4	4.3
45.	11.7	11.2	8.9	8.3	6.5	5.7	5.7	4.3	4.2
46.	12.5	11.6	9.2	8.5	6.5	5.7	5.7	4.2	4.1
47.	13.3	12.1	9.4	8.7	6.6	5.7	5.7	4.1	4.0
48.	14.2	12.7	9.7	9.0	6.7	5.7	5.7	3.9	3.9
49.	15.2	13.3	10.1	9.2	6.7	5.7	5.7	3.8	3.7
50.	16.4	14.0	10.4	9.6	6.8	5.7	5.7	3.6	3.6
∞.	9.7	8.0	6.9	6.7	6.0	5.7	5.7	5.2	5.2

constant throughout the 50 year period, equal to 5.7 percent of salary. The normal cost during the first year ranges from zero under the CDCM to a high of 7.2 under the ^{CA}PBCM. At the other end of the projection period, the CDCM is seen to equal 16.4 percent of salary while the ^{CA}PBCM is only 3.6 percent. Interestingly, the cost under each cost method, except the CDCM, is nearly the same around the 25th year of the financial projection, totaling 5 to 6 percent of salary.

The various modifications of the accrued benefit cost method tend to moderate the increase in costs under the conventional ABCM. Also the costs under the ^{CA}PBCM and ^{CA}APBCM are seen to decrease substantially over the 50-year period as a percentage of salary. The cost increase under the accrued benefit cost methods, and the decrease under the CA version of the projected benefit cost method, are the result of extreme structural shifts in the underlying population, and it is quite likely that a given plan would have a more stable maturity status than that depicted by the population used in Table 16–1. This being the case, the cost trends brought about by changes in the underlying population would not be as great as those shown.

The normal cost percentage for a perfectly mature population is given at the bottom of Table 16–1. Here one can see that the CDCM is about twice as expensive as the projected benefit cost methods, and that the accrued benefit cost methods as a percentage of salary are about 1 percent more costly than the projected benefit cost methods.

The costs presented in this section are not as general as one might initially believe. The rate of inflation plays a significant role in the relationship between benefits paid out and current salary. The higher the rate of inflation the lower will be the costs under the CDCM when expressed as a percentage salary—provided retirement benefits are not increased along with inflation. The benefit formula of the plan would also have an important bearing on the relative cost among actuarial cost methods and, of course, each of the actuarial assumptions plays some role in generating different normal costs among the various measures. There is, however, one parameter change under a stationary population assumption that causes all methods to develop the same normal cost, namely, a zero rate of interest. The cost for this special case is 9.7 percent of salary under the standard assumptions used in Table 16–1, that is, the cost under the CDCM for the mature population. As the interest rate exceeds zero, the equilibrium costs under each method are a function of the degree to which each method funds the retirement benefit in advance. Since the projected benefit cost methods advance fund to a greater extent than other methods, the long-run normal cost is the least under these methods. Thus, even though the data in Table 16–1 are not as general as one would like to have them, they nevertheless portray the dominant pattern of normal cost among actuarial cost methods for various population maturity statuses.

Normal Cost Plus Supplemental Cost Comparisons

It is not sufficient, for the typical plan, to analyze only the normal cost, since there is generally an associated supplemental cost. The purpose of this section is to present the total costs of the pension plan during the 50-year period, first under the assumption that the initial supplemental liability is amortized on a level basis over a 30-year period, and second, assuming that the initial supplemental liability is amortized by precisely the same methodology as the particular cost method amortizes the non-supplemental liability of the plan, that is, each cost method on a "without supplemental liability" basis.

The results under the 30-year amortization procedure are set forth in Table 16–2. The costs under both the CDCM and the TBCM— neither of which has a supplemental cost for the model plan—are provided for comparison purposes, as are the normal cost values under all methods beyond the 30-year amortization period. Since the supplemental liability is amortized on a level basis, while costs are expressed as a percentage of an ever-increasing salary, the impact of the supplemental cost is the greatest in the first year and diminishes in importance thereafter. The ABCM in the first year shows a total cost of 3.8 percent, up from a normal cost of 2.7 percent of salary, and the ^{CA}PBCM shows a cost of 12.2 percent, up from 7.2 percent. The increase is greater for the latter method because the initial actuarial liability is substantially greater under the projected benefit cost methods than it is under the accrued benefit cost methods.

The 30-year amortization procedure causes the ^{CA}ABCM to develop the smoothest 50-year cost pattern, beginning at 7.7 percent of salary, decreasing to a low of 6.1 and increasing again to 6.8 at the end of 50 years. Both of the projected benefit cost methods are seen to develop rather steeply decreasing total costs as a percentage of salary during the first ten years of the amortization period, after which the decrease becomes more gradual until the supplemental liability is fully amortized in the 30th year of the plan operation.

It was pointed out in earlier chapters that the various individual accrued benefit and projected benefit cost methods could be designed

TABLE 16–2

Normal Cost Plus Supplemental Cost (on a level 30-year amortization basis) as a Percentage of Salary

Year	CDCM	TBCM	ABCM	$^{CS}ABCM$	$^{CA}ABCM$	$^{CS}PBCM$	$^{CS}APBCM$	$^{CA}PBCM$	$^{CA}APBCM$
0.....	0.0	1.1	3.8	4.7	7.7	9.4	9.4	12.2	12.2
1.....	0.1	1.1	3.7	4.6	7.4	9.0	9.0	11.6	11.6
2.....	0.1	1.2	3.7	4.5	7.2	8.6	8.6	11.0	11.0
3.....	0.2	1.3	3.7	4.5	7.0	8.3	8.3	10.5	10.6
4.....	0.3	1.4	3.7	4.5	6.9	8.1	8.0	10.1	10.1
5.....	0.4	1.5	3.8	4.5	6.7	7.8	7.8	9.7	9.8
6.....	0.4	1.6	3.9	4.5	6.6	7.6	7.6	9.4	9.4
7.....	0.5	1.7	3.9	4.6	6.6	7.5	7.4	9.0	9.1
8.....	0.6	1.8	4.0	4.6	6.5	7.3	7.3	8.8	8.8
9.....	0.7	1.9	4.1	4.7	6.5	7.2	7.2	8.5	8.6
10.....	0.8	2.1	4.2	4.7	6.4	7.1	7.0	8.3	8.3
11.....	0.9	2.3	4.3	4.8	6.4	7.0	6.9	8.0	8.1
12.....	1.0	2.4	4.4	4.9	6.4	6.9	6.8	7.8	7.9
13.....	1.1	2.6	4.5	5.0	6.3	6.8	6.8	7.7	7.7
14.....	1.2	2.8	4.6	5.1	6.3	6.7	6.7	7.5	7.5
15.....	1.3	3.0	4.8	5.2	6.3	6.7	6.6	7.3	7.4
16.....	1.5	3.2	4.9	5.2	6.3	6.6	6.6	7.2	7.2
17.....	1.6	3.4	5.0	5.3	6.3	6.6	6.5	7.0	7.1
18.....	1.8	3.6	5.1	5.4	6.3	6.5	6.5	6.9	6.9
19.....	1.9	3.7	5.3	5.5	6.3	6.5	6.4	6.8	6.8
20.....	2.1	4.0	5.4	5.6	6.3	6.4	6.4	6.6	6.7
21.....	2.3	4.2	5.5	5.7	6.3	6.4	6.3	6.5	6.6
22.....	2.5	4.4	5.6	5.8	6.3	6.3	6.3	6.4	6.5
23.....	2.7	4.6	5.8	5.9	6.3	6.3	6.3	6.3	6.4
24.....	3.0	4.9	5.9	6.0	6.3	6.3	6.2	6.2	6.3
25.....	3.2	5.1	6.0	6.1	6.3	6.2	6.2	6.1	6.2
26.....	3.5	5.3	6.2	6.2	6.3	6.2	6.2	6.1	6.1
27.....	3.7	5.6	6.3	6.3	6.3	6.2	6.2	6.0	6.0
28.....	4.0	5.8	6.4	6.4	6.3	6.2	6.1	5.9	5.9
29.....	4.3	6.1	6.6	6.5	6.3	6.1	6.1	5.8	5.8
30.....	4.6	6.4	6.6	6.5	6.1	5.7	5.7	5.2	5.2
31.....	4.9	6.6	6.7	6.6	6.1	5.7	5.7	5.2	5.1
32.....	5.3	6.9	6.9	6.7	6.1	5.7	5.7	5.1	5.1
33.....	5.6	7.2	7.0	6.8	6.1	5.7	5.7	5.1	5.0
34.....	6.0	7.4	7.1	6.9	6.1	5.7	5.7	5.0	5.0
35.....	6.4	7.8	7.3	7.0	6.2	5.7	5.7	5.0	4.9
36.....	6.8	8.1	7.4	7.1	6.2	5.7	5.7	4.9	4.9
37.....	7.2	8.3	7.5	7.2	6.2	5.7	5.7	4.8	4.8
38.....	7.7	8.6	7.7	7.3	6.2	5.7	5.7	4.8	4.8
39.....	8.2	9.0	7.8	7.5	6.3	5.7	5.7	4.7	4.7
40.....	8.7	9.3	8.0	7.6	6.3	5.7	5.7	4.7	4.6
41.....	9.2	9.6	8.2	7.7	6.3	5.7	5.7	4.6	4.6
42.....	9.8	10.0	8.3	7.9	6.4	5.7	5.7	4.5	4.5
43.....	10.4	10.3	8.5	8.0	6.4	5.7	5.7	4.5	4.4
44.....	11.0	10.7	8.7	8.2	6.5	5.7	5.7	4.4	4.3
45.....	11.7	11.2	8.9	8.3	6.5	5.7	5.7	4.3	4.2
46.....	12.5	11.6	9.2	8.5	6.5	5.7	5.7	4.2	4.1
47.....	13.3	12.1	9.4	8.7	6.6	5.7	5.7	4.1	4.0
48.....	14.2	12.7	9.7	9.0	6.7	5.7	5.7	3.9	3.9
49.....	15.2	13.3	10.1	9.2	6.7	5.7	5.7	3.8	3.7
50.....	16.4	14.0	10.4	9.6	6.8	5.7	5.7	3.6	3.6
∞.....	9.7	8.0	6.9	6.7	6.0	5.7	5.7	5.2	5.2

to amortize each individual participant's initial actuarial liability over a period from his attained age until his retirement age. In the case of the accrued benefit cost methods, this involves allocating B_r over the ages z to r if the plan starts when the participant is age z, while in the case of the projected benefit cost methods, the entire cost of the projected benefit is accounted for over this period. Furthermore, the aggregate methods can be operated without freezing the supplemental liability at the outset, by simply amortizing the difference between the aggregate $(PVFB)_x$ and the assets of the plan over the future lifetimes (or salaries) of all plan participants.

Table 16–3 shows total plan costs under this procedure as a percentage of the total cost under the level 30-year amortization procedure as analyzed in Table 16–2. A substantial difference exists between the two procedures for handling the plan's supplemental liability, with the 30-year approach being considerably less costly in the first few years. An exception to this is the cost under the ^{CS}APBCM where the cost difference is less than 5 percent for any year during the projection period. The cost differences given in Table 16–3, for all practical purposes are minor after five years. The "without" supplemental liability procedure is seen to be more expensive for about ten years, to be less expensive for the next 20 years, and then to be more expensive until the last orginal employee leaves the plan (that is, after 45 years). Exceptions to the latter are the aggregate methods which approach the cost of the plan under the 30-year amortization asymptotically and are never actually equal to their individual counterparts.

Funding Status Comparisons

The data in Table 16–4 show the assets under each actuarial cost method as a percentage of the method's actuarial liability. A percentage is not shown for the CDCM since it develops neither assets nor an actuarial liability. The percentages are not shown for the aggregate methods either, since they do not develop an actuarial liability in the conventional sense. However, since their asset positions are nearly identical to those of their individual counterparts, and their actuarial liabilities—if indeed they have them—are probably best determinable from their individual counterparts, the percentages under the ^{CS}PBCM and ^{CA}PBCM are sufficient to describe the funding statuses of the two aggregate methods.

Assets are measured at the beginning of the year, prior to the normal cost and supplemental costs then due, and they are compared to the

TABLE 16–3

Normal Cost Plus Supplemental Cost (on an actuarial cost method basis) as a Percentage of Normal Cost Plus Supplemental Cost (on a level 30-year amortization basis)

Year	ABCM	$^{CS}ABCM$	$^{CA}ABCM$	$^{CS}PBCM$	$^{CS}APBCM$	$^{CA}PBCM$	$^{CA}APBCM$
0.	120.3	116.0	116.0	118.4	104.2	141.3	142.9
1.	108.3	106.4	109.1	110.9	103.1	128.6	132.9
2.	103.9	102.8	106.0	107.2	102.2	120.3	124.1
3.	101.7	101.1	104.3	104.9	101.4	114.3	117.2
4.	100.7	100.3	103.1	103.3	100.7	109.7	111.7
5.	100.2	100.0	102.3	102.2	100.2	106.1	107.1
6.	99.8	99.7	101.5	101.3	99.7	103.2	103.5
7.	99.5	99.6	100.9	100.6	99.3	100.8	100.6
8.	99.4	99.5	100.4	100.0	99.0	98.9	98.2
9.	99.3	99.5	100.0	99.6	98.7	97.3	96.3
10.	99.4	99.5	99.7	99.2	98.5	96.1	94.8
11.	99.3	99.5	99.4	98.9	98.3	95.1	93.6
12.	99.3	99.5	99.1	98.6	98.1	94.2	92.7
13.	99.3	99.5	98.9	98.3	98.0	93.5	91.9
14.	99.3	99.5	98.7	98.1	97.9	93.0	91.4
15.	99.3	99.5	98.5	97.9	97.8	92.5	91.0
16.	99.2	99.4	98.3	97.7	97.7	92.2	90.7
17.	99.2	99.3	98.1	97.5	97.7	91.9	90.5
18.	99.1	99.3	97.9	97.3	97.7	91.7	90.4
19.	99.1	99.2	97.8	97.1	97.6	91.5	90.4
20.	99.1	99.1	97.6	96.9	97.6	91.4	90.4
21.	99.0	99.1	97.5	96.7	97.6	91.3	90.4
22.	99.0	99.0	97.3	96.6	97.6	91.2	90.5
23.	98.9	98.9	97.2	96.4	97.6	91.2	90.6
24.	98.9	98.8	97.0	96.2	97.6	91.2	90.7
25.	98.9	98.7	96.9	96.1	97.6	91.2	90.9
26.	98.9	98.7	96.8	96.0	97.6	91.3	91.0
27.	98.9	98.6	96.8	95.9	97.6	91.4	91.2
28.	98.8	98.6	96.7	95.8	97.6	91.4	91.3
29.	98.8	98.5	96.6	95.7	97.7	91.5	91.5
30.	100.5	100.8	101.2	101.9	104.1	100.8	101.4
31.	100.4	100.7	101.0	101.6	103.8	100.7	101.2
32.	100.3	100.5	100.8	101.3	103.6	100.5	101.1
33.	100.2	100.4	100.6	101.0	103.4	100.4	101.0
34.	100.2	100.3	100.5	100.8	103.2	100.3	100.9
35.	100.1	100.3	100.4	100.7	103.0	100.2	100.8
36.	100.1	100.2	100.3	100.5	102.8	100.2	100.7
37.	100.1	100.1	100.2	100.4	102.6	100.1	100.6
38.	100.0	100.1	100.1	100.3	102.5	100.1	100.5
39.	100.0	100.1	100.1	100.2	102.4	100.0	100.5
40.	100.0	100.0	100.1	100.1	102.3	100.0	100.4
41.	100.0	100.0	100.0	100.1	102.2	100.0	100.4
42.	100.0	100.0	100.0	100.0	102.1	100.0	100.4
43.	100.0	100.0	100.0	100.0	102.0	100.0	100.3
44.	100.0	100.0	100.0	100.0	101.9	100.0	100.3
45.	100.0	100.0	100.0	100.0	101.8	100.0	100.3
46.	100.0	100.0	100.0	100.0	101.8	100.0	100.3
47.	100.0	100.0	100.0	100.0	101.7	100.0	100.2
48.	100.0	100.0	100.0	100.0	101.7	100.0	100.2
49.	100.0	100.0	100.0	100.0	101.6	100.0	100.2
50.	100.0	100.0	100.0	100.0	101.6	100.0	100.2

TABLE 16–4

Plan Assets as a Percentage of the Actuarial Liability (on a level 30-year amortization basis)

Year	TBCM	ABCM	$^{CS}ABCM$	$^{CA}ABCM$	$^{CS}PBCM$	$^{CA}PBCM$
0	0.0	0.0	0.0	0.0	0.0	0.0
1	100.0	22.2	20.8	18.4	17.3	16.4
2	100.0	38.5	36.4	32.9	31.3	29.8
3	100.0	50.8	48.5	44.4	42.6	40.8
4	100.0	60.2	57.9	53.8	51.7	49.9
5	100.0	67.6	65.4	61.3	59.3	57.4
6	100.0	73.4	71.3	67.5	65.5	63.6
7	100.0	78.0	76.2	72.6	70.7	68.8
8	100.0	81.8	80.1	76.8	75.0	73.2
9	100.0	84.8	83.3	80.3	78.6	77.0
10	100.0	87.3	86.0	83.2	81.7	80.1
11	100.0	89.4	88.2	85.7	84.3	82.8
12	100.0	91.1	90.0	87.8	86.5	85.2
13	100.0	92.5	91.6	89.6	88.4	87.1
14	100.0	93.7	92.9	91.1	90.0	88.9
15	100.0	94.7	93.9	92.4	91.4	90.4
16	100.0	95.5	94.9	93.5	92.6	91.7
17	100.0	96.2	95.7	94.4	93.7	92.8
18	100.0	96.8	96.4	95.3	94.6	93.8
19	100.0	97.4	96.9	96.0	95.4	94.7
20	100.0	97.8	97.4	96.6	96.1	95.5
21	100.0	98.2	97.9	97.1	96.7	96.2
22	100.0	98.5	98.2	97.6	97.3	96.8
23	100.0	98.8	98.6	98.1	97.7	97.4
24	100.0	99.0	98.9	98.4	98.2	97.9
25	100.0	99.2	99.1	98.8	98.6	98.3
26	100.0	99.4	99.3	99.1	98.9	98.7
27	100.0	99.6	99.5	99.3	99.2	99.1
28	100.0	99.8	99.7	99.6	99.5	99.4
29	100.0	99.9	99.9	99.8	99.8	99.7
30	100.0	100.0	100.0	100.0	100.0	100.0
31	100.0	100.0	100.0	100.0	100.0	100.0
32	100.0	100.0	100.0	100.0	100.0	100.0
33	100.0	100.0	100.0	100.0	100.0	100.0
34	100.0	100.0	100.0	100.0	100.0	100.0
35	100.0	100.0	100.0	100.0	100.0	100.0
36	100.0	100.0	100.0	100.0	100.0	100.0
37	100.0	100.0	100.0	100.0	100.0	100.0
38	100.0	100.0	100.0	100.0	100.0	100.0
39	100.0	100.0	100.0	100.0	100.0	100.0
40	100.0	100.0	100.0	100.0	100.0	100.0
41	100.0	100.0	100.0	100.0	100.0	100.0
42	100.0	100.0	100.0	100.0	100.0	100.0
43	100.0	100.0	100.0	100.0	100.0	100.0
44	100.0	100.0	100.0	100.0	100.0	100.0
45	100.0	100.0	100.0	100.0	100.0	100.0
46	100.0	100.0	100.0	100.0	100.0	100.0
47	100.0	100.0	100.0	100.0	100.0	100.0
48	100.0	100.0	100.0	100.0	100.0	100.0
49	100.0	100.0	100.0	100.0	100.0	100.0
50	100.0	100.0	100.0	100.0	100.0	100.0

actuarial liability at this point. This explains why a zero ratio exists at the outset of the projection period. The funding status under each of the actuarial cost methods is somewhat higher for those methods that have the *smallest* total cost and vice versa. The TBCM shows full funding after one year, while the CAPBCM shows assets equal to 16.4 percent of its actuarial liability, the smallest funding rate of all.

The actuarial liability under each method except the TBCM is about 50 percent funded after only three or four years, and 75 percent funded after seven or eight years.[2] In spite of this rapid beginning, the actuarial liability is not fully funded until the end of 30 years due to the level amortization procedure.

The data in Table 16–4 point out quite clearly the deceptive nature of using the actuarial liability under a particular actuarial cost method as a measure of its funding status. That the least costly method is also the one that has a highest funding ratio is inconsistent indeed. These results suggest that perhaps the funding status of a plan should be measured by a liability independent of the actuarial cost method. Two liability measures could be used in this regard, the continuation-of-plan liability (CPL) and a termination-of-plan liability (TPL). The CPL turns out to be equal to the actuarial liability under the CAABCM, while the TPL must be calculated separately, as discussed earlier. Table 16–5 shows the funding status of the nine actuarial cost methods by comparing the assets under each method to the TPL.[3]

The CDCM, which has a zero funding status, is given for emphasis. The TBCM, contrary to the previous results, develops assets far below those that are needed on a plan termination basis. At the bottom of Table 16–5 the funding status for a perfectly mature plan is given, for which the TBCM produces a 61 percent funding level. The funding percentage of the remaining cost methods is significantly different, with the ABCM generating just enough assets to cover the TPL after 19 years. At the other extreme, the CAPBCM has assets 23 percent in excess of the TPL after only two years, and 144 percent in excess after ten years. In general, the projected benefit cost methods generate assets that exceed the plan termination liability and in many cases assets are more than double this liability. The funding level for the mature plan, as shown at the bottom of Table 16–5, is 147 percent

---

[2] These rapid funding results obtain because of no plan changes during this period, because projection assumptions are identical with valuation assumptions, because the population is relatively under mature at the outset, and because the population growth assumptions cause the plan's initial supplemental liability to dwindle in importance fairly rapidly.

[3] The TPL is calculated for all employees irrespective of their vesting status.

TABLE 16-5

Plan Assets as a Percentage of the Termination-of-Plan Liability (on a level 30-year amortization basis)

Year	CDCM	TBCM	ABCM	$^{CS}ABCM$	$^{CA}ABCM$	$^{CS}PBCM$	$^{CS}APBCM$	$^{CA}PBCM$	$^{CA}APBCM$
0. 0	0	0	0	0	0	0	0	0
1. 0	6	22	28	45	55	55	71	71
2. 0	11	38	48	78	95	94	123	122
3. 0	15	51	63	102	123	123	160	159
4. 0	18	60	75	120	145	144	186	186
5. 0	20	68	84	134	161	160	206	206
6. 0	23	74	91	144	172	172	220	220
7. 0	25	79	96	152	181	180	230	230
8. 0	26	83	101	158	187	186	237	237
9. 0	28	86	104	162	191	190	241	242
10. 0	29	89	107	165	194	193	243	244
11. 0	31	91	109	167	196	194	244	245
12. 0	32	93	111	168	196	195	244	245
13. 0	33	94	112	169	196	195	243	244
14. 0	34	96	113	169	196	195	241	242
15. 0	35	97	114	169	195	194	239	240
16. 0	37	98	115	169	194	192	236	237
17. 0	38	98	115	168	192	191	233	234
18. 0	39	99	116	167	190	189	230	231
19. 0	40	100	116	166	189	187	227	228
20. 0	41	100	116	165	187	185	224	225
21. 0	42	101	116	164	185	183	220	221
22. 0	43	101	116	163	183	181	217	218
23. 0	44	101	116	162	181	179	214	215
24. 0	44	101	116	160	179	177	211	212
25. 0	45	102	116	159	177	175	208	209
26. 0	46	102	116	158	175	174	205	206
27. 0	47	102	115	157	173	172	202	203
28. 0	48	102	115	155	171	170	199	200
29. 0	49	102	115	154	169	168	196	197
30. 0	49	102	115	153	168	166	194	194
31. 0	50	102	114	151	166	164	190	191
32. 0	51	102	114	150	164	162	188	188
33. 0	52	102	114	149	162	161	185	186
34. 0	52	102	113	147	160	159	182	183
35. 0	53	102	113	146	158	157	180	181
36. 0	54	102	113	145	157	155	177	178
37. 0	54	102	112	144	155	154	175	176
38. 0	55	102	112	143	154	152	173	174
39. 0	56	102	112	142	152	151	171	172
40. 0	56	102	112	141	151	150	169	170
41. 0	57	102	111	140	150	148	167	168
42. 0	58	102	111	139	148	147	165	166
43. 0	58	102	111	138	147	146	163	164
44. 0	59	102	111	137	146	145	161	162
45. 0	59	102	111	136	145	144	160	160
46. 0	60	102	110	135	144	142	158	159
47. 0	61	102	110	134	142	141	156	157
48. 0	61	102	110	134	141	140	155	155
49. 0	62	102	110	133	140	139	153	154
50. 0	62	102	110	132	139	138	152	152
∞. 0	61	102	110	137	147	147	164	164

and 164 percent, respectively, for the CS and CA versions of the projected benefit cost methods. The accrued benefit cost methods also generate a favorable funding status after a few years of the plan's operation and a 2 percent, 10 percent, and 37 percent redundancy in assets, respectively, are generated by the ABCM, CSABCM, and CAABCM for the mature plan.

Table 16–6 shows the funding status of the plan as measured by the CPL. Since the actuarial liability under the CAABCM is equal to the CPL, the funding status of this actuarial cost method is precisely the same (although rounded to the nearest integer) as it was in Table 16–4, where assets were compared to the actuarial liability of each method. The funding status for the mature case, which tends to be fairly representative, is 45 percent for the TBCM, 107 percent for the individual and aggregate CS versions of the projected benefit cost method, and 120 percent for the CA versions.

The marked differences between the funding statuses, as measured in Tables 16–4, 16–5, and 16–6, show that measuring the funding of a pension plan is importantly a function of the actuarial cost method *and* the liability chosen for the analysis.

TABLE 16-6

Plan Assets as a Percentage of the Continuation-of-Plan Liability (on a level 30-year amortization basis)

Year	CDCM	TBCM	ABCM	$^{CS}ABCM$	$^{CA}ABCM$	$^{CS}PBCM$	$^{CS}APBCM$	$^{CA}PBCM$	$^{CA}APBCM$
0. 0	0	0	0	0	0	0	0	0
1. 0	3	9	11	18	22	22	29	29
2. 0	5	16	20	33	40	40	52	52
3. 0	6	22	27	44	54	54	70	69
4. 0	8	27	33	54	65	65	83	83
5. 0	9	31	38	61	74	73	94	95
6. 0	11	35	43	67	81	80	103	103
7. 0	12	38	46	73	86	86	110	110
8. 0	13	40	49	77	91	91	115	116
9. 0	14	43	52	80	95	94	120	120
10. 0	15	45	54	83	98	97	123	123
11. 0	16	47	56	86	100	100	125	126
12. 0	17	48	58	88	102	102	127	128
13. 0	18	50	60	90	104	103	129	129
14. 0	18	51	61	91	105	105	130	130
15. 0	19	53	62	92	106	106	130	131
16. 0	20	54	64	93	107	106	131	131
17. 0	21	55	65	94	108	107	131	131
18. 0	22	56	66	95	108	108	131	131
19. 0	23	57	67	96	109	108	131	131
20. 0	24	58	68	97	109	108	131	131
21. 0	25	59	69	97	109	109	130	131
22. 0	26	60	70	98	109	109	130	131
23. 0	26	61	70	98	110	109	130	130
24. 0	27	62	71	98	110	109	129	130
25. 0	28	63	72	99	110	109	129	129
26. 0	29	64	73	99	110	109	128	129
27. 0	30	65	73	99	110	109	128	129
28. 0	31	66	74	100	110	109	128	128
29. 0	31	66	75	100	110	109	127	128
30. 0	32	67	75	100	110	109	127	127
31. 0	33	68	76	100	109	109	126	126
32. 0	34	68	76	100	109	108	125	126
33. 0	35	69	77	100	109	108	124	125
34. 0	36	69	77	100	109	108	124	124
35. 0	36	70	77	100	108	108	123	124
36. 0	37	71	78	100	108	107	122	123
37. 0	38	71	78	100	108	107	122	122
38. 0	39	72	79	100	108	107	121	122
39. 0	39	72	79	100	108	107	121	121
40. 0	40	73	79	100	107	106	120	121
41. 0	41	73	80	100	107	106	120	120
42. 0	42	74	80	100	107	106	119	120
43. 0	42	74	81	100	107	106	118	119
44. 0	43	75	81	100	107	106	118	118
45. 0	44	75	81	100	106	106	117	118
46. 0	44	75	82	100	106	105	117	117
47. 0	45	76	82	100	106	105	116	117
48. 0	46	76	82	100	106	105	116	116
49. 0	46	77	83	100	106	105	115	116
50. 0	47	77	83	100	105	105	115	115
∞. 0	45	74	80	100	107	107	120	120

Chapter 17

Illustrative Pension
Cost Forecasts

The objective of this chapter is to develop several illustrative pension cost projections, each of which is designed to analyze the cost impact of either a plan change or a deviation in the actual experience of the plan relative to the actuarial assumptions. The population used for the forecasts is an adaptation of the population used in the previous chapter, its characteristics being given in Table 4–8 of Chapter 4. This population is assumed to grow for a period of ten years and then remain constant for 40 years. This growth pattern creates a series of year-to-year populations that conform to many plan populations in practice, having an average age of about 40 and an average service period of about ten years. This growth pattern is in sharp contrast to the one assumed in the previous chapter, where a gradually decreasing rate of growth for 25 years followed by a gradually increasing rate of decline for 25 years was assumed. This caused the population to pass from an undermature through a mature and into an overmature status. While this maturity pattern is instructive for analyzing the cost differences between actuarial cost methods, it adds an undesirable complication for the analyses in this chapter.

The analysis is based on costs under the ABCM, the ^{CS}PBCM, and the ^{CS}APBCM. The initial supplemental liability (past service liability) is amortized on a level basis over 30 years, and for the ^{CS}APBCM the initial supplemental liability is defined to be equal to the supplemental liability under the ^{CS}PBCM. Under the ABCM and the ^{CS}PBCM, the supplemental liability created during the forecast by plan amendments is amortized on a level basis over 30 years, while the supplemental liability created by actuarial gains and losses is

216

amortized over 15 years. Under the ^{CS}APBCM, however, the supplemental liability created during the forecast from both plan amendments and actuarial gains and losses is amortized over the future salaries of plan participants. While it is true that the various forecasts given in this chapter show general trends that would hold for nearly all plans, the absolute value of the various costs analyzed would not be correct for any particular plan. By this point the reader should be well aware of the many factors that can cause pension costs to deviate among plans and for a given plan over time.

EFFECT OF CHANGE IN BENEFIT FORMULA

In Chapter 14 the long-run cost relationship between a plan with a final five-year average benefit formula and one with a career average benefit formula was analyzed. At that point the it was found that the plan's $\sum(PVFB)_x$ function under a career average plan was 52.3 percent of the liability under a final five-year average plan. Thus, the cost of amending the career average plan to a final average plan, based on this information, would be an increase of 91 percent. This estimate, however, does not consider the supplemental cost associated with the liability created by the plan amendment for service rendered prior to the year in which the amendment is made. The purpose of this section is to analyze the cost impact over a 50 year period of amending a career average plan to a final five-year average plan in the tenth year of the forecast, taking into account the supplemental costs created by the plan amendment.

Figure 17–1 shows the costs under the ^{CS}APBCM for the amended career average plan as a percentage of the costs for the final average plan, the latter costs shown as 100 percent in each year. Since the plan amendment is not made until the tenth year of the forecast, the costs of the career average plan are only about one-half as large as the cost of the final average plan. However, at the point of plan amendment, the costs of the amended career average plan become over 35 percent greater than the costs of the base plan as a result of the supplemental costs associated with the amendment. This transitional cost scales downward each year, except during the thirtieth year of the forecast, at which point the costs of the amended plan are seen to become larger percentages of the cost of the base plan. This occurs because the supplemental cost associated with the past service liability of the two plans is paid off after 30 years.

FIGURE 17–1

Costs under an Amended Career Average Plan as a Percentage of the Costs under a Final Average Plan (based on the ᶜˢAPBCM)

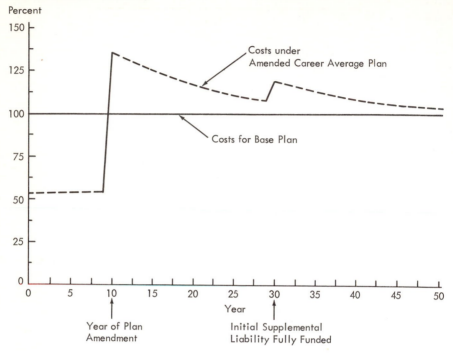

Table 17–1 shows the costs under the amended career average plan as a percentage of the costs of the base plan for all three cost methods at various points during the forecast. These data show that the cost difference between a career average plan and a final five-year average plan is less for the ABCM than for either version of the PBCM, and that the ABCM has a considerably smaller transitional cost than the two versions of the PBCM. Also, the ᶜˢAPBCM shows the greatest impact on costs at the point of plan amendment, and because of the manner in which this method amortizes the supplemental liability created by the plan amendment, a transitional cost exists beyond the 40th year of the forecast (that is, 30 years after the plan amendment).

The results in this section illustrate the deceptive nature of both short-term cost estimates of plan changes (that is, the impact on total costs for the current year) and long-term cost estimates (that is, the impact on the plan's normal cost exclusive of supplemental cost). In other words, the cost impact of a plan amendment can be analyzed properly only by projecting the plan's costs over a period of time.

TABLE 17–1

Costs under an Amended Career Average Plan as a Percentage of the Costs under a Final Average Plan

Year of Forecast	Cost Method		
	ABCM	$^{CS}PBCM$	$^{CS}APBCM$
0	66	55	54
5	63	55	54
10	114	128	136
15	110	123	126
20	108	120	118
25	106	116	112
30	107	127	119
35	106	121	113
40	100	100	109
45	100	100	106
50	100	100	104

EFFECT OF C-O-L PLAN AMENDMENT

It was observed in Chapter 14 that a 3 percent cost-of-living provision increased the $\sum(PVFB)_x$ function of active employees by 18.2 percent. In this section the analysis turns to the cost impact of amending the standard plan in the tenth year of the forecast to provide a 3-percent cost-of-living provision from that point onward. Figure 17–2 shows the results under the $^{CS}APBCM$. At the time the plan is amended, costs are increased by 36 percent, which is more than double the long-run cost of the 3 percent C-O-L provision. The cost impact each year thereafter gradually declines, except during the 30th year of the forecast, at which point the initial supplemental liability is fully funded. Forty years after the plan amendment, costs are 19 percent greater than the costs of the base plan, which is only about 2 percent greater than the true long-run cost increment under this actuarial cost method.

Table 17–2 gives the details of the cost impact under all three actuarial cost methods. Once again the ABCM is seen to have the lowest transitional cost, and the $^{CS}APBCM$ is the most sensitive to the plan amendment in the initial year. However, the differences among the three cost methods are not nearly as great as the difference associated with amending a career average plan to a final average plan. As was the case in the previous section, the results in this section point out quite clearly that the short-term and intermediate-term cost impact of a plan amendment providing a cost-of-living benefit is considerably different from the long-term cost impact of such a provision.

FIGURE 17–2

Costs under a Plan Amended to Provide a 3 Percent Cost-of-Living Benefit as a Percentage of Costs under a Plan without a Cost-of-Living Benefit (based on the ^{CS}APBCM)

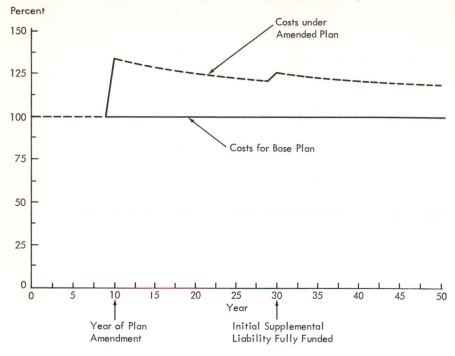

TABLE 17–2

Costs under a Plan Amended to Provide a 3 Percent Cost-of-Living Benefit as a Percentage of Costs under a Plan without a Cost-of-Living Benefit

Year of Forecast	Cost Method		
	ABCM	$^{CS}PBCM$	$^{CS}APBCM$
0	100	100	100
5	100	100	100
10	127	131	134
15	125	129	130
20	123	127	126
25	122	126	123
30	123	129	126
35	122	127	123
40	118	117	121
45	118	117	120
50	118	117	119

EFFECT OF VESTING-RELATED PLAN AMENDMENT

Figure 17–3 shows the cost increase associated with a plan that does not have a vesting provision during the first ten years and is then amended (retroactively) to provide full vesting after ten years of service. This graph depicts the costs of the amended plan as a percentage of the costs under the standard plan, the latter assuming ten-year vesting from the outset of the forecast.

FIGURE 17–3

Costs under a Plan Amended to Provide Full Vesting after Ten Years as a Percentage of Costs under a Plan with Ten-Year Vesting (based on ^{CS}APBCM)

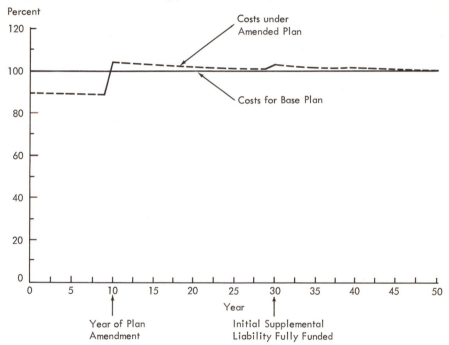

Costs of the amended plan are 90 percent of the base plan's costs in the first year of the forecast. In the tenth year of the forecast when the plan is amended to provide full vesting after ten years service, costs increase to 104 percent of the base plan's costs and gradually decrease to the costs of the base plan during the remainder of the forecast period.

Two important points are revealed by Figure 17–3. The first point is that the cost under a plan without vesting increases by only 11 percent in the long-run as a result of ten-year vesting (since the costs of the plan without vesting are 90 percent of those of the plan with vesting) and these results were obtained also for the ^{CS}PBCM. This increase is in sharp contrast to the values given in Chapter 14, where the ^{CS}PBCM had a 17.5 percent increase in its normal cost and a 7.4 percent increase in its actuarial liability for an identical plan change. Thus, in this case total costs are increased by a percentage that falls midway between the impact on the plan's normal cost and actuarial liability, a result caused by the existence of a supplemental cost based on the past service of the two plans.

The second point of interest is that there is little difference between the immediate cost impact and the long-run cost impact of a plan amendment associated with vesting, unlike the results of a change in the plan's benefit formula as analyzed in the two previous sections. The reason for the relatively minor transitional cost of vesting is the fact that the plan's actuarial liability is not significantly affected by the change in the vesting provision, and this causes the supplemental cost associated with the plan change to be relatively minor. Thus, for this particular plan change, the transitional costs are not nearly as important as they are for other plan changes.

EFFECT OF TERMINATION-BASED ACTUARIAL DEVIATIONS

It was pointed out earlier in this book that an increase in the assumed rates of termination reduces total costs in spite of the fact that the cost of vesting usually increases and vice versa. In this section we consider, for a plan providing full vesting after ten years of service, the cost effect of experiencing termination rates among active employees that are different from the assumed rates. Of particular interest is the cost consequence of an increase in termination rates, since such an increase could possibly be brought about by the more liberal vesting provisions under ERISA.

Figure 17–4 shows the costs under the ^{CS}APBCM, expressed as a percentage of the base plan's costs, for two separate cases: (1) where the actual rates of termination among active employees are 50 percent lower than the assumed rates and (2) where the actual rates are 50 percent greater than the assumed termination rates. The actuarial gains or losses generated by these deviations are assumed to be amortized over the future salaries of plan participants.

Figure 17–4 shows that if employees terminate according to lower rates than those assumed, pension costs increase, and vice versa. The

FIGURE 17–4

Costs under Plans Experiencing Termination-Based Actuarial Gains and Losses as a Percentage of Costs under the Base Plan with No Actuarial Deviations Assumed (based on the CSAPBCM)

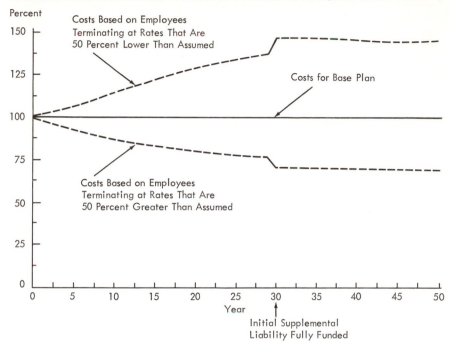

cost impact associated with fewer-than-expected terminations is larger than the impact associated with greater-than-expected terminations. For example, costs after ten years are 15 percent larger if the plan experiences 50 percent fewer terminations than assumed, while contributions are 12 percent smaller if 50 percent more employees terminate than expected. The cost increase after fifty years is 46 percent while the cost reduction is 31 percent. The cost impact under the ABCM was found to be very similar to that of the CSAPBCM, whereas the CSPBCM experienced a larger cost impact. For example, after 50 years, the cost increase associated with lower-than-expected terminations amounted to 64 percent, while the cost decrease associated with higher-than-expected terminations amounted to 43 percent.

The results presented in Figure 17–4 are not designed to illustrate what might actually occur in practice, since the plan actuary would undoubtedly change the assumed rates of terminations after several years of experiencing a persistent actuarial deviation of this magnitude

(50 percent). Rather, the results illustrate two points. The first point is that it takes a fairly long time before even substantial termination-based actuarial deviations begin to have a significant impact on plan costs. For example, after five years plan costs are affected by less than 10 percent and after ten years by less than 20 percent. We will see subsequently that deviations in the rates of salary increase and investment return have a far more substantial impact on costs than the 50 percent deviation in termination rates.

The second point brought out by Figure 17–4 is that costs eventually reach a plateau when the plan experiences termination-based deviations year after year. Although the plateau associated with a 50 percent deviation in termination rates is not precisely equal to a 50 percent deviation (in the opposite direction) in costs, it nevertheless represents a fairly good approximation to the long-run cost impact.

EFFECT OF INVESTMENT-BASED ACTUARIAL DEVIATIONS

In this section the analysis considers the impact on plan costs if the investment earnings on plan assets are 2 percent greater and 2 percent less than the assumed interest rates. It will be remembered that the base plan costs are determined under a 7 percent interest rate. Thus, the effects of both a 9 percent and a 5 percent yield rate are analyzed. As noted earlier, actuarial gains and losses are amortized over a period of 15 years under the ABCM and the ^{CS}PBCM, and over the future salaries of plan participants under the ^{CS}APBCM.

Figure 17–5 shows the costs under the ^{CS}APBCM, assuming that the investment yield is 9 percent under one plan and 5 percent under another plan from the tenth year of the forecast onward. Costs decline rapidly towards zero when 9 percent is earned on the plan's portfolio and they increase by about the same pattern when 5 percent is earned on the portfolio. From Figure 17–5 it appears that the 9 percent yield on assets will cause costs to eventually reach zero, while a 5 percent yield causes costs to reach a level of about two-thirds greater than the base plan, the latter assumed to earn 7 percent on investments.

Table 17–3 shows the results under all three actuarial cost methods. These data show that the ^{CS}PBCM is more sensitive to deviations in the investment assumption than either the ABCM or the ^{CS}APBCM. The ^{CS}PBCM is more sensitive than the ^{CS}APBCM simply because of the difference in the length of the period over which these two methods are assumed to amortize the supplemental liability created by the investment yield. The individual version amortizes this liability

FIGURE 17–5

Costs under Plans Yielding 5 and 9 Percent as a Percentage of the Costs under the Base Plan Yielding 7 Percent (based on the ^{CS}APBCM)

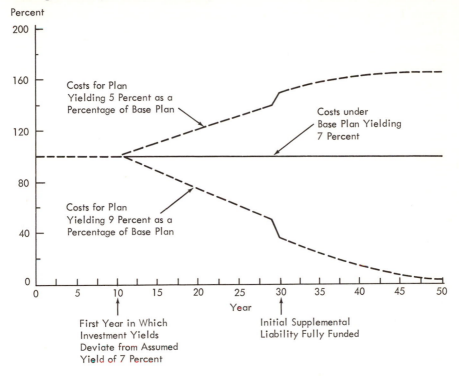

TABLE 17–3

Cost Rates under Plans Experiencing 5 and 9 Percent Salary Rates as Percentages of the Cost Rate under the Base Plan Experiencing a 7 Percent Salary Rate

Year of Forecast	9 Percent Yield			5 Percent Yield		
	ABCM	$^{CS}PBCM$	$^{CS}APBCM$	*ABCM*	$^{CS}PBCM$	$^{CS}APBCM$
10.	100	100	100	100	100	100
15.	91	87	89	109	112	110
20.	80	70	76	118	127	121
25.	69	51	62	126	142	132
30.	55	16	37	138	171	150
35.	44	−2	25	147	185	157
40.	35	−16	15	154	197	162
45.	32	−20	8	159	204	165
50.	31	−20	4	162	209	166

over 15 years, while the aggregate version amortized it over the future salaries of active employees, the latter spreading the gains and losses over a longer period. The ^{CS}PBCM is more sensitive than the ABCM to investment deviations simply because it generates a larger level of assets, which in turn amplifies the effects of investment deviations. After 25 years of persistent actuarial gains (that is, after 35 years of the forecast), the ^{CS}PBCM shows the costs are negative, implying that the plan is fully funded and the investment yield is of such magnitude that costs equalling a given percentage of the base plan's costs could could theoretically be taken out of the plan.

The results in this section are affected by the initial level of assets at the point where the investment yields begin to deviate. If, for example, the plan had no assets at this point, the impact on costs would be less that shown in Figure 17–5 for a period of time. By the same token, if plan assets were greater than those of the base plan at the point where deviations begin to occur, then the impact on costs would be larger.

EFFECT OF SALARY-BASED ACTUARIAL DEVIATIONS

In this section pension costs over a 50 year period are analyzed under the assumptions that the actual salaries of plan participants increase at both a lower and a higher rate than the assumed rate of increase. In particular, a 2 percent deviation between the assumed salary rate increase and the actual salary rate increase is considered. Since the base plan has a salary assumption that includes a 3 percent inflation component, a 2 percent positive and negative deviation in the salary experience of the plan can be viewed as a change in this component, that is, the exposure of salaries to a 5 percent and 1 percent inflation factor rather than the 3 percent. The deviation of the plan's salary experience is assumed to begin during its tenth year of operation, an assumption also used in connection with analyzing the effects of investment yield deviations in the previous section.

Figure 17–6 shows the effects of the positive and negative 2 percent deviation in the salary experience of the plan in relation to the costs of the base plan, for which the salary experience conforms to the 7 percent salary assumption. It is clear from this figure that the impact on costs of a 2 percent deviation in the plan's salary is far greater than the impact of a 2 percent deviation in the investment yield. Costs are nearly zero after 20 years of favorable salary experience, and four times greater that the base plan under unfavorable salary experience.

FIGURE 17–6

Costs under Plans Experiencing Salary Increases of 5 and 9 Percent as a Percentage of the Costs under the Base Plan with Salary Increases of 7 Percent (based on the ^{CS}APBCM)

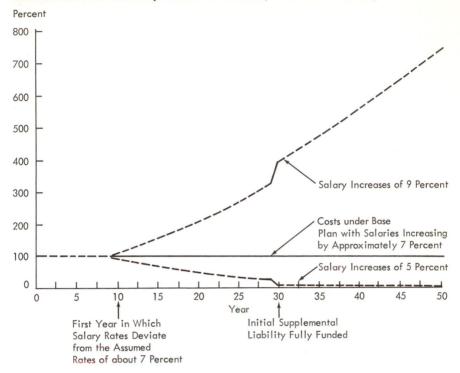

By the end of the 50-year forecast, costs are still zero under the favorable salary experience and over seven times greater than the base plan under unfavorable salary experience. The results under the ABCM were found to be somewhat less sensitive than those of the ^{CS}APBCM which are portrayed in Figure 17–6, while the results of the ^{CS}PBCM were somewhat more sensitive.

The results given in Figure 17–6 portray the impact on the plan's *dollar* costs. However, unlike the previous simulations in this chapter, the salary base of the three pension plans shown in Figure 17–6 become different after the tenth year of the forecast. Under these circumstances it may be more meaningful to compare the cost *rate* of the plans (that is, total costs as a percentage of the underlying salary base) rather than dollar costs.[1] Table 17–4 shows the costs rates of

---

[1] If the cost impact is given as a percentage of the cost under the base plan, and if the salary base among the plans is the same, then the analysis will be the same whether dollar costs or the cost rate is used.

TABLE 17–4

Cost Rates under Plans Experiencing 5 and 9 Percent Salary Rates as Percentages of the Cost Rate under the Base Plan Experiencing a 7 Percent Salary Rate

Year of Forecast	5 Percent Salary Rate			9 Percent Salary Rate		
	ABCM	$^{CS}PBCM$	$^{CS}APBCM$	ABCM	$^{CS}PBCM$	$^{CS}APBCM$
0.	100	100	100	100	100	100
5.	100	100	100	100	100	100
10.	103	100	100	92	97	97
15.	114	94	97	76	96	95
20.	117	79	87	74	101	97
25.	114	59	75	77	107	101
30.	92	−20	16	86	132	123
35.	75	−48	5	94	137	126
40.	54	−65	2	103	142	129
45.	42	−58	4	112	146	133
50.	38	−43	8	118	149	136

the two plans experiencing a 5 or 9 percent rate of salary increase, expressed as a percentage of the cost rate of the base plan, which experiences a 7 percent rate of salary increase. The results are given for all three costs methods at five-year intervals during the 50-year forecast period.

If salaries increase by 5 percent instead of the assumed rate of 7 percent, the cost rate of the plan decreases relative to the cost rate of the base plan. The exception to this is the ABCM during the first 20 years of salary deviations, where the cost rate is somewhat larger than that of the base plan. This occurs because under this method salaries are not projected to retirement, but rather projected backwards for a period of five years in order to calculate each participant's current five-year average salary. As the underlying salary base begins to increase at a slower pace than expected, the effect of projecting backwards five years under the ABCM has a considerably smaller impact on the plan's dollar costs than the effect of projecting forward to each participant's retirement age as required under the projected benefit cost methods. The net result is that when the ABCM costs are expressed as a percentage of the continually shrinking salary base, a higher cost rate is developed as compared to the cost rate of the base plan. Eventually, however, the actuarial gains generated from the 5 percent salary rate increase accumulate and cause the ABCM cost rate to be less than that of the base plan. Unlike the ABCM, the two versions of the projected benefit cost method have cost rates less than the base plan from the outset of the salary deviation. The $^{CS}PBCM$

is seen to be considerably more sensitive to favorable salary increases than the ^{CS}APBCM. In fact, after approximately 20 years of favorable salary experience, a negative cost rate obtains and reaches a level of nearly two thirds of the positive cost rate under the base plan.

If salaries increase by 9 percent instead of the assumed rate of 7 percent, the cost rate of the plan first becomes smaller and then becomes larger than the cost rate of the base plan. The cost rate is smaller for nearly 30 years under the ABCM, for about 20 years under the ^{CS}PBCM, and for almost 25 years for the ^{CS}APBCM. A smaller cost rate occurs for a period of time after the salary begins to deviate because the salary base of the plan increases in direct proportion to the assumed salary deviation, while the increase in plan costs lag behind. The lag is caused in part by the fixed supplemental cost associated with the initial past service supplemental liability, and in part because the actuarial loss created by the salary deviation is spread over future years instead of being recognized entirely in the year it occurs.

EFFECT OF INFLATION-BASED ACTUARIAL DEVIATIONS

In the previous two sections we considered the impact on plan costs if the investment yield or the salary increase deviated from its assumed rate. In this section the analysis turns to the effects on plan costs when the salary and investment experience deviate simultaneously in the same direction. Since both the salary rate and interest rate assumptions include an inflation component, the results can be viewed as the effects of experiencing inflation-based actuarial deviations. The deviations, which begin in the tenth year of the forecast, are equal to either a positive or a negative 2 percent. This implies that one plan experiences a 2 percent rate of inflation and the other experiences a 6 percent rate of inflation, whereas the base plan experiences a 4 percent rate.

As was the case in the previous section, the salaries of the two plans becomes different from the salaries of the base plan. Thus, it is more meaningful to examine the relative change in the cost *rates* of the plans rather than the change in the dollar costs of the plans. Although not shown in this section, the dollar costs of the plan experiencing a 2 percent rate of inflation are *lower* than the dollar costs of the base plan, while the costs of the plan experiencing a 6 percent rate of inflation are *higher* than those of the base plan. In fact, a graph of the dollar costs as a percentage of the base plan's dollar costs under the ^{CS}APBCM looks quite similar to Figure 17–6 with the *y*-axis scaled to a maximum of 500 percent instead of 800 percent. In other words, the dollar impact of a 2 percent unfavorable salary experience is offset to some extent by a 2 percent favorable investment yield, and vice versa.

TABLE 17–5

Cost Rates under Plans Experiencing 2 and 6 Percent Inflation Rates as a Percentage of the Cost Rates under the Base Plan Experiencing a 4 Percent Inflation Rate

Year of Forecast	2 Percent Inflation Rate*			6 Percent Inflation Rate†		
	ABCM	$^{CS}PBCM$	$^{CS}APBCM$	*ABCM*	$^{CS}PBCM$	$^{CS}APBCM$
0.	100	100	100	100	100	100
5.	100	100	100	100	100	100
10.	103	100	100	92	97	97
15.	126	111	111	70	88	88
20.	146	123	124	64	85	85
25.	166	140	139	63	84	84
30.	180	135	131	67	94	94
35.	196	159	147	71	91	92
40.	208	187	160	76	88	90
45.	211	208	167	81	85	88
50.	210	220	169	83	82	86

* Equivalent to a 5 percent rate of salary increase and a 5 percent rate of investment return.
† Equivalent to a 9 percent rate of salary increase and a 9 percent rate of investment return.

Table 17–5 gives the results of the inflation-based actuarial deviations, where the percentages represent the cost *rate* of the plan expressed as a percentage of the base plan's cost rate.[2] If the plan experiences a 2 percent rate of inflation instead of the expected 4 percent rate, the cost rate becomes progressively larger than the base plan's cost rate.[3] On the other hand, if the plan experiences a 6 percent rate of inflation instead of the expected 4 percent rate, the cost rate becomes progressively lower than the base plan's cost rate under the two versions of the projected benefit cost method and under the ABCM they follow a saucer shape, decreasing for about 15 years and increasing thereafter. By the end of the forecast period, the effect on the cost rates of all three cost methods is quite similar for positive and negative deviations in the inflation parameter.

---

[2] It will be remembered that the cost rate is defined as the dollar cost as a percentage of the plan's aggregate salary.

[3] There is a discontinuity in the gradually increasing contribution rate during the thirtieth year of the forecast due to the past service supplemental liability being fully funded at this point. The results given for every five years only does not properly show this discontinuity.

While the results presented in this section are not sufficient by themselves to ascertain the general relationship of the effects of inflation on a plan's costs, it appears that inflation greater than expected increases the dollar costs of the plan and decreases the cost rate of the plan relative to the dollar cost and cost rate of a plan experiencing the expected rate of inflation. If this generalization were to hold true under all circumstances, as the rate of inflation approaches infinity, dollar costs also approach infinity while the cost rate approaches zero. In other words, pension costs lag the increase in salaries brought about by the unexpected inflation.

EFFECT OF NON-OFFSETTING SALARY AND INVESTMENT DEVIATIONS

In this section the effect on plan costs of non-offsetting deviations in both the salary and investment experience of the plan are considered. In particular, there is considered the result of allowing salaries to increase by 2 percent less than the assumed rate while at the same time allowing the investment yield to exceed the assumed rate by 2 percent. Another experiment assumes just the opposite, that is, salaries increase by 2 percent more than the assumed rate and investment yields are 2 percent less than the assumed rate. Again the analysis focuses on the change in the plan's cost rate rather than the change in dollar costs because of the different salary bases that develop during the forecast. Although the dollar cost impact is not shown, a graph of the costs as a percentage of the costs under the base plan is quite similar to Figure 17–6 with the *y*-axis scaled from negative 100 to positive 1,100 percent. In other words, favorable salary and investment experience allows costs to become negative after about 15 years of persistent deviations, while unfavorable salary and investment experience causes costs to increase to more than nine times the costs under the base plan by the end of the projection period.

Table 17–6 gives the results of the experiment. If the investment yield is 9 percent instead of the assumed 7 percent and if salaries increase by 5 percent instead of the assumed 7 percent, the cost rate of the plan decreases significantly. After a period of about 15 years the costs under the plan become negative and in some cases reach a negative level more than three and one-half times the cost rate of the base plan.

If the investment yield is 5 percent instead of the assumed 7 percent and if salaries increase by 9 percent instead of the assumed 7 percent,

TABLE 17–6

Cost Rates under Plans Experiencing Non-Offsetting Salary and Investment Deviations as a Percentage of the Cost Rates under the Base Plan

Year of Forecast	9 Percent Investment Yield 5 Percent Salary Rate			5 Percent Investment Yield 9 Percent Salary Rate		
	ABCM	$^{cs}PBCM$	$^{cs}APBCM$	ABCM	$^{cs}PBCM$	$^{cs}APBCM$
0.	100	100	100	100	100	100
5.	100	100	100	100	100	100
10.	103	100	100	92	97	97
15.	101	76	82	81	104	101
20.	83	29	46	82	115	108
25.	52	−37	−3	88	128	116
30.	−13	−207	−133	102	165	146
35.	−72	−299	−187	113	177	153
40.	−130	−367	−224	126	188	160
45.	−152	−361	−242	138	198	167
50.	−139	−303	−248	148	209	173

the cost rate of the plan increases significantly. In some cases the cost rate is more than double the cost rate of the base plan. The ^{cs}PBCM, as in previous analyses, is more sensitive to the non-offsetting investment and salary deviations than the other cost methods, and the ABCM is the least sensitive.

The experiements designed to test the sensitivity of pension costs to deviations in actuarial assumptions presented in this chapter are extreme cases in that they show the effects of a persistent deviations for an extended period of time. As noted earlier, these experiments are not intended to analyze what might happen in a given pension plan, since the plan actuary would most assuredly make a modification in the plan's actuarial assumptions after a period of substantial and reoccurring actuarial gains or losses. Rather, the experiments are designed to test the general sensitivity of pension costs to such actuarial gains and losses, and to ascertain the long-run relationship between actuarial assumptions and pension plan costs.

Glossary of Mathematical Notation

$\ddot{a}_{\overline{n}|}$ present value of an n-year annuity certain, with payments made at the beginning of the year

$\ddot{a}_x$ present value, at age x, of a life annuity, with payments made at the beginning of the year

$\ddot{a}_x^d$ present value of a life annuity based on disabled-life mortality, with payments made at the beginning of the year

$\ddot{a}_x^{rm}$ present value of an annuity payable for life or until the annuitant remarries, with payments made at the beginning of the year

$\ddot{a}_{x:\overline{n}|}^T$ present value of an employment-based annuity, with payments made at the beginning of the year

$^s\ddot{a}_{x:\overline{n}|}^T$ present value of an employment-based annuity, with payments made at the beginning of the year equal in value to the employee's attained age salary, based on a unit salary at age x

$\ddot{a}_{x:\overline{n}|}$ present value of an annuity payable until age n or the annuitant's death, whichever occurs first, with payments made at the beginning of the year

$_{n|}\ddot{a}_x$ present value of an annuity payable for life, with the first payment deferred n years

$^k\ddot{a}_{xy}^{\ 1}$ present value of a joint life annuity paying \$1 per year while the life age x is alive and \$$k$ per year to the life age y if the life age x dies first

$^{MCR}\ddot{a}_x$ present value of a modified cash refund annuity with lump sum death payment equal to the difference, if any, between the employee's pension contributions and the benefits received at date of death

$^{\text{MIR}}\ddot{a}_x$ present value of a modified installment refund annuity with payments at least until the employee's pension contributions are returned and thereafter until the annuitant's death

ABCM   individual accrued benefit cost method with supplemental liability

^{CA}ABCM   modified individual accrued benefit cost method with supplemental liability, with benefits allocated by years of service

^{CS}ABCM   modified individual accrued benefit cost method with supplemental liability, with benefits allocated as a constant percentage of attained age salary

$(\text{AC})_x$ annual cost for plan participant at age x under a specified actuarial cost method without supplemental liability

$(\text{AC})_t$ annual cost for plan under specified actuarial cost method without supplemental liability during year t

^{CA}APBCM   aggregate projected benefit cost method with supplemental liability and with costs that represent a constant dollar amount

^{CS}APBCM   aggregate projected benefit cost method with supplemental liability and with costs that represent a constant percentage of salary

$(\text{Assets})_x$ assets associated with an employee age x

$(\text{Assets})_t$ plan assets during year t

$(\text{AL})_x$ actuarial liability for individual at age x under a specified actuarial cost method

$(\text{AL})_t$ actuarial liability for plan at time t under a specified actuarial cost method

$(\text{AL})'_x$ special notation to denote the accumulation of past normal costs under the plan

$^{r'}(\text{AL})_x$ actuarial liability under an early retirement assumption

$^{*r'}(\text{AL})_x$ actuarial liability under an actuarially reduced early retirement assumption

$(\text{AVPNC})_x$ accumulated value of past normal costs at age x for an age-y entrant

$(\text{AVPSC})_x$ accumulated value of past supplemental costs at age x for an age-y entrant

$(AVPSL)_x$ accumulated value of past supplemental liability at age x for an age-y entrant

b_x benefit accrual at age x for an age-y entrant

$b_{y,x}$ b_x but where the entry age variable is explicit

b'_x the implicit benefit accrual as defined by any actuarial cost method's normal cost amount

b_x^T benefit accrual as defined under the ABCM without supplemental liability

$^{CA}b_x$ benefit accrual under the ^{CA}ABCM, that is, the projected benefit prorated by years of service

$^{CA}b_x^d$ benefit accrual associated with disability benefits under a special version of the ^{CA}ABCM

$^{CA}b_x^r$ benefit accrual associated with retirement benefits under a special version of the ^{CA}ABCM

$^{CA}b_x^s$ benefit accrual associated with a surviving spouse benefit under a special version of the ^{CA}ABCM

$^{CA}b_x^T$ benefit accrual under the ^{CA}ABCM without supplemental liability

$^{CA}b_x^v$ benefit accrual associated with vesting benefits under a special version of the ^{CA}ABCM

$^{CS}b_x$ benefit accrual under the ^{CS}ABCM, that is, the projected benefit prorated by attained age salary

$^{CS}b_x^T$ benefit accrual under the ^{CS}ABCM without supplemental liability

B_x accrued benefit at age x for an age-y entrant

$B_{y,x}$ B_x but where the entry age variable is explicit

B'_x the implicit accrued benefit as defined by any actuarial cost method's normal cost amount

B_x^T accrued benefit as defined under the ABCM without supplemental liability

$^{CA}B_x$ accrued benefit as defined under the ^{CA}ABCM, that is, the projected benefit pro-rated by years of service

$^{CA}B_x^T$ accrued benefit under the ^{CA}ABCM without supplemental liability

$^{CS}B_x$ accrued benefit as defined under the ^{CS}ABCM, that is, the projected benefit pro-rated by attained age salary

$^{CS}B_x^T$ accrued benefit as defined under the ^{CS}ABCM without supplemental liability

$\sum B_t$ total benefit payments during year t

CDCM current dispursements cost method

$(CPL)_x$ continuation-of-plan liability at age x

$(Cont)_t$ plan contributions at time t

$d_x^{(d)}$ number of participants becoming disabled during age x in a service table

$d_x^{(m)}$ number of participants dying during age x in a service table

$d_x^{(r)}$ number of participants retiring during age x in a service table

$d_x^{(T)}$ total number of participants decrementing from active service during age x in a service table

$d_x^{(w)}$ number of participants withdrawing during age x in a service table

d iv = rate of discount

$(DCR)_x$ disability cost ratio at age x

$E(AL)_t$ expected plan actuarial liability at time t

$E(Assets)_t$ expected plan assets at time t

$E(B)$ expected retirement benefit based on retirement decrements only

$E(Cont)_t$ expected plan contributions at time t

$(ERCR)_x$ early retirement cost ratio at age x for multiple early retirement ages

$*(ERCR)_x$ early retirement cost ratio at age x for multiple early retirement ages under actuarially reduced early retirement

$_k(ERCR)_x$ early retirement cost ratio at age x for retirement at age k

$_k^*(ERCR)_x$ early retirement cost ratio based on actuarially equivalent early retirement at age k

$E(S)$ expected salary based on retirement decrements only

$E^{AL}(UL)_t$ expected plan unfunded liability, based on the plan actuarial liability, at time t

$E(Y)$ expected years of service based on retirement decrements only

$g_x^{(d)}$ disability-related benefit grading function

$g_x^{(r)}$ retirement-related benefit grading function

$*g_x^{(r)}$ actuarially equivalent early retirement benefit grading function

$g_x^{(s)}$ survivor benefit grading function

$g_x^{(v)}$ vesting-related benefit grading function

I inflation rate assumed in salary function

i rate of interest

i' rate of interest used to accumulate employee contributions

k proportion of attained age salary which denotes the benefit accrual under the ^{CS}ABCM

k_x proportion of the difference between the present value of future benefits and the actuarial liability that a specified actuarial cost method defines as its normal cost

K proportion of the attained age salary that represents the normal cost under the individual ^{CS}PBCM

$l_{y,x}$ number of active plan participants at age x who entered at age y

$l_x^{(T)}$ number of participants in active service at age x who entered at age y from a service table

$l_{y,x}^{(T)}$ $l_x^{(T)}$ but where the entry age variable is explicit

m maximum of age x or the first age in the summation

M the probability that a participant has a spouse

$(NC)_x$ normal cost for plan participant at age x under a specified actuarial cost method

$(NC)_t$ normal cost for plan at time t under a specified actuarial cost method

$^d(NC)_x$ disability-related normal cost under a specified actuarial cost method

$^{r'}(NC)_x$ normal cost under an early retirement assumption for a specified actuarial cost method

$^{*r'}(NC)_x$ normal cost under an actuarially reduced early retirement assumption for a specified actuarial cost method

$^s(NC)_x$ survivor benefit-related normal cost under a specified actuarial cost method

$^T(NC)_x$ normal cost associated with all benefits under a specified actuarial cost method

$^v(NC)_x$ vesting-related normal cost under a specified actuarial cost method

P rate of productivity increase as reflected in salary rate increases

$p_x'^{(d)}$ probability of surviving one year when only the disability decrement is considered

$_np_x'^{(d)}$ probability of surviving n years when only the disability decrement is considered

$p_x'^{(m)}$ probability of surviving one year when only the mortality decrement is considered

$_np_x'^{(m)}$ probability of surviving n years when only the mortality decrement is considered

$^dp_x'^{(m)}$ probability of surviving one year when only the disabled life mortality is considered

$p_x'^{(r)}$ probability of surviving one year when only the retirement decrement is considered

$p_x^{(T)}$ probability of surviving in employment one year with all decrement except early retirement being considered

$_np_x^{(T)}$ probability of surviving in employment n years with all decrements being considered

$^rp_x^{(T)}$ probability of surviving in employment one year with all decrements including early retirement being considered

$p_x'^{(w)}$ probability of surviving one year when only the withdrawal decrement is considered

$_np_x'^{(w)}$ probability of surviving n years when only the withdrawal decrement is considered

^{CA}PBCM individual projected benefit cost method with supplemental liability and with costs that represent a constant dollar amount

^{CS}PBCM individual projected benefit cost method with supplemental liability and with costs that represent a constant percentage of salary

PTCM plan termination cost method

$(PVAB)_x$ present value of accrued benefits at age x for an age-y entrant

$(PVFB)_x$ present value of future benefits at age x for an age-y entrant

$(PVFB)_{y,x}$ $(PVFB)_x$ but where the entry age variable is explicit

$\sum(PVFB)_x$ present value of future benefits for the entire plan

$^d(PVFB)_x$ present value of future disability benefits at age x for an age-y entrant

$^r(PVFB)_x$ present value of future retirement benefits at age x, based on normal retirement only, for an age-y entrant

$^{r'}(\text{PVFB})_x$	present value of future retirement benefits at age x, based on early and normal retirement, for an age-y entrant
$^{*r'}(\text{PVFB})_x$	present value of future retirement benefits at age x, based on actuarial reduced early retirement and normal retirement, for an age-y entrant
$^{s}(\text{PVFB})_x$	present value of future surviving spouse benefits at age x for an age-y entrant
$^{T}(\text{PVFB})_x$	present value of all future benefits at age x for an age-y entrant
$^{v}(\text{PVFB})_x$	present value of future vesting benefits at age x for an age-y entrant
$(\text{PVFC})_x$	present value of future employee contributions at age x for an age-y entrant
$(\text{PVFNC})_x$	present value of future normal costs at age x for an age-y entrant
$(\text{PVFSC})_x$	present value of future supplemental costs at age x for age-y entrant
$q_x'^{(d)}$	rate of decrement due to disability during age x
$q_x^{(d)}$	probability of decrement due to disability during age x
$q_x'^{(m)}$	rate of decrement due to morality during age x
$q_x^{(m)}$	probability of decrement due to mortality during age x
$^{d}q_x'^{(m)}$	rate of decrement due to disabled life mortality during age x
$q_x'^{(r)}$	rate of decrement due to retirement during age x
$q_x^{(r)}$	probability of decrement due to retirement during age x
$q_x'^{(w)}$	rate of decrement due to withdrawal during age x
$q_x^{(w)}$	probability of decrement due to withdrawal during age x
r	normal retirement age
r'	first age at which the employee qualifies for early retirement
s_x	salary at age x for an age-y entrant
$s_{y,x}$	s_x but where the entry age variable is explicit
S_x	cumulative salary from y to $x-1$ for an age-y entrant
$S_{y,x}$	S_x but where the entry age variable is explicit
$(\text{SCR})_x$	survivor benefit cost ratio at age x
$(\text{SL})_x$	supplemental liability at age x
$(\text{SLI})_x$	supplemental liability increment at age x

$^{\text{AD}}(\text{SLI})_x$ supplemental liability increment due to an actuarial deviation at age x

$^{\text{AL}}(\text{SLI})_x$ supplemental liability increment based on the actuarial liability at age x

$(\text{SS})_x$ salary scale at age x

TBCM   terminal benefit cost method

$^{d}(\text{TC})_x$ disability term cost at age x

$^{r}(\text{TC})_x$ retirement term cost at age x

$^{s}(\text{TC})_x$ survivor benefit term cost at age x

$^{v}(\text{TC})_x$ vesting term cost at age x

$(\text{TPL})_x$ termination-of-plan liability at age x

$^{\text{AL}}(\text{UL})_t$ unfunded liability based on the actuarial liability of the plan at time t

$^{\text{CPL}}(\text{UL})_t$ unfunded liability based on the CPL of the plan at time t

$^{\text{TPL}}(\text{UL})_t$ unfunded liability based on the TPL of the plan at time t

u the number of years that, when added to the participant's age, yields the assumed age of the spouse

$(\text{USL})_x$ unamortized supplemental liability at age x

$(\text{USL})_t$ unamortized supplemental liability of the plan during time t

$(\text{VCR})_x$ vesting cost ratio at age x

v^n present value of \$1 due n years from the present time, based on a specified interest rate

x attained age

y entry age

Index

241

*This book is set in 11 and 10 point Times
Roman, leaded 2 points. Chapter numbers are
18 point Univers Medium and 24 point (small)
Univers Medium. Chapter titles are 24 point
(small) Univers Medium. The size of the type
page is 27 by 46 picas.*